Van Zoeren Library

MAY 27 1981

Hope College
Holland, Michigan

WITHDRAWN

Statistics on radio and television 1960-1976

Division of Statistics on Culture and Communication Office of Statistics

Paris, 1978

Unesco

ISBN 92-3-101681-4

Published in 1979
by the United Nations Educational,
Scientific and Cultural Organization,
7, place de Fontenoy, 75700 Paris

Printed by Joseph Floch, Mayenne

© Unesco 1979.

Table of contents

		Page
Introduction		6
Part I	Radio broadcasting	7
	1. Organization	
	2. Sound broadcasting transmitters	
	3. Sound broadcasting radio receivers	
Part II	Television broadcasting	21
	4. Organization	
	5. Television broadcasting transmitters	
	6. Television receivers	
Part III	Radio and television broadcasting programmes	31

Tables

	Page
A. Distribution of countries according to main types of domestic radio broadcasting system (around 1960) by continents	7
B. Distribution of countries and territories according to number of sound broadcasting transmitters in use, by continents (circa 1960 and circa 1973)	8
C. Number of sound broadcasting transmitters	8
D. Countries operating ultra-short wave transmitters having a total transmitting power of more than 30 kw, around 1960	10
E. Countries operating ultra-short wave transmitters having a total transmitting power of more than 30 kw, around 1972	11
F. Countries with more than 100 sound broadcasting transmitters around 1960	11
G. Countries with more than 100 sound broadcasting transmitters around 1973	11
H. Distribution of countries according to the number of radio receivers per 1,000 inhabitants, by continents (around 1960, 1970 and 1976)	12
I. Estimated number of radio receivers in use and of receivers per 1,000 inhabitants, by continents (circa 1960, 1970 and 1976)	14
J. Countries with more than 2,500,000 radio receivers in 1960	14
K. Countries with more than 4,000,000 radio receivers in 1976	16
L. Countries having between 200-500 radio receivers per 1,000 inhabitants in 1976	17
M. Countries having more than 500 radio receivers per 1,000 inhabitants in 1976	16

N. Total number of radio receivers for the years 1960-1976, by continents 17

O. Estimated number of television transmitters operating on a regular basis, by continents (1960 and around 1974) . 23

P. Distribution of countries according to the number of television receivers per 1,000 inhabitants, by continents (1960, 1976) 23

Q. Estimated number of television receivers in use and of receivers per 1,000 inhabitants, by continents (circa 1960, 1970 and 1976) 24

R. Countries with more than one million television receivers in 1960 24

S. Countries with more than one million television receivers in 1976 24

T. Countries with more than 40 television receivers per 1,000 inhabitants in 1960 25

U. Countries between 40-100 television receivers per 1,000 inhabitants in 1976 25

V. Countries between 100-200 television receivers per 1,000 inhabitants in 1976 25

W. Countries with more than 200 television receivers per 1,000 inhabitants in 1976 25

X. Estimated number of television receivers in use 1960-1976 30

Charts

1. Distribution of sound broadcasting transmitters . . . 9

2. Total number of radio receivers by continents 1960, 1970 and 1976 13

3. Distribution of radio receivers by continents. Estimated percentages 1960, 1970, 1976 15

4. Distribution of number of television broadcasting by continents 22

5. Total number of television receivers by continents 1960, 1970 and 1976 26

6. Distribution of television receivers by continents. Estimated percentages 1960, 1970, 1976 27

Graphs

1. Total number of radio receivers (America - North and Europe) 18

2. Total number of radio receivers (America - South, Asia, Africa and Oceania) 19

3. Total number of television receivers (Europe, Asia and America - North) 28

4. Total number of television receivers (America - South, Oceania and Africa) 29

Annex Tables 33

1. Number of sound broadcasting transmitters 35

2. Number of radio receivers and receivers per 1,000 inhabitants 39

3. Number of television transmitters 47

4. Number of television receivers 51

5. Composition of domestic radio broadcasting programmes according to national classification during a typical week in 1959 57

6. Composition of television broadcasting programmes according to national classifications, during a typical week in 1960 59

7. Domestic radio classified by main type of programmes, in hours of broadcasting (latest data available for the period 1968-1971). 61

8. Television classified by main type of programmes, in hours of broadcasting (latest data available for the period 1968-1971). 62

9. Domestic radio classified by main type of programmes: total hours of broadcasting and percentage distribution (latest data available for the period 1968-1973) 63

10. Television classified by main type of programmes: total hours of broadcasting and percentage distribution (latest data available for the period 1968-1973) 64

11. Radio broadcasting: programmes by type 65

12. Television broadcasting: programmes by type 66

13. Radio broadcasting: programmes by type (1971-1974) . 67

14. Radio broadcasting: total hours of broadcasting per year and percentage distribution by type of programme (latest data available 1972-1975) 75

15. Radio broadcasting: programmes by type for a typical week in the year 1973 82

16. Television broadcasting: programmes by type (1972-1974) 86

17. Television broadcasting: total hours of broadcasting per year and percentage distribution by type of programme (latest data available 1972-1975) 91

18. Television broadcasting: programmes by type for a typical week in the year 1973 95

Recommendation concerning the international standardization of statistics on radio and television adopted by the General Conference at its nineteenth session - Nairobi, 22 November 1976 . . 99

Questionnaire on Statistics of Communication
Part III: Radio and television broadcasting 1977
(Unesco/STC/Q/782, March 1978) 105

Introduction

The main purpose of this report is to present international statistics concerning broadcasting and receiving facilities for both radio and television for the period 1960-1976. The report also deals with aspects of programme contents as they have evolved during the period of reference. The report is the follow-up to a similar report which was published in 1963 and which referred to the period 1950-1960. Up-dating of the previous report has been a long-felt need. Further, it has appeared worthwhile to present a review of the statistics of the past years before entering the new era opened by the adoption of the Recommendation by the General Conference of Unesco in 1976 on the international standardization of statistics on radio and television. The first survey to be carried out on the basis of that Recommendation was in progress at the time of writing.

The Recommendation of 1976 on these statistics is reproduced in the Annex, which also groups a number of statistical tables which have not been included in the body of the Report. The questionnaire which has been prepared for the 1978 survey, which is under way, is also reproduced in that Annex, so as to give an idea of the new tables which will result from that first survey. The Tables which are contained in the present Report, based upon past surveys, will illustrate in this context the difference between the type of information collected so far and that which the Recommendation of 1976, it is hoped, will help collect and which will better serve the purpose of international comparison.

I. Radio broadcasting

1. ORGANIZATION

Organization and control of broadcasting, for both sound and visual, are in all countries subject to special government regulations, more generally for such technical reasons as the allocation of wave-lengths, and also for a majority of countries for reasons of public order, considering the wide impact of these media.

For the practical purposes of the world statistical surveys carried out by Unesco in the period 1960-1976, the various types of domestic radio broadcasting systems have been classified in the following three main groups.

(a) *Broadcasting as a public service*

Broadcasting organized on a non-commercial basis and largely financed through licence fees and/or government subsidies, although some countries may include a limited amount of commercial advertising. Services may be operated:

(i) Under direct State control as a national institution or government department.

(ii) By a public corporation, under State control but enjoying a certain degree of operational independence, including independence with respect to the arrangement of programmes and administration.

(b) *Radio broadcasting as a private enterprise*

Broadcasting carried out by commercial companies entirely financed by income from advertising or including also private concerns operated on a non-commercial basis such as stations belonging to universities, religious associations, and other non-profit-making institutions.

(c) *Combined systems*

(i) Radio broadcasting mainly based on the principle of private commercial enterprise, but including State-operated stations. Such systems may include private stations operated on a non-commercial basis and publicly owned stations operated on a commercial basis.

(ii) Radio broadcasting as a public service (either under direct State control or operated by a public corporation), with a parallel system of commercial radio.

The majority of countries have a mix of the two broad categories of services mentioned under (a) and (b), with still further complexity being created by "hybrid" types made up by these two broad categories. The United States of America, Canada and most of the Latin American countries have their sound broadcasting mainly based on the principle of private enterprise, whether profit-making (commercial), or non-profit-making (universities, religious associations). In these countries that type of broadcasting more often than not runs parallel to services offered by State-operated stations. In Antigua a commercial station provides the only broadcasting services, and is run with government participation.

Broadly the situation around 1960 was as illustrated in Table A:

Table A — Distribution of countries according to main types of domestic radio broadcasting systems (circa 1960) by continents

Continent	Total number of countries	Government control of public corporation	Private enterprise	Coexistence of government (or public) and private enterprise
Africa	48	41	4	3
America, North	24	8	9	7
America, South	14	2	5	7
Asia (excl. USSR)	40	31	3	6
Europe (incl. USSR)	31	26	3	2
Oceania	17	14	1	2
World total	174	122	25	27

Since 1960, the situation has evolved greatly. There seems to be no point now of classifying countries according to the above categories, since more and more countries tend to fall within what is termed above "coexistence of government (or public) and private enterprise". The classification of countries, with the implication that they fall into either of the two broad categories above, is no longer a worthwhile exercise. What is important, which the statistical survey of broadcasting being presently carried out will hopefully show, will be the description of broadcasting institutions in countries, by their constitutional status. Broadcasting institutions in countries could fall within one or more of the following types, defined as follows:

Government broadcasting institution: a broadcasting institution operated in all respects by a government (central or federal, State, provincial, local, etc.) either directly or through a separate institution created by it;

Public service broadcasting institution: a broadcasting institution created or licensed by a legislative act or regulation (central or federal, State, provincial, local, etc.) and which constitutes an autonomous body;
(This category includes cases of private ownership where the purpose is not profit-making and which qualify for the status of public utility);

Commercial broadcasting institution: a broadcasting institution corporately or privately owned and operating for financial profit.

In future reports, the first of which will be based on results of the on-going survey, data for countries will show in each country the total number of sound broadcasting institutions, divided into government, public service and commercial, as defined above.

2. SOUND BROADCASTING TRANSMITTERS

In 1950, some 50 countries in the world had no broadcasting facilities; 23 of these were in Africa. Around 1960, the number of countries having no radio transmitters had shrunk to 12, seven of which were countries of Africa. Around 1973, of the 187 countries and territories considered in this survey which could claim to cover nearly the whole world, two countries only had no transmitting facilities; they were Leichtenstein and San Marino, in Europe.

From Table B it can be seen that the number of countries having from 2 to 20 transmitters has remained fairly constant over the years, i.e. 102 in 1960 and 98 in 1973. The 34 countries which in 1960 had either one transmitter or none at all were only 13 in 1973. In the upper ranges i.e. 20 to 200 or more, we find 25 more countries than in 1960, 12 of which having moved into the group "over 200 transmitters".

Table C which follows, presents world and regional data for the sound broadcasting transmitters in use over the period 1960-1974.

Table C — Number of sound broadcasting transmitters

Continent	circa 1960*	circa 1965	circa 1970	circa 1974
Africa (excl. South Africa	305	390	520	567
South Africa	45	102	177	182
America, North	5 700	7 359	8 256	10 432
America, South	1 900	2 217	2 653	2 802
Asia	1 200	1 420	1 965	2 752
Europe	2 600	4 171	5 209	6 568
Oceania	250	290	308	343
USSR	407		3 034	(3 034)

* Estimates
= According to various sources (Unesco Statistical Yearbook, Special World Communication Questionnaire (Unesco)

Table B — Distribution of countries and territories according to number of sound broadcasting transmitters in use, by continents (circa 1960 and circa 1973)

Continent	Year	Total number of countries	Countries with the following number of transmitters						
			0	1	2 to 5	6 to 20	21 to 50	51 to 200	more than 200
Africa	circa 1960	55	7	7	25	12	4	—	—
	1973	55	—	2	22	21	8	2	
America, North	circa 1960	25	1	2	6	5	5	4	2
	1973	25		2	6	5	—	9	3
America, South	circa 1960	14	—	1	3	1	1	6	2
	1973	14	—	—	2	2	1	3	6
Asia (exclu. USSR and China)	circa 1960	40	—	3	18	11	3	4	1
	1973	40	—	—	10	14	7	7	2
Europe (incl. USSR)	circa 1960	35	3	—	5	10	6	7	4
	1973	35	2	1	2	5	8	7	10
Oceania	circa 1960	18	1	9	6	—	1	1	—
	1973	18	—	6	7	2	1	2	—
World totals	1960	187	12	22	63	39	20	22	9
	1973	187	2	11	49	49	25	30	21

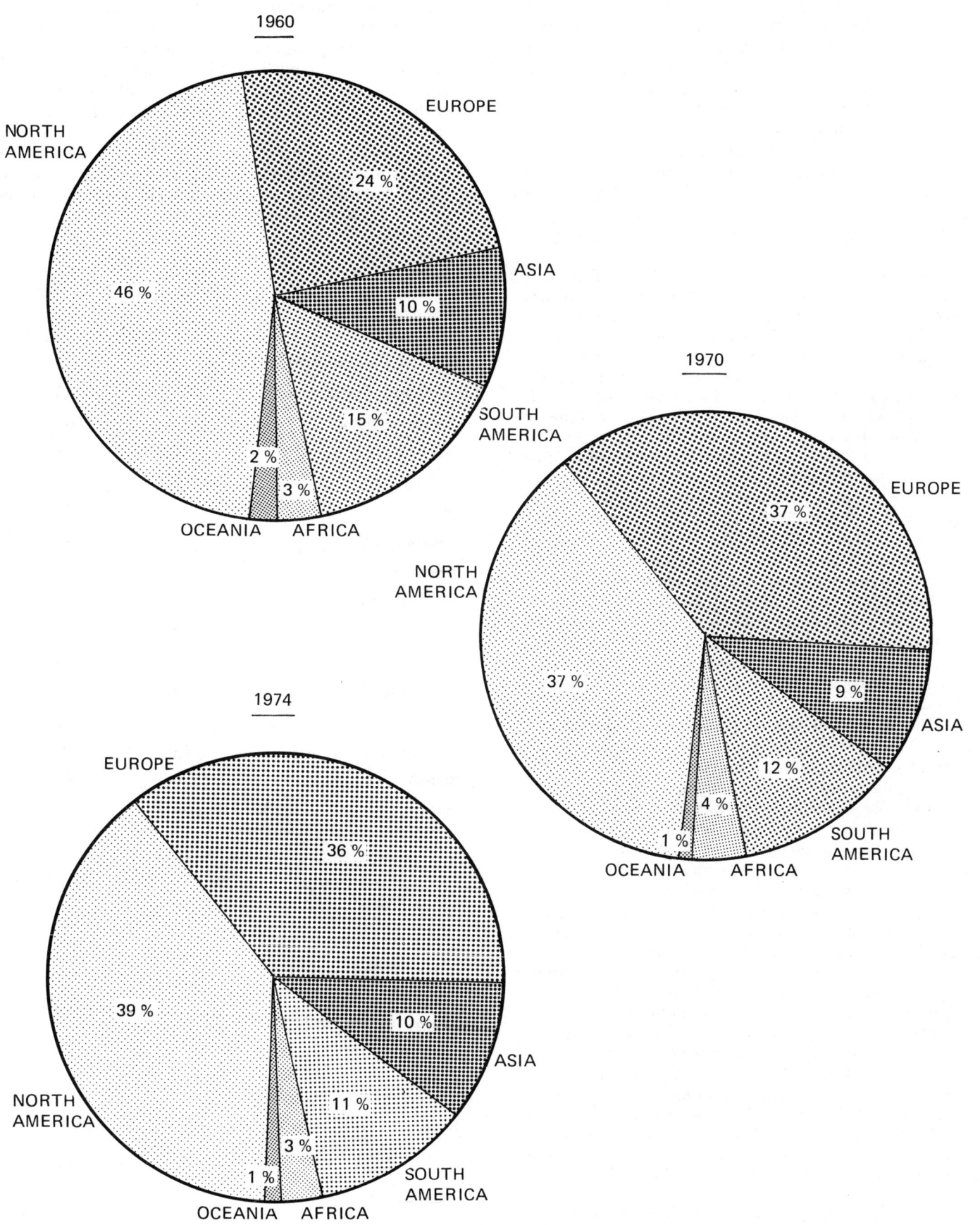
Chart 1 — Distribution of sound broadcasting transmitters by continents (circa 1960, 1970, 1974)

During the last fifteen years or so, the number of transmitters in service throughout the world has increased considerably. Around 1975, for the whole of Africa excluding South Africa, the number of transmitters is shown as being 567. This figure may itself be smaller than the real figure, because of the conservative estimates made in a number of cases. In Angola radio transmitters which were reported at one time to number 48 in 1970 and 77 around 1972 was down to 19 in 1974. Despite this big drop for Angola and a less important one for Mozambique, the increase in the number of transmitters for the period 1965-1974 has been of the order of 40%, excluding South Africa. The latter was reported to have, around 1970, some 177 transmitters operating, including 78 FM transmitters forming the special Radio Bantu network which broadcast is seven main African languages for altogether a total of 592 hours per week around that same year.

For countries of North America, as listed in Table 1 of the Annex, the increase in the number of transmitters has been 85% for the period 1960-1974, the increase for the United States of America accounting for 73% of the increase for the group as a whole. For the 14 countries of South America the increase has been of the order of 50% for the same period. Contrary to what happened in North America, where the United States, the high-flier of the group, accounted for nearly ¾ of the increase, as stated above, Brazil which outdistances the other members of its group in the number of transmitters has not seen much increase for the period under review. That number climbed from 920 in 1960, to 999 in 1974, i.e. less than 10% for the period. Bolivia and Peru have trebled their number of transmitters, Argentina and Chile has doubled theirs, with Ecuador registering an intermediary achievement. From available figures, the transmitting power for Argentina has more than doubled during that period. For Brazil a decrease in transmitting power is registered. That may be due to under-reporting of all the stations operating in that vast country. Ecuador is shown to have more than trebled its transmitting power.

The countries of Asia as a group have doubled their number of transmitters in the span of 15 years. Japan has multiplied the number of its transmitters by 2.5. The same holds for the Philippines. Thailand is supposed to register a ten-fold increase. However, in the last case, the figures reported at the last survey may have been exaggerated.

For Europe, the increase in the number of transmitters has been over 130% compared with an increase of some 110% for the world as a whole. Among those countries of Europe where there has been at least a three-fold increase, figure Portugal (5.6), Austria (3.33), France (3.02) and Sweden (2.94). Italy had 1,003 transmitters in 1960, of which 872 were reported as being ultra-short-wave. Around 1974 the figure was 1964, of which 1,835 were ultra-short-wave transmitters. Italy is far ahead in this group, with the second country Yugoslavia trailing far behind with 487 transmitters. However, transmitting power gives a different picture. The Federal Republic of Germany with 346 transmitters had a transmitting power of 21,079 kw, while Italy, the high-flier in the number of transmitters, mustered 2,939 kw only. It remains that in this group Italy stands out with the largest number, even if low-powered, of VHF transmitters i.e. 1,835, Norway ranking second with 307, and Sweden with 274.

In Oceania, where Australia, New Zealand and Papua New Guinea had more than 10 transmitters around 1973, with 219, 58 and 22 transmitters respectively, the increase since 1960 has been slower than for the other groups. It has amounted to 40% for the period, with an increase of barely 11% for Australia but one of 60% for New Zealand. Papua New Guinea is reported to have increased the number of its transmitters from 3 to 22 (see Table I).

Tables D and E illustrate how countries have increased their transmitting power for ultra-short wave sound broadcasting. Only 16 countries in 1960 had a total transmitting power of more than 30 kw. Around 1972 there were 35 of those countries, including a number of the developing countries.

Table D — Countries operating ultra-short wave transmitters having a total transmitting power of more than 30 KW, around 1960

Country	Number of ultra-short wave transmitters	Total transmitting power (in KW)
United States of America	817	12 637
Germany, Fed. Rep. of	155	3 775
United Kingdom	126	1 260
Austria	28	746
Yugoslavia	8	741
Finland	44	637
Sweden	35	595
Denmark	8	360
Netherlands	12	283
Canada	89	237
Italy	872	210
Germany, Eastern	22	143
Spain	9	59
Switzerland	43	48
Japan	5	41
Brazil	54	34

Table E — Countries operating ultra-short wave transmitters having a total transmitting power of more than 30 KW, around 1972

Country	Number of ultra-short wave transmitters	Total transmitting power (in KW)	Country	Number of ultr-short wave transmitters	Total transmitting power (in KW)
United States of America*	2 901	—	Italy	1 835	249.59
Germany, Fed. Rep. of	271	7 412	Greece	37	244
United Kingdom	266	4 704.05	Spain	213	240
Canada	415	4 113	Turkey	3	200.25
Austria	252	2 398.39	Japan	451	154.4
Yugoslavia	154	2 290	Czechoslovakia	123	144
Finland	83	1 983	France	239	140
Norway	307	1 512	Hungary	18	129
Mexico	82	1 134.13	Iran	17	114
Belgium	32	876.5	Israel	18	90
Netherlands	23	858	Bulgaria	15	90
Ireland	12	847	Thailand	76	83.20
Monaco	2	600	Brazil	35	72.9
Portugal	85	517.28	Philippines	14	49.25
Denmark	13	410.41	Singapore	4	40.0
Switzerland	196	361	Romania	62	35
German Democratic Rep.	43	310.5	Peru	10	33.45

* The total transmitting power is unavailable. However the U.S.A. should occupy first place in this ranking by transmitting power; in 1960, U.S.A. had 817 ultra-short transmitting with total transmitting power of 12 637 KW. In 1960 Sweden had 165 ultra-short transmitters with total transmitting power of 5 594 KW. With 282 transmitters in 1972 she should occupy at least third place in this ranking.

Tables F and G show respectively the countries which had more than 100 sound broadcasting transmitters around 1960 and around 1973.

Table F shows the countries in which there were more than 100 sound broadcasting transmitters operating around 1960. The number of these countries has increased by 22 around 1973 (see Table G).

Table F — Countries with more than 100 sound broadcasting transmitters (circa 1960)

Country	Number of transmitters	Country	Number of transmitters
United States of America	4 281	Colombia	281
Italy	1 003	Germany, Fed. Rep. of	236
Brazil	924	United Kingdom	222
USSR	407	Cuba	190
Mexico	377	Australia	185
Canada	363	Ecuador	135
Japan	358	Philippines	127
Spain	318	Austria	120

Table G — Countries with more than 100 sound broadcasting transmitters (circa 1973)

Country	Number of transmitters	Country	Number of transmitters
Unites States of America	7 785	Sweden	282
		Columbia	244
USSR	3 034	Venezuela	235
Italy	1 964	Chile	229
Brazil	999	Australia	219
Japan	911	Switzerland	211
Canada	811	Cuba	184
Mexico	668	Portugal	180
Indonesia	586	Korea, Rep. of	172
Yugoslavia	487	Argentina	163
Spain	406	Honduras	151
Austria	399	India	146
United Kingdom	397	Nicaragua	137
Thailand	361	Bolivia	133
Germany, Fed. Rep. of	346	Czechoslovakia	123
		Panama	117
Norway	343	Dominica	110
Ecuador	336	German, Dem. Rep. of	106
Philippines	327		
Peru	304	Uruguay	101
France	290		

3. SOUND BROADCASTING (RADIO) RECEIVERS

Statistics on radio listening facilities, and on the number of receivers, in any given country can only be accurate if they are obtained by listener survey methods (censuses or annual surveys). However, such statistics are compiled only in a limited number of countries. For the majority of countries, statistics on radio listening facilities can only be obtained through secondary sources. The statistics relate to (a) the number of licences issued (or, in some cases, number of declarations made) in countries where the owners of radio receivers are legally required to pay a licence fee or to declare possession of receivers; (b) the number of subcribers to wired broadcasting systems where such systems are in use.

Statistics which have been available on radio receivers do not distinguish between the various existing types of these receivers, from the light portable transistor sets, or even merely loudspeakers connected to a wired broadcasting network or variations on that theme, to sophisticated tuners in separate units or combined with various units of High Fidelity reproducing equipment, tape recorders, the so-called music centres, etc. Moreover such statistics rarely indicate the location of such receivers, whether they are installed in private homes, in automobiles or in public places, whether they are portable sets, etc. Further, the statistics do not differentiate between the sets equipped for receiving very high or ultra-high frequencies. The Unesco Recommendation concerning the international standardization of statistics on radio and television has provision for the collection of data on radio receivers differentiated according to whether they are equipped with amplitude modulation (AM) only, or are also equipped for frequency modulation (FM). If statistics are ever obtained to show that distinction they would become available hopefully through the Unesco survey on Radio and Television Statistics being presently carried out (1978). Data on radio receivers given in the tables refer either to the number of licences issued and, in some cases, the number of sets declared (L), or to the estimated number of receivers in use (E). In many countries, a licence may cover the ownership or use of more than one radio receiver.* It is for this reason among others that the figures should be treated with reserve. Furthermore, estimates of the number of receivers in use vary widely in reliability. With due regard to the difficulty of assessing the degree of reliability of the statistics available and the lack of information for a number of countries, approximate estimates of the total number of radio receivers for continents and the world, for the years 1960, 1970 and 1976, are given in Tables H to I. It is seen from Table I that North America and Europe

---

* It is estimated that for those countries, when the number of licences is given, the corresponding number of radio receivers is between two and three times that number. Examples are Sweden, Austria, Netherlands, Denmark, etc.

Table H — Distribution of countries according to the number of radio receivers per 1,000 inhabitants, by continents (circa 1960, 1970 and 1976)

Continent	Year	Total number of countries	Number of countries with number of receivers by thousand, as indicated below				
			Up to 10 receivers	11-50	51-100	101-200	More than 200
Africa	circa 1960	50	30	15	5	—	—
	1970	53	7	25	12	8	1
	1976	53	2	23	12	12	4
America, North	circa 1960	22	1	8	6	5	2
	1970	30	—	3	6	6	15
	1976	30	—	3	6	1	20
America, South	circa 1960	12	—	7	3	2	—
	1970	13	—	—	3	6	4
	1976	13	—	—	3	4	6
Asia (excluding USSR and China)	circa 1960	38	11	15	9	3	—
	1970	37	4	12	5	9	7
	1976	37	3	12	6	6	10
Europe (including USSR)	circa 1960	28	—	1	4	6	17
	1970	34	—	—	1	6	27
	1976	34	—	—	1	2	31
Oceania	circa 1960	9	2	2	1	2	2
	1970	17	—	—	4	5	8
	1976	17	—	—	1	5	11
Totals	1960	159	44	42	32	19	22
	1970	184	11	40	31	40	62
	1976	184	5	38	29	30	82

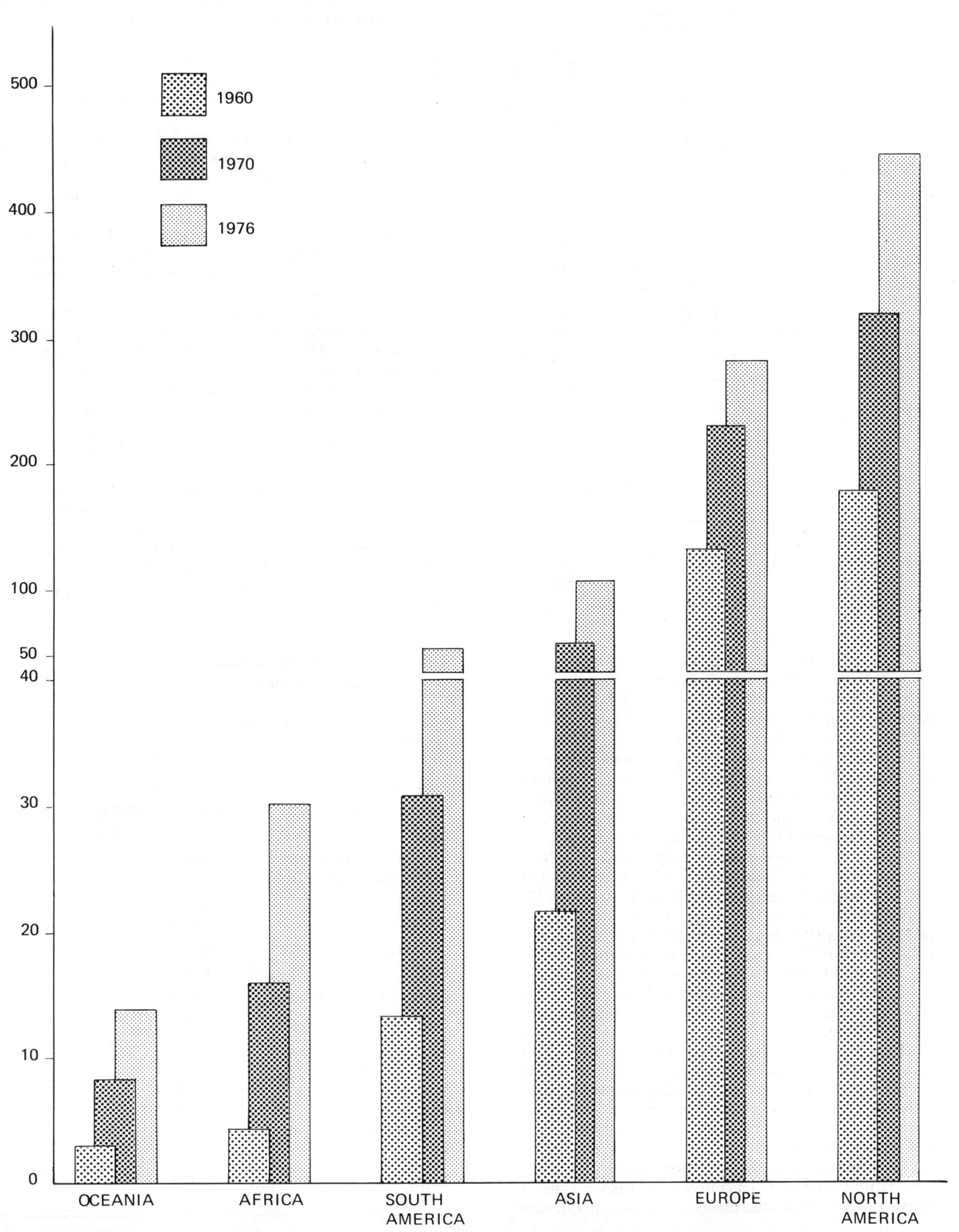

Table I — Estimated number of radio receivers in use and of receivers per 1,000 inhabitants, by continents (circa 1960, 1970 and 1976)

Continent	Year	Total number (million)	Percent of world total	Number of receivers per 1,000 inhabitants
Africa	circa 1960	4	1.1	15
	1970	16	2.4	45
	1976	30	3.1	72
America, North	circa 1960	184	50.7	688
	1970	326	48.5	1 027
	1976	454	47.7	1 310
America, South	circa 1960	14	3.8	93
	1970	31	4.6	164
	1976	58	6.0	259
Asia	circa 1960	22	6.1	23
	1970	58	8.6	48
	1976	113	11.8	81
Europe	circa 1960	136	37.5	213
	1970	233	34.7	332
	1976	284	30.0	387
Oceania	circa 1960	3	.8	184
	1970	8	1.2	428
	1976	14	1.4	632
World total	circa 1960	363		122
	1970	672		241
	1976	953		305

held in 1960 over 88% of the total number of receivers in the world. That figure has come down to 78% in 1976. South America, Asia and Oceania have each doubled the percentage they held in that span of some 15 years. Africa has trebled its share from just over 1% in 1960 to 3% in 1976. The disparities between countries remain very wide, just as probably those within individual countries themselves.

Chart 2 illustrates the increase in numbers of receivers over the period. From 1960 to 1970 there has been nearly a four-fold increase for receivers held by Africa, and a seven-fold increase for the period 1960 to 1976. For North America the increase from 1960 to 1970 has been around 77% and for the period 1970 to 1976 the increase was 39%. South America has registered an increase of 130% for the period 1960 to 1970 and another of 82% for the period running from 1970 to 1976. Asia had an increase of 170% for the period 1960 to 1970 and one of 91% from 1970 to 1976. For Europe the increase during the first period was 70% and for the second was 22% only. For that second period (re 1970 to 1976) the increase for Europe has been much lower than the other well-endowed continent - North America - which has registered an increase of 39%. Despite the higher increase for the other continents, the gap with North America and Europe, where the big majority of developed countries are located, is closing only slightly. The percentages held by the continents for circa 1960, 1970 and 1976 are shown on the "pie-charts" of Chart 3.

Relative figures on number of sets per 1,000 population, as exact indicators of accessibility of broadcasting services may be misleading. Beside the diversity of methods used for obtaining estimates on which the rates are based, various factors can in fact make for substantial differences in the actual utilization of radio receivers in different areas. For instance a household in developed countries may hold more than one receiver, which consequently reduces in these cases the accessibility factor these unweighted rates are purported to represent. On the other hand in countries where collective listening on an organized basis or otherwise is developed to a certain extent (e.g. India, Egypt) these rates should be inflated to reflect a more correct accessibility factor. But it is accepted that, within the limits imposed by these reservations, the number of receivers per thousand inhabitants is a valid indicator for a rough measurement of accessibility to radio receiving facilities.

Every country in the world has radio receivers, but vast areas are still inadequately equipped. Table 2 in the Annex presents information on the availability of radio receivers per 1,000 inhabitants for a good number of countries, which altogether nearly cover the whole world. In 1950, half of the countries considered in a previous survey had not more than 10 receivers per 1,000 inhabitants. Around 1960, 28 per cent of the countries (two-thirds of which were in Africa) were still in this category. In 1970, of the 184 countries considered, under 6% of the countries (two-thirds of which were in Africa) were in this category representing 11 countries. In 1976, that number had dwindled to five, two in Africa and three in Asia.

In 1976, the percentage of countries with more than 200 receivers per 1,000 inhabitants was approximately 45%, having climbed from barely 7% in 1960. Table I presents in summary form estimates of the number of radio receivers in the world. Because of the relative inadequacy of available statistics the data should be regarded as rough estimates only.

Table J — Countries having more than 2,5000,000 radio receivers in 1960

Country	Total number of radio receivers (in thousands)
United States of America	168 500 (1959)
USSR	40 818 (1959)
Germany, Federal Rep. of	16 441
United Kingdom	15 163
Japan	12 410
France	10 981
Canada	8 050
Italy	8 005
German, Democratic Rep.	5 574
Poland	5 268
Brazil	4 570*
Czechoslovakia	3 530
Argentina	3 500
Mexico	3 300
Netherlands	3 126
Sweden	2 744
Spain	2 717

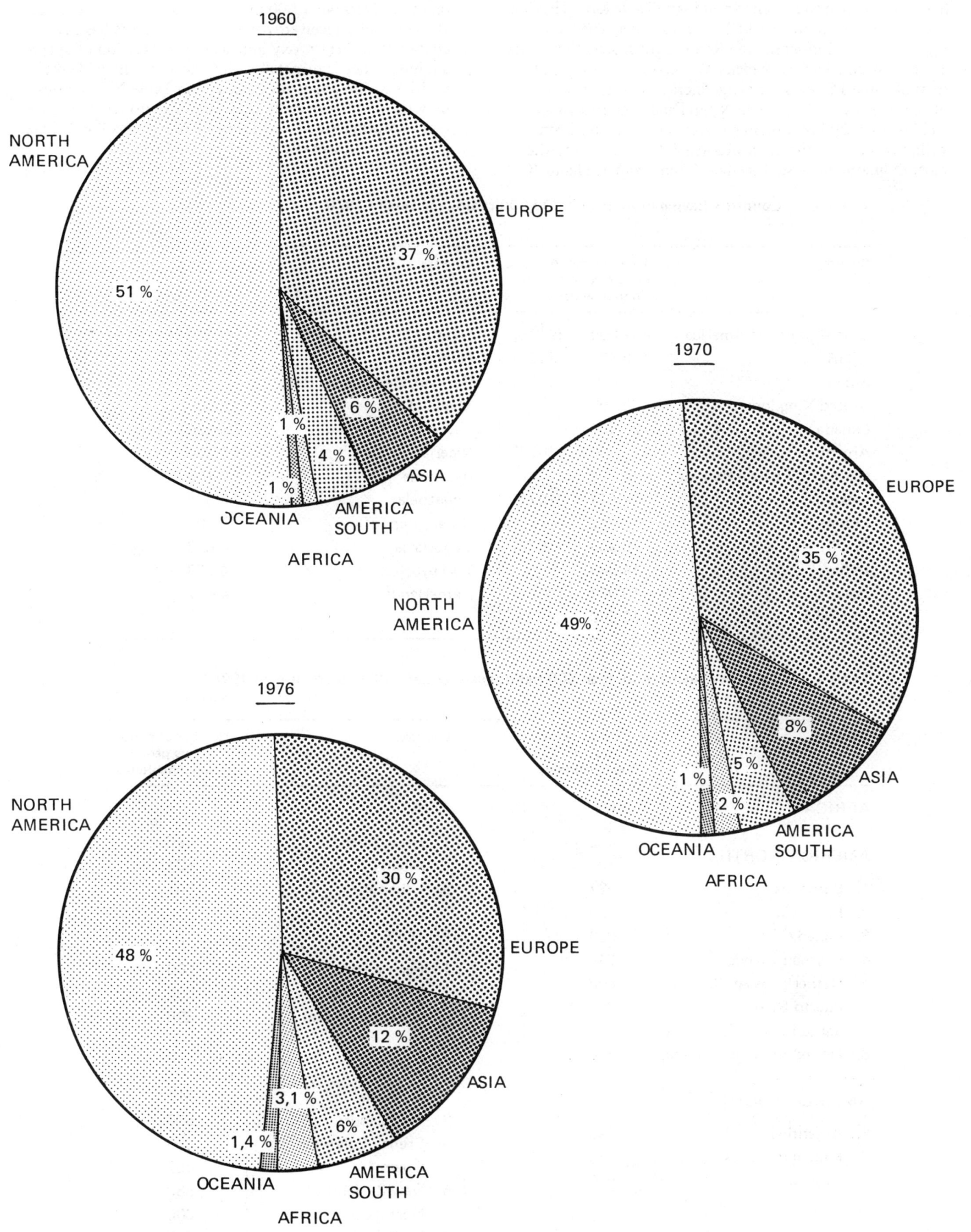

In 1960, 17 countries had more than 2½ million radio receivers (Table J). In 1976, with the exception of Czechoslovakia and Sweden with 3.9 and 3.2 million radio receivers respectively, all these countries form now a group having more than four million radio sets (Table K) and having been joined by countries like India, Australia, Thailand, Egypt, Nigeria, Indonesia, the Republic of Korea, Venezuela, Yugoslavia and Turkey, which have recorded within that span of some 15 years very large increases in the number of radio receivers they hold. Nigeria and Thailand which had less than 200,000 radio receivers in 1960 have been, within this group, the countries which have registered the most dramatic increase, Nigeria, 35 times and Thailand 30. Then come India with seven times, the Republic of Korea over six times, Australia with five times, Thailand and Egypt over three-and-a-half times.

Tables L and M group countries according to ranges of radio receivers per 1,000 inhabitants in 1976. The range 200-500 radio receivers per 1,000 inhabitants has been chosen as a rough proxy indicator of possession of at least a radio set per family, taking into account the wide disparities within countries themselves. Table N illustrates how the number of radio receivers by continents has progressed during the period 1960-1976. Graphs I and II are graphical representations of the same facts.

Table K — Countries having more than 4,000,000 radio receivers in 1976

Country	Total number of radio receivers (in thousands)		Country	Total number of radio receivers (in thousands)
United States of America	402 000	(9175)	Spain	9 300
USSR	122 477	(9175)	Poland	8 228
Japan	59 650		German, Democratic Rep.	6 167
United Kingdom	39 500		Thailand	5 500
Canada	23 400		Egypt	5 250
Argentina	21 000	(1974)	Nigeria	5 100
Germany, Federal Rep. of	20 224		Indonesia	5 100
Mexico	17 514	(1974)	Venezuela	5 034
France	17 442		Korea, Rep. of	5 000
Brazil	16 980	(1975)	Yugoslavia	4 526
India	14 848		Turkey	4 228
Italy	13 024		Netherlands	4 017
Australia	10 500			

Table L — Countries having more than 500 radio receivers per 1,000 inhabitants in 1976

Country	Number of radio receivers per 1,000 inhabitants	Country	Number of radio receivers per 1,000 inhabitants
AFRICA	Nil	ASIA	
		1. Hong Kong	586
AMERICA, NORTH		2. Japan	531
1. Barbados	527	3. Lebanon	541
2. Bermuda	895		
3. Canada	999	EUROPE	
4. Cayman Islands	546	1. Faeroe Islands	600
5. Netherlands Antilles	608	2. Luxembourg	598
6. Puerto Rico	602	3. United Kingdom	698
7. Santa Lucia	746		
8. United States of America	1 870	OCEANIA	
		1. Australia	747
AMERICA, SOUTH		2. Fiji Islands	510
1. Argentina	895	3. French Polynesia	960
2. Falkland Islands	550	4. Guam	853
3. Uruguay	510	5. New Zealand	883
		6. Norfolk Islands	600
		7. Pacific Islands	617

Table M — Countries having between 200 - 500 radio receivers per 1,000 inhabitants in 1976

Country	Number of radio receivers per 1,000 inhabitants	Country	Number of radio receivers per 1,000 inhabitants
AFRICA		**EUROPE**	
1. Equatorial Guinea	254	1. Andorra	287
2. Mauritius	219	2. Austria	290
3. Sao Tomé and Principe	247	3. Belgium	409
4. Seychelles	284	4. Bulgaria	311
5. Western Sahara	214	5. Czechoslovakia	265
		6. Denmark	368
AMERICA, NORTH		7. Finalnd	468
1. Antigua	220	8. France	327
2. Bahama	462	9. German Democratic Rep.	358
3. Belize	487	10. Germany, Federal Rep.	328
4. Cuba	217	11. Gilbraltar	367
5. Dominica	224	12. Greece	307
6. El Salvador	331	13. Hungary	241
7. Greenland	237	14. Iceland	293
8. Grenade	229	15. Ireland	300
9. Jamaica	270	16. Italy	236
10. Mexico	319	17. Liechstenstein	364
11. St Pierre and Miquelon	440	18. Monaco	313
12. Trinidad and Tobago	265	19. Netherlands	294
13. Turks and Caicos	500	20. Norway	320
		21. Poland	241
AMERICA, SOUTH		22. San Marino	300
1. Ecuador	301	23. Spain	260
2. Guyana	341	24. Sweden	384
3. Surinam	259	25. Switzerland	321
4. Venezuela	400	26. Yugoslavia	211
		27. USSR	492
ASIA		**OCEANIA**	
1. Kuwait	435	1. Cook Islands	280
2. Macau	254	2. Nauru	450
3. Qatar	421	3. New Caledonia	462
4. United Arab Emirates	241	4. Western Samoa	295

Table N — Total number of radio receivers for the years 1960-1976, by continents (in millions)

Continents	1960	1961	1962	1963	1964	1965	1966	1967	1968	1969	1970	1971	1972	1973	1974	1975	1976
Africa	4	5	6	7	8	10	12	13	14	15	16	17	19	23	27	28	30
America, North	184	193	202	211	246	265	288	312	317	322	326	374	395	411	447	450	454
America, South	14	16	18	19	20	21	21	23	24	25	31	34	44	48	51	55	58
Asia	22	29	32	35	37	42	45	48	52	55	58	61	64	90	94	108	113
Europe	136	152	167	174	179	184	190	197	203	210	233	240	250	259	268	277	284
Oceania	3	3	3	3	3	3	3	4	4	6	8	9	11	11	12	13	14
TOTAL	363	398	428	449	493	525	559	597	614	633	672	735	783	842	899	931	953

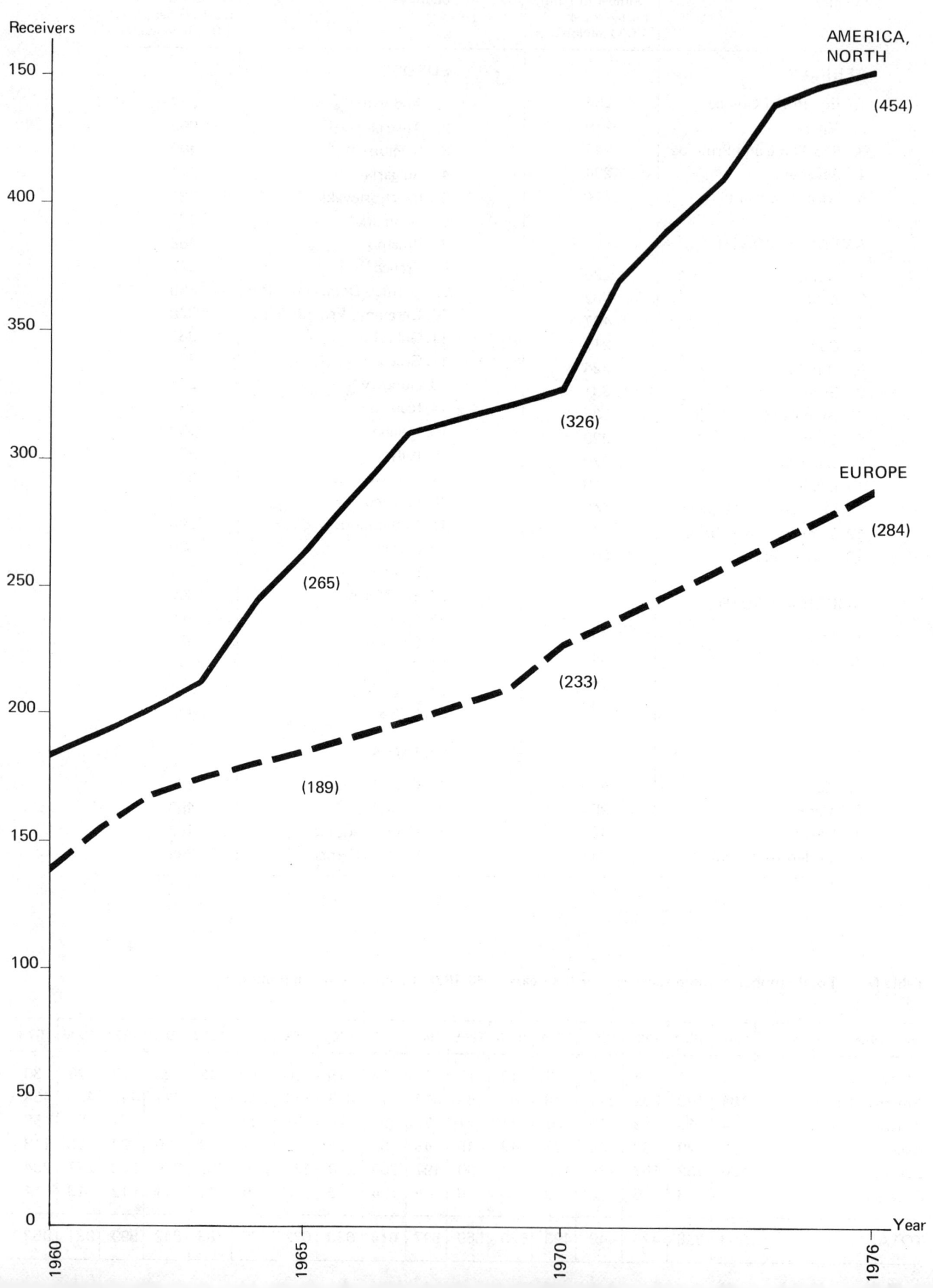

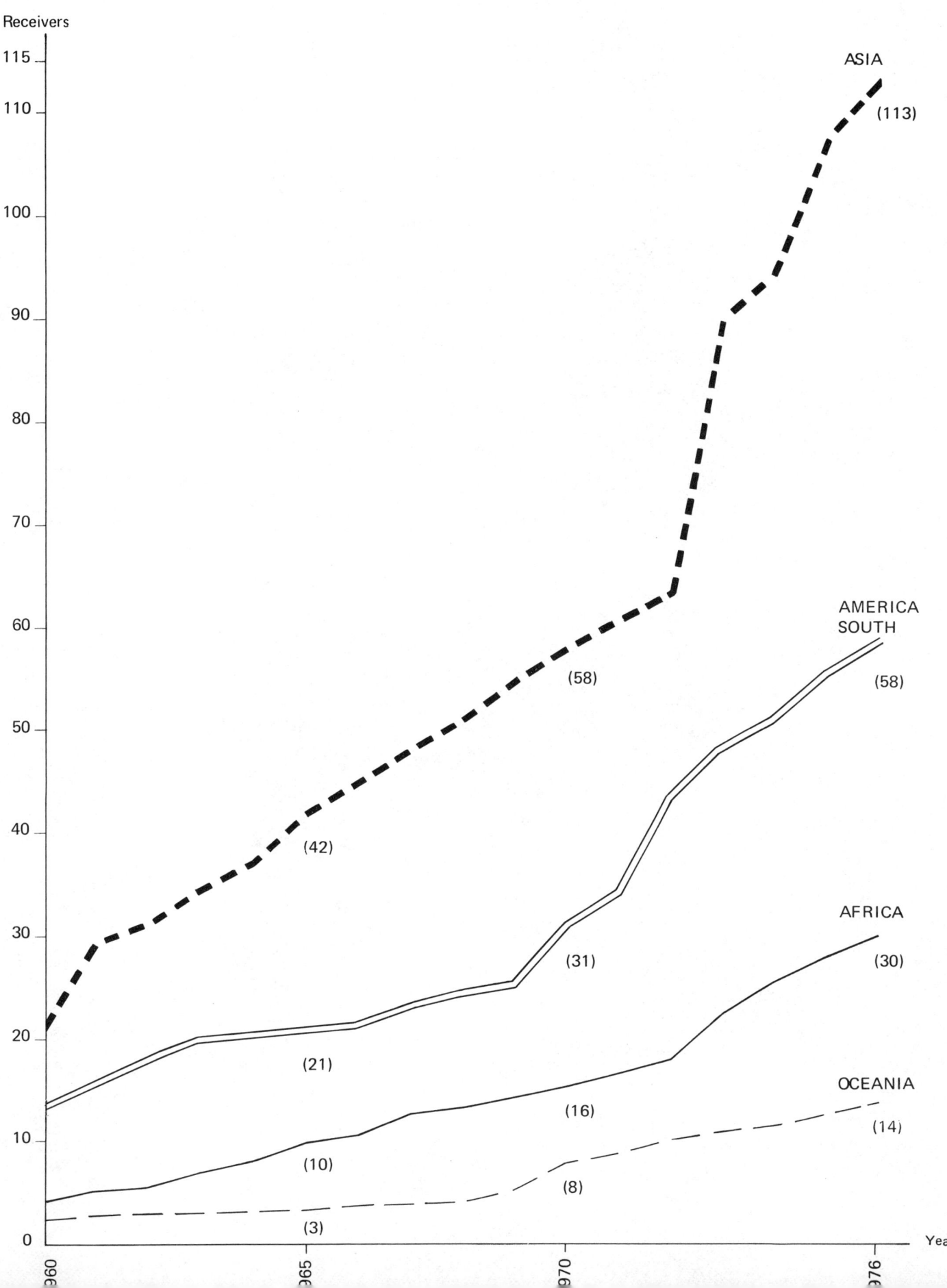

II. Television broadcasting

4. ORGANIZATION

The organization of television in the different countries of the world in general has followed a similar path as for sound broadcasting services. These are mainly organized by governmental or public service institutions or by private enterprises. As private enterprises there should be the further distinction between those which are solely motivated by public service concerns, and others which are mainly profit-oriented. All that is said on page 7 in this regard on sound broadcasting applies also to television broadcasting.

History

Television broadcasting has been expanding rapidly throughout the world during the last fifteen years or so. In 1936 only one country, the United Kingdom, was transmitting regular programmes. In 1950, the number was five; in 1955, 17; in 1960, 63 countries were making regular television broadcasts to the public. The distribution up to 1960 was as follows:

	Number of countries making regular TV broadcasts		
	1950	1953	1960
Africa	—	—	4
America, North	2	5	14
America, South	—	3	8
Asia (excl. USSR)	—	2	12
Europe (incl. USSR)	3	7	24
Oceania	—	—	2
World total	5	17	63

In 1960, six African countries (Algeria, Egypt, Morocco, Nigeria, Southern Rhodesia and Tunisia) had television. By 1962 they were seven, having been joined by Kenya. Since then there has been progressive increase, and in 1976 the number of African countries having television services stood at 31 (see Table 4).

In North America from 14 in 1960, the number of countries having television crept to 27 in 1976 (see Table 4).

In South America, there were eight countries with television in 1960. In 1976 there were 12, i.e. covering all the countries within this group with the exception of the Falkland Islands and Guyana (see Table 4).

In North America 14 countries of the group of 27 constituting that region had television services in 1960. In 1967, of that group, only Puerto Rico had no television. Antigua, Barbados, Guadeloupe, Martinique, Panama Canal Zone joined the "TV club" in 1965, St. Lucia and St. Pierre and Miquelon in 1967. The group was complete in 1970 (see Table 4).

In Asia, 13 countries had television in 1960. Indonesia, Israel, Singapore and Yemen inaugurated their television services in 1963; Malaysia and Pakistan in 1964, Jordan in 1966, the Viet-Nam Socialist Republic in 1969, Mongolia in 1970 and Brunei in 1975, thereby completing their group of 30 (see Table 4).

In Europe, 26 countries had television in 1960. Monaco started television services in 1961, Gibraltar in 1962, Albania in 1964, Andorra in 1965, Greece in 1966, Iceland in 1967 thereby completing the European group of 32, including the USSR (see Table 4).

In Oceania two countries had television in 1960, Australia and New Zealand. Guam and New Caledonia joined them in 1965, French Polynesia in 1966 and American Samoa in 1968, when the group of six countries for the region was complete (see Table 4).

5. TELEVISION BROADCASTING TRANSMITTERS

In 1953 only three of the countries with television services had more than 10 transmitters: the United States 351; the Federal Republic of Germany 13 and Canada 12.

Around 1960, fourteen countries had each more than 20 television transmitters, including seven countries who had over 90. They were: the United States, 579; Italy 425 (of which 397 were auxiliary transmitters); the Federal Republic of Germany, 325 (280 auxiliary transmitters); the USSR, 169 (76 auxiliary transmitters); Japan, 127 (12 auxiliary transmitters); Canada 98, (24 auxiliary transmitters); France, 91 (59 auxiliary transmitters).

Around 1960, there were 19 countries operating one transmitter only on a regular basis; eight of them were in Latin America, six in Asia, three in Europe (Bulgaria, Luxembourg and Monaco), one in Africa (the former Federation of Rhodesia and Nyasaland) and one in Oceania (New Zealand).

Since 1960, the spread of television has been very rapid, especially in the newly independent countries of Africa. It is true that most of the television services provided by newcomers into the "club" do not have full national coverage. Table 4 in the Annex shows that the number of African countries with television services has grown from six in

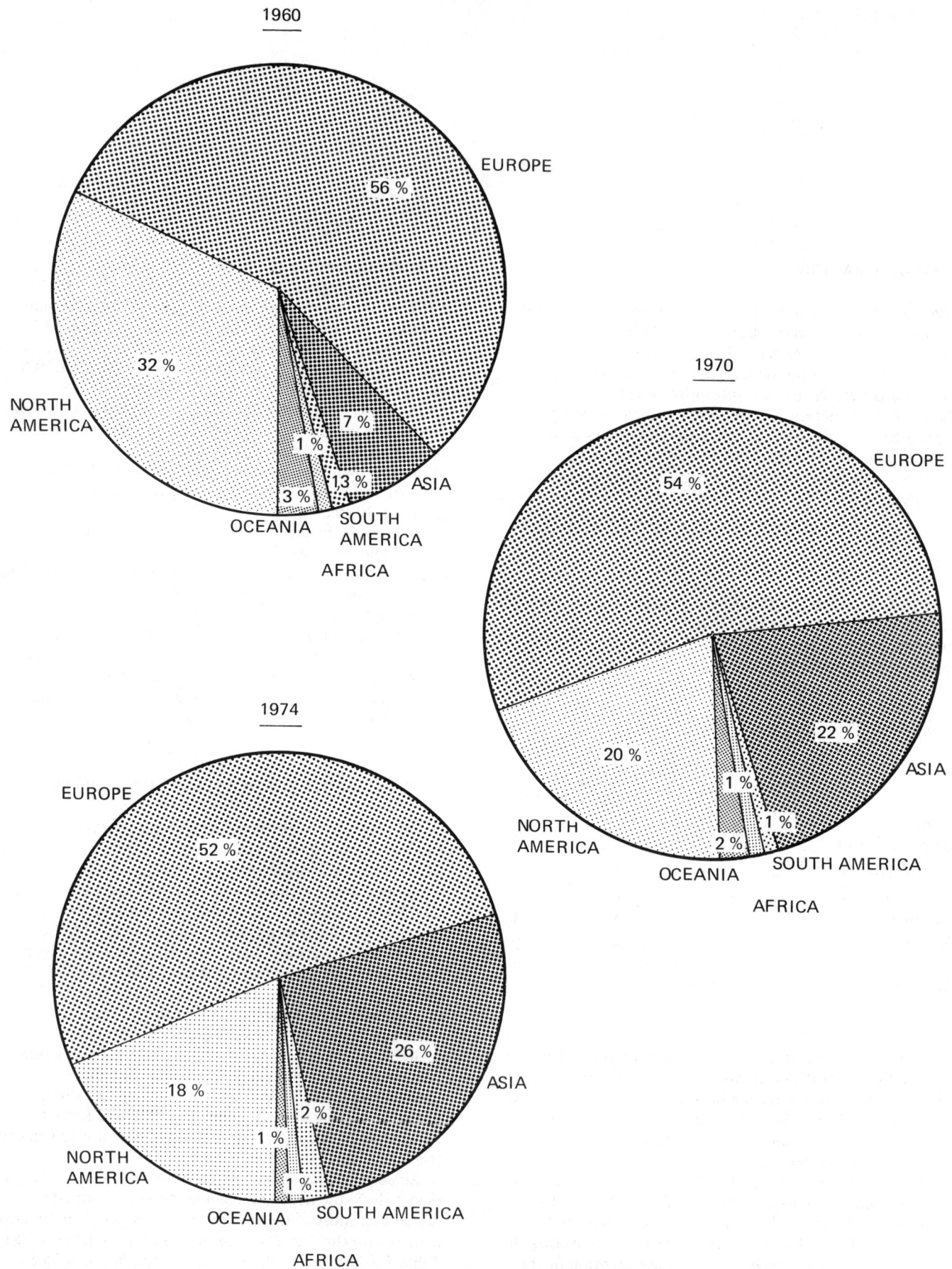

Chart 4 — Distribution of number of television broadcasting transmitters by continents (circa 1960, 1970, 1974)

1960 to at least 32 around 1972. Data in Table 3 do not refer to the same date. Data for every single year are unavailable. But the Table gives a rough picture of the transmitters in regular use in these countries over a period stretching from the end of the last decade to the middle of the present one. International comparability based on the number of transmitters is not a valid exercise especially as the breakdown into principal and auxiliary transmitters and the power of the transmitters themselves are not given. However the growth in the number of transmitters in a region is indicative of the importance taken by television in the region.

Table O — Estimated number of television transmitters operating on a regular basis, by continents (1960 and circa 1974)

Continent	1960		1974	
	Total	Auxiliary	Total	Auxiliary
Africa	22	(10)	242	(117)
America, North	731	(43)	4 595	(2 010)
America, South	81	(35)	463	(199)
Asia, (excl. USSR)	160	(26)	6 639	(6 086)
Europe (incl. USSR)	1 270	(900)	11 222	(9 711)
Oceania	17	—	367	(250)
World totals	2 281	(1 044)	25 464	(12 287)

The rapid growth since 1960 in the number of television transmitters is well illustrated by the above table, especially in Asia where the number of transmitters has increased by over 40 times. Japan held 127 of the 160 transmitters, shown against Asia in 1960. In 1974 of the estimates of 6,639 transmitters shown as going to Asia, 6,117 went to Japan. In North America, where a host of "small" countries are grouped with the U.S.A. and Canada, the U.S.A. has like Japan in Asia the lion's share: 3,695 of the total of 4,595 for the region. In Europe, France shoots far ahead of the other countries with over 3,000 transmitters followed by USSR with some 1,749 transmitters, by Italy 1,200 and by Germany, Federal Republic with 1,153. In South America, Argentina and Brazil have together nearly 50% of the transmitters held by that group of 13 countries. In Oceania, Australia (198) and New Zealand (144) hold together over 90% of the transmitters of the group.

6. TELEVISION RECEIVERS

Statistics on television receivers, like those on radio receivers, are derived from secondary sources and refer either to the number of licences issued (or in a few cases of declarations made) or to the estimated number of receivers in use. This fact should be borne in mind when trying to make any kind of comparison between countries.

In the Annex, Table 4 gives data on the number of television receivers per 1,000 inhabitants for the years 1960-1976 for all those countries for which time series are available, which comprise the great majority of the countries of the world which have television services. When comparing the data, on top of the fact that secondary sources have been tapped and that one has had recourse more often than not to estimates which vary with reality,

Table P — Distribution of countries according to the number of television receivers per 1,000 inhabitants, by continents (1960-1976)

Continent	Year	Total number of countries	Number of countries with the following numbers of receivers per 1,000 inhabitants						
			at least one	2 to 10	11 to 20	21 to 50	51 to 100	101 to 200	more than 200
Africa	1960	5	3	2	—	—	—	—	—
	1976	31	11	9	3	6	2	—	—
America, North	1960	14	2	6	3	—	1	—	2
	1976	27	—	3	2	4	6	4	8
America, South	1960	8	2	2	2	2	—	—	—
	1976	12	—	1	1	2	5	3	—
Asia	1960	17	7	9	—	—	1	—	—
	1976	30	2	5	4	6	4	7	2
Europe	1960	24	—	5	3	8	5	2	1
	1976	32	—	1	—	—	1	9	21
Oceania	1960	2	1	—	—	—	—	1	—
	1976	6	—	—	—	—	1	2	3
World totals	1960	70	15	24	8	10	7	3	3
	1976	138	13	19	10	18	19	25	34

one should take into account another factor, i.e. that in a large number of countries television sets are installed in cafes, bars, restaurants and other public places for public or communal viewing. For such countries, information based on number of receivers may not do justice to the real size of television audiences. However, for television as for radio, the number of sets per 1,000 inhabitants may give a rough indication of the availability of television receiving facilities.

The distribution of countries according to the number of television receivers per 1,000 inhabitants in 1960 and 1976 is shown in Table P.

In 1953, of the 19 countries which had television receivers, only four had more than 10 receivers per 1,000 inhabitants; in 1960 out of 70 countries, 31 had more than 10 receivers per 1,000 inhabitants, including 13 which had more than 50 receivers per 1,000 inhabitants. Television in Africa, Asia and Oceania was, in 1960, still in its beginnings. In these regions only two countries had more than 10 sets per 1,000 inhabitants: Australia (108) and Japan (64).

Tables P and Q illustrate the general improvement which has occurred since 1960 for all the world regions in this new media.

In 1976 out of 138 countries, 106 had more than 10 receivers per 1,000 inhabitants, and 78, i.e. more than half the number of countries, having more than 50 sets per 1,000 inhabitants.

Table Q — Estimated number of receivers in use and of receivers per 1,000 inhabitants, by continents (circa 1960, 1970 and 1976)

Continent	Year	Total number (thousands)	Number of receivers per 1,000 inhab.
Africa	circa 1960	122	0.4
	1970	1 206	3.4
	1976	2 757	6.8
America, North	circa 1960	60 782	228
	1970	96 541	302
	1976	142 700	412
America, South	circa 1960	2 111	14
	1970	12 571	68
	1976	20 300	89
Asia	circa 1960	7 064	7.5
Asia	1970	27 428	22
	1976	39 400	28
Europe	circa 1960	20 973	36
	1970	125 255	178
	1973	174 200	237
Oceania	circa 1960	1 126	70
	1970	3 480	200
	1976	5 733	259
World totals	circa 1960	92 178	
	1970	266 481	
	1976	385 090	

Table R — Countries with more than 1 million television receivers in 1960

Country	Number of receivers (in thousands)	Country	Number of receivers (in thousands)
United States of America	56 000	Italy	2 124
Un. Kingdom	11 076	France	1 902
Japan	5 990	Brazil	1 200
USSR	5 000	Australia	1 122
Germany, Fed. Rep. of	4 635	German Dem. Rep.	1 035
Canada	3 930	Sweden	1 030

Table S — Countries with more than 1 million television receivers in 1976

Country	Number of receivers (in thousands)	
United States of America	121 000	(1974)
USSR	55 181	(1975)
Japon	26 545	(1975)
Germany, Fed. Rep. of	19 226	(1975)
United Kingdom	17 729	
France	14 500	
Italy	12 377	
Brazil	10 525	
Canada	9 895	
Poland	6 820	
Spain	6 640	
German, Dem. Rep.	5 180	
Mexico	4 885	(1974)
Australia	4 785	
Argentina	4 500	(1975)
Czechoslovakia	3 793	
Netherlands	3 774	
Yugoslavia	3 463	
Sweden	2 988	
Romania	2 963	
Belgium	2 646	
Hungary	2 495	
Korea, Republic of	2 300	
Switzerland	1 809	
Austria	1 772	
Turkey	1 769	
Iran	1 720	
Finland	1 714	
Columbia	1 700	
Denmark	1 637	
Bulgaria	1 546	
Venezuela	1 431	
Greece	1 165	
Norway	1 087	

For Africa, Asia and Oceania, from two countries in 1960 which had over 10 sets per 1,000 inhabitants, the number has reached 40 in 1976.

The pie-charts on page 27 show how the share of North America in the world estimates of television receivers has dwindled from 66% to 36% from 1960 to 1970, due mainly to the great expansion registered by Europe. The percentage for Asia has remained fairly stable, 8% of the world estimates in 1960, and 10% in both 1970 and 1976. The percentage for South America has been 5% throughout the period 1970-1976. Europe's share has shown little change from 1970 to 1976: the drop from 47% to 45% being due for half to gains in North America, and half to gains in Africa and Oceania.

Table R presents data for the 12 countries with more than one million television receivers in 1960, and Table S for the 34 countries finding themselves in that category by 1976.

Table T lists countries which had more than 40 television receivers per 1,000 inhabitants in 1960. Tables U to V list countries according to arbitrarily set ranges of possession of television receivers per 1,000 inhabitants in 1976.

Table X gives the estimated number of television receivers by continents for the period 1960-1976. Graphs 3 and 4 illustrate the changes during that period.

Table T — Countries with more than 40 television receivers per 1,000 inhabitants in 1960

Country	Number of receivers per 1,000 inhabitants	Country	Number of receivers per 1,000 inhabitants
United States of America	310	Cuba	74
Canada	218	Netherlands	69
United Kingdom	211	Belgium	68
Sweden	137	Japan	64
Denmark	119	German, Dem. Rep.	60
Australia	108	Czechoslovakia	58
Germany, Fed. Rep. of	83	Italy	43
		Malta	43
		France	41

Table U — Countries between 40-100 television receivers per 1,000 inhabitants in 1976

Country	Number of receivers per 1,000 inhabitants	Country	Number of receivers per 1,000 inhabitants
French Polynesia	99	Korea, Rep. of	66
Brazil	93	Columbia	64
Surinam	88	Martinique	55
Mexico	85 (1974)	Jamaica	54
Cyprus	84	St Vincent	52 (1974)
Portugal	82	Ivory Coast	51
French Guinea	81	Iran	51
United Arab Emirates	79	Mauritius	45
Costa Rica	76	Jordan	45
Reunion	72	Malaysia	45
Chile	68	Turkey	43
Cuba	67	Guadeloupe	42
		Ecuador	41

Table V — Countries between 100 - 200 television receivers per 1,000 inhabitants in 1976

Country	Number of receivers per 1,000 inhabitants	Country	Number of receivers per 1,000 inhabitants
Poland	200	Lebanon	144
San Marino	200	Romania	139
Hong Kong	196	Israel	135
Barbados	194	Brunei	134
Malta	191	Andorra	130
Spain	186	Greece	130
Kuwait	179 (1974)	Singapore	129
Argentina	177 (1975)	Bahrain	120
Bulgaria	175	New Caledonia	117
American Samoa	173	Venezuela	114
Yugoslavia	161	Uruguay	113
Netherlands Antilles	146	Panama	108
		Trinidad and Tobago	108

Table W — Countries with more than 200 television receivers per 1,000 inhabitants in 1976

Country	Number of receivers per 1,000 inhabitants	Country	Number of receivers per 1,000 inhabitants
Guam	990	Netherlands	275
Monaco	667	Switzerland	275
U.S.A.	571	France	272
Virgin Islands (U.S.)	485	Norway	270
Panama Canal Zone	455	Belgium	268
Canada	428	New Zealand	264
Qatar	421	Czechoslovakia	256
St Pierre and Miquelon	400	Iceland	242
Bermuda	368	Japan	237
Finland	368	Gibraltar	236
Sweden	358	Hungary	236
Denmark	325	Austria	231
United Kingdom	313	Italy	224
Germany, Fed. Rep. of	312	USSR	216 (1975)
German, Dem. Rep.	301	Puerto Rico	215
Australia	279	Iraland	207
		Antigua	206

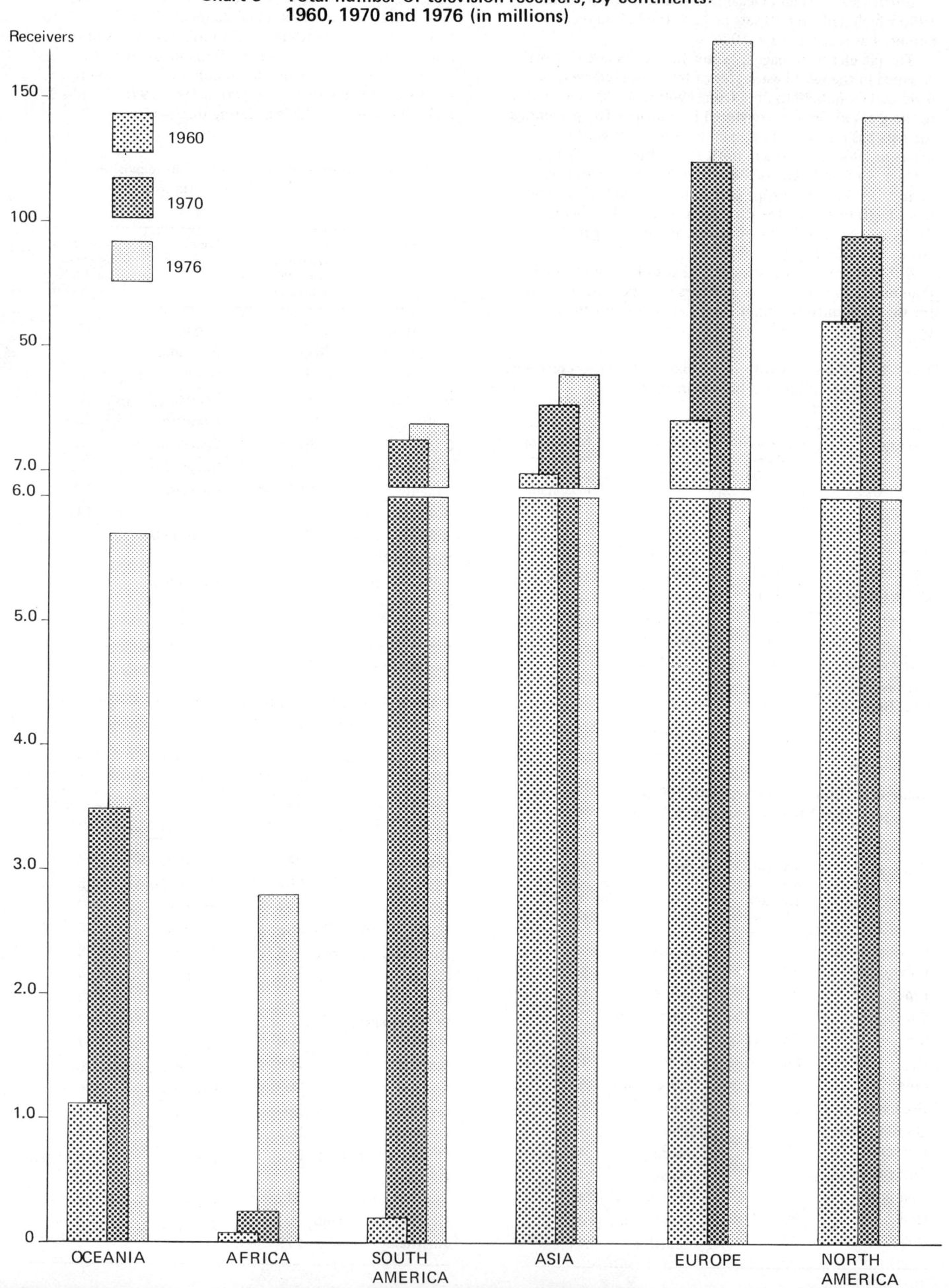

Chart 6 — Distribution of television receivers by continents
Estimated percentages 1960, 1970 and 1976

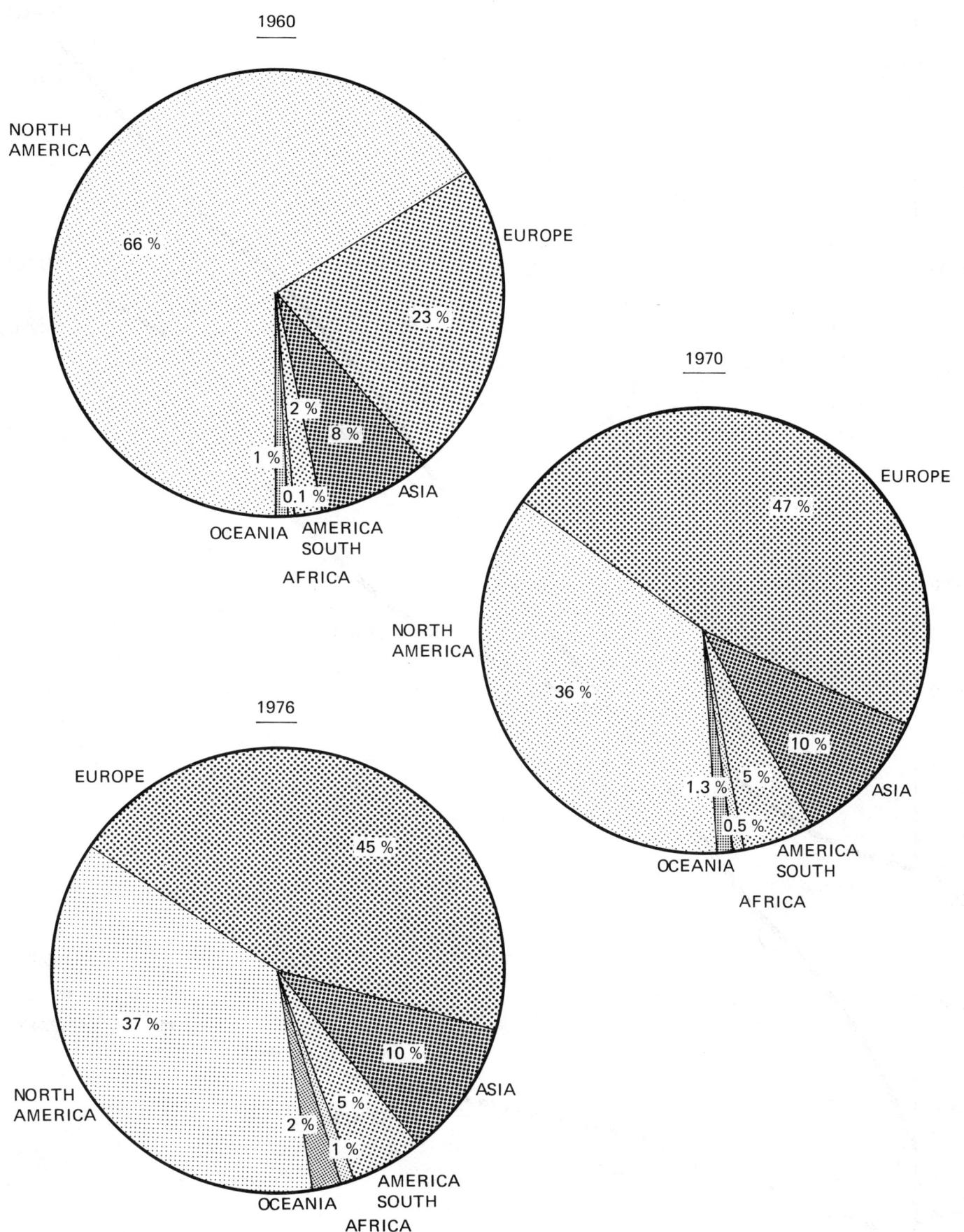

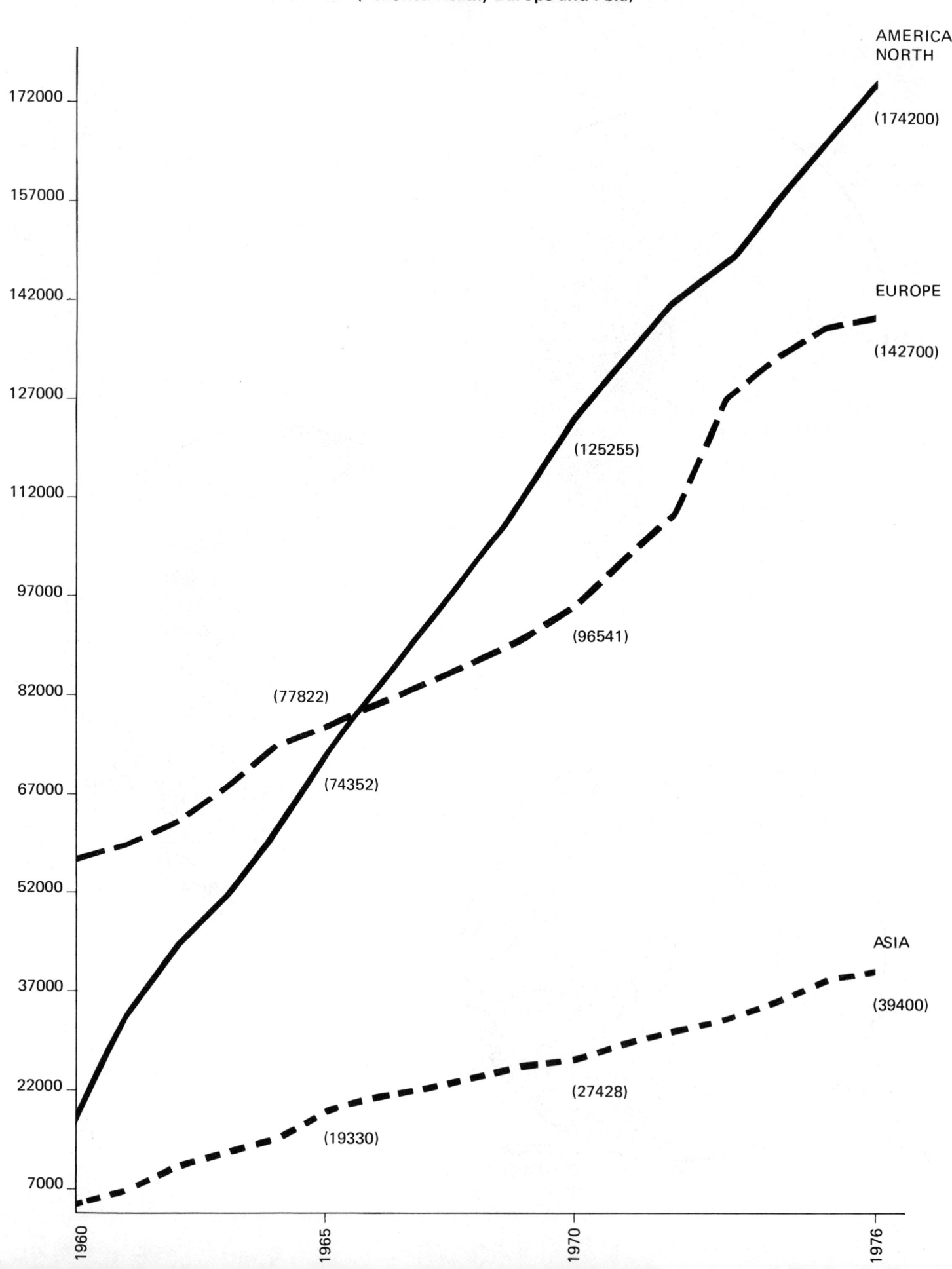

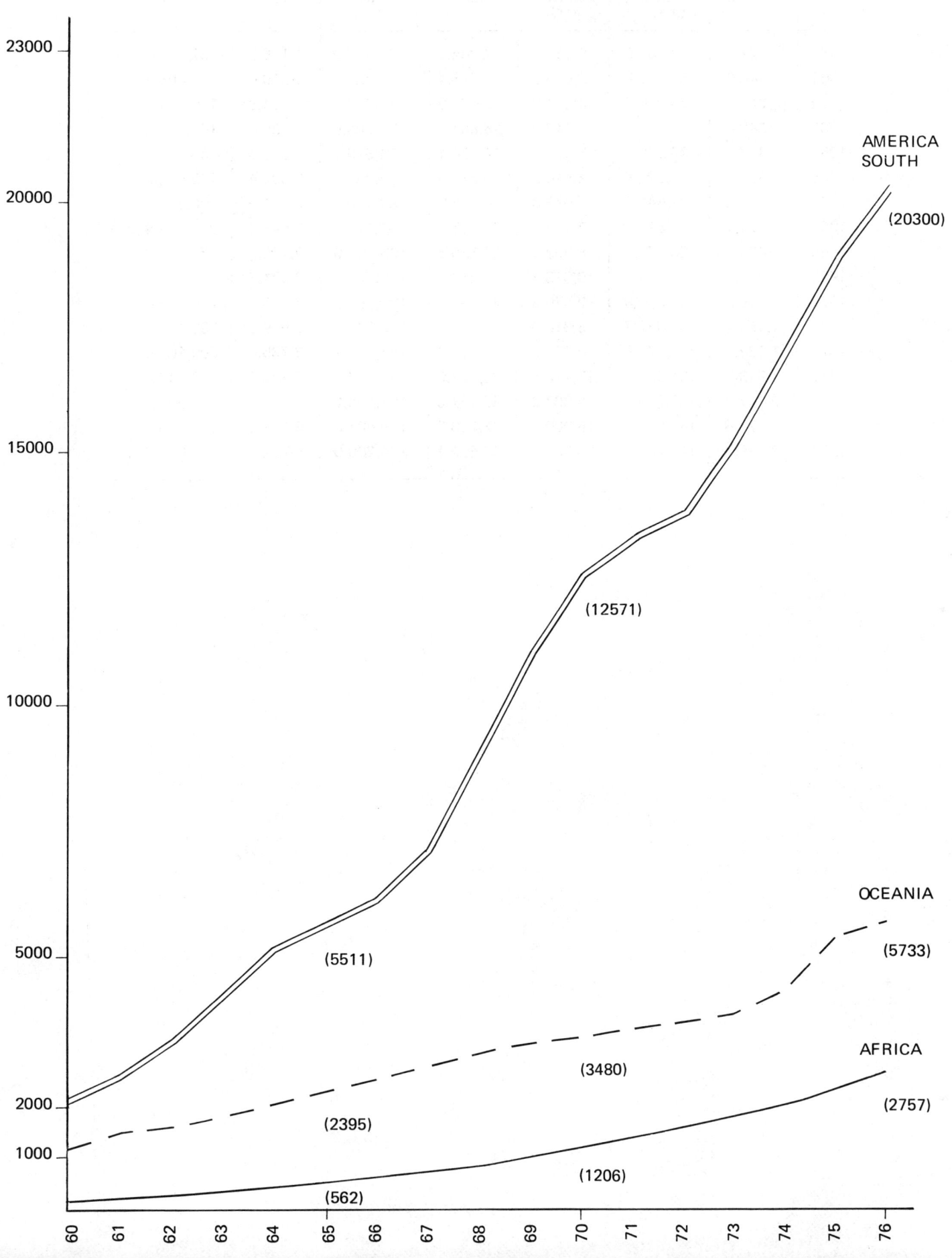

Graph 4 — Total number of television receivers (in thousands) (America-South, Oceania and Africa)

Table X — Estimated number of television receivers in use (1960-1976) (in thousands)

Year	AFRICA	AMERICA, NORTH	AMERICA, SOUTH	ASIA	EUROPE	OCEANIA	TOTAL
1960	122.4	60,781.6	2,110.5	7,064.0	20,973.0	1,125.5	92,177.5
1961	145.0	62,630.6	2,669.0	9,715.4	36,326.2	1,519.0	113,005.2
1962	244.2	65,020.5	3,244.0	13,021.9	46,022.8	1,634.0	129,187.4
1963	340.5	67,803.7	4,143.0	15,851.0	54,764.0	1,839.0	144,741.2
1964	457.0	74,045.2	5,123.0	17,736.1	64,546.2	2,076.0	163,983.5
1965	562.2	77,821.8	5,510.8	19,330.4	74,352.2	2,395.4	179,972.8
1966	661.8	82,541.1	6.023.0	20,485.5	84,465.9	2,631.5	196,808.8
1967	774.1	86,817.6	7,178.1	21,785.2	95,020.5	2,843.4	214,418.9
1968	859.5	88,972.6	8,932.9	23,185.5	105,748.0	3,176.5	230,875.0
1969	1,021.5	91,504.4	10,815.3	25,219.3	115583.9	3,321.7	247,466.1
1970	1,205.9	96,540.9	12,570.9	27,427.5	125,254.8	3,479.6	266,479.6
1971	1,455.4	105,632.7	13,310.5	29,020.2	135,081.0	3,609.5	288,109.3
1972	1,668.1	112,375.9	13,734.5	30,751.9	146,837.7	3,735.8	309,103.9
1973	1,943.5	131,399.3	15,173.5	32,707.0	151,977.9	3,842.1	337,043.3
1974	2,227.7	136,546.4	16,862.0	35,437.0	161,166.2	4,369.0	356,608.3
1975	2,473.5	141,000.0	18,909.6	37,723.3	169,081.0	5,481.0	374,668.4
1976	2,756.7	142,700.0	20,300.0	39,400.1	174,200.0	5,732.8	385,089.6

III. Radio and television broadcasting programmes

Statistics on radio and television broadcasting programmes have been difficult to present in an international tabulation mainly because of the lack of uniformity in national definitions and classifications.

As an illustration of the diversity of classification of these programmes, Tables 5 and 6 of the Annex give data around 1960 for 43 and 26 countries respectively, concerning the proportion of broadcast time (in percentage broadcasting hours) devoted to different categories of radio and television programmes, according to the original schemes of classification employed by the different countries. The information has come mainly from the replies to Unesco questionnaires.

In order to harmonize reporting of data on programme content, a classification of programmes was later adopted to include seven types as follows:
1. Information
2. Advertising
3. Education
4. Light entertainment
5. Arts, letters and sciences
6. Broadcasts for ethnic minorities
7. Broadcasts for special audiences.

The data published in the Unesco Yearbooks referred for the reporting countries either to broadcasting hours for a week that was considered typical or for an average week of a given year, and further distinguished between the time allocated to nationally produced and to foreign programmes. The Table giving information on domestic radio programmes in hours of broadcasting per week, according to the type of programme, was presented for the first time in the 1971 Unesco Yearbook. The seven main groups of programmes were established on their content basis and the data referred to a given year in the period 1968-1971.

Tables 7 and 8 of the Annex illustrate for radio and television the type of tables published on this topic in the Unesco Yearbook. (For the data on the other reporting countries, refer to the 1971 Unesco Yearbook.)

A few years later, eight main groups were used for classifying both radio and television programmes as follows:
1. Information
2. Education
3. Culture
4. Sciences
5. Entertainment
6. Programmes for special audiences
7. Advertising
8. Other programmes not elsewhere classified.

Tables 9 and 10 of the Annex illustrate the change to the new classification used when data were collected for 1974 or for the latest year available, and published in the 1974 Unesco Yearbook. (Data for the other reporting countries can be obtained from the 1974 Unesco Yearbook.)

Using the same classification the 1975 Unesco Yearbook has adopted a new presentation of the data, as illustrated by Tables 11 and 12 of the Annex, for radio and television programmes.

Tables 13 and 16 give programme content of radio and television broadcasting respectively for two or more of the years 1971-1975, according to eight categories, namely (1) Information, (2) Education, (3) Culture, (4) Sciences, (5) Entertainment, (6) Programmes for Special Audiences, (7) Advertising and (8) Other programmes not elsewhere classified. Even though replies to the questionnaire on radio broadcasting for 1971 have referred to the earlier classification into seven types, a breakdown and a regrouping of the data for 1971 have been effected for countries for which data are available, in order to obtain the classification into eight types and thereby lengthen the series in a number of cases, so as to give more substance for comparison.

Tables 14 and 17 show programme content for radio and television respectively for the latest year available, and distinguish nationally produced programmes from the rest.

Tables 15 and 18 illustrate for radio and television respectively programme content by type during a typical week in 1973.

It should be admitted that all these classifications which have attempted to obtain the best possible measure of international comparability have not been very successful, because of the nature of the problem itself. Definitions of the groups would vary widely within countries. Even with the best delineation of programmes it has been difficult to assign precisely a programme to its proper group. Further, overlapping occurs all the time between some of the groups. Not only definitions used as a basis for classification also differ, the same term often is employed to designate different categories of programmes. A few examples may be offered as an illustration. The term "educational" may be used to refer to programmes exclusively prepared by or on behalf of educational organizations, or to include not only programmes of purely didactic content, but also educational programmes in the broad sense of the term such as cultural talks, documentaries, and other programmes designed to further the popularization of knowledge. Similarly, the designation "programmes for children", normally applied to entertainment programmes for this type of audience, may sometimes include school broadcasts as well. Such difficulties are attendant upon any classification system, and the classification of radio and television programmes even within the same country does not claim any special privilege for avoiding these difficulties. When it comes to a classification to serve the purpose of international comparison, the problem is rendered more complex still. However, an effort has been made, within the provision of the Recommendation concerning the international standardization of statistics on radio and television, in order to streamline definitions and classifications so as to avoid some of the problems linked up with the reporting of data in this area. The classification which has been adopted in the Recommendation is as follows:

---

21. *Total annual broadcasting time (in hours) or broadcasting institutions referred to in paragraph 14(a).*

(a) By function, as percentage of total broadcasting time:
  (i) Informative programmes:
    News bulletins and news commentaries (including sports news);
    Other informative programmes.
  (ii) Educational, cultural and religious programmes:
    Educational programmes:
    - Educational programmes related to a specific curriculum (excluding those for rural development purposes);
    - Educational programmes for rural development purposes;
    - Other educational programmes.
    Cultural programmes:
    - Cultural programmes or activities;
    - Programmes about culture.
    Religious programmes.
  (iii) Advertisements
  (iv) Entertainment programmes and unclassified programmes
    Entertainment programmes:
    - Cinema films
    - Plays
    - Music
    - Sport programmes (but excluding sports news)
    - Other entertainment programmes
    Unclassified programmes

(b) By language of programme, as percentage of total broadcasting time
  (i) Official language(s)
  (ii) Dialects of the official language(s)
  (iii) Languages of ethnic minorities
  (iv) Other languages.

(c) By origin of programme, as percentage of total broadcasting time
  (i) National production
  (ii) Imported programmes
  (iii) International co-productions.

It is noticed that this new classification goes beyond former classifications which concentrated on "function" only, to include classification by language and origin of programme. The survey which is at present under way will alone provide the answer to the question whether the new classification will have proved more useful in supplying more significant data on these programmes while achieving a sounder basis for international reporting and comparison. A publication providing an evaluation of that first survey based on the Recommendation of 1976 is envisaged.

Annex

For tables 1 to 18 the following symbols are used:
- — Magnitude nil
- ---- Data not available
- * Estimated data

Table 1 — Number of sound broadcasting transmitters
Number of countries and territories presented in this table: 174
LMW = long and medium wave; SW = short wave; USW = ultra short wave

COUNTRY	CIRCA 1965				CIRCA 1970				CIRCA 1974			
	Total	LMW	SW	USW	Total	LMW	SW	USW	Total	LMW	SW	USW
AFRICA												
Algeria	20	15	5	-	25	20	5	-	25	...	...	...
Angola	50	...	...	...	48	16	32	-	19	...	...	...
Benin	4	1	3	-	4	2	2	-	4	2	2	-
Botswana	...	...	...	...	4	1	2	1	4	1	2	1
Burundi	3	1	2	-	6	2	4	-	7	2	4	1
Cape Verde Islands	3	-	3	-	4	-	4	-	4	...	...	...
Central African Rep.	3	1	2	-	4	2	2	-	...	...	...	...
Chad	3	1	2	-	3	1	2	-	6	2	3	1
Comoro Islands	1	-	1	-	2	-	1	1	3	1	1	1
Congo	4	2	2	-	4	2	2	-	10	2	5	3
Djibouti	3	1	2	-	3	2	1	-	4	2	1	1
Egypt	29	15	14	-	42	26	16	-	42	26	16	-
Ethiopia	6	-	6	-	8	4	4	-	5	3	2	-
Gabon	3	1	2	-	8	...	...	...	10	6	4	-
Gambia	1	-	1	-	2	...	...	...	4	2	1	1
Ghana	16	-	15	1	17	-	16	1	10	-	6	4
Guinea	...	...	...	...	3	...	...	...	5	1	4	...
Ivory Coast	8	6	2	-	12	...	...	...	17	...	...	...
Kenya	...	...	...	...	12	...	...	...	18	6	11	1
Lesotho	...	...	...	...	1	...	...	...	...	...	...	...
Liberia	9	5	4	-	...	...	...	...	15	6	9	-
Libyan Arab Jamahiriya	...	...	...	...	8	...	...	...	12	8	4	-
Madagascar	6	2	4	-	9	3	6	-	16	9	7	-
Malawi	4	3	1	-	15	7	3	5	15	8	3	4
Mali	8	4	4	-	14	4	10	-	14	4	10	-
Mauritania	6	1	5	-	6	...	...	...	4	2	2	-
Mauritius	2	1	1	-	3	2	1	-	3	2	1	-
Morocco	35	25	4	6	35	22	7	6	33	26	3	4
Mozambique	39	14	24	1	46	...	...	...	36	15	19	2
Namibia	...	...	...	...	2	...	...	...	4	...	...	...
Niger	8	5	3	-	9	5	4	-	13	10	3	-
Nigeria	27	19	7	1	36	17	15	4	46	25	21	-
Portuguese Guinea	...	...	...	...	...	...	...	...	2	1	1	-
Reunion	5	2	3	-	5	2	3	-	4	2	2	-
Rhodesia	...	...	...	...	...	...	...	...	22	12	10	-
Rwanda	1	-	1	-	5	4	1	-	5	4		
St. Helena									1	1		
Sao Tomé e Principe	3	1	2	-	2	1	1	-	4	...		
Senegal	10	3	7	-	12	...	...	...	14	10		
Seychelles	1	-	-	1	4	2	2	-	2	2		
Sierra Leone	6	1	2	3	3	2	1	-	3	2		
South Africa	102	...	...	...	177	...	...	...	182	...		
Sudan	4	1	3	-	9	3	6	-	7	2	5	-
Swaziland	...	...	...	...	2	1	-	1	7	2	3	2
Togo	4	1	3	-	5	2	3	-	5	2	3	-
Tunisia	9	5	1	3	7	3	3	1	8	4	3	1
Uganda	5	2	3	-	6	3	3	-	7	6	1	-
United Republic of Cameroon	7	3	4	-	9	4	5	-	4	4	-	-

COUNTRY	CIRCA 1965				CIRCA 1970				CIRCA 1974			
	Total	LMW	SW	USW	Total	LMW	SW	USW	Total	LMW	SW	USW
AFRICA (cont'd.)												
United Republic of Tanzania									9	4	5	-
Upper Volta	3	1	2	-	4	1	3	-	4	1	3	-
Western Sahara	2[1]	2	-	-	3	2	1	-	7	4	2	1
Zaire	20	...	...	...	27	4	18	5	22	6	15	1
Zambia	9	5	4	-	22	12	6	4	22	8	10	4
AMERICA, NORTH												
Antigua	2	2	-	-	3		...	...	3	...	...	...
Bahama	2	2	-	-	6	4	-	2	6	4	-	2
Barbados	1	1	-	-	3	2	-	1	3	2	-	1
Belize	...	...	...	...	4	3	1	-	6	6	-	-
Bermuda	1	1	-	-	3	2	-	1	3	2	-	1
Canada	345	267	22	56	415	311	22	82	811	522	9	280
Costa Rica	48	...	...	...	51	35	4	12	51	35	4	12
Cuba	...	...	...	...	110	94	16	...	110	94	16	...
Dominica	...	...	...	...	...	...	...	...	2	...	...	...
Dominican Republic	137	99	12	26	141	...	...	...	184	108	38	38
El Salvador	67	48	11	8	67	...	...	...	65	62	3	...
Greenland	4	3	-	1	11	4	4	3	13	3	3	7
Grenada	4	2	2	-	4	2	2	-	5	3	2	-
Guadeloupe	3	3	-	-	2	2	-	-	2	2	-	-
Guatemala	92	62	30	-	89	85	4	-	94	87	2	5
Haiti	26	22	4	-	40	-	-	-	57	25	27	5
Honduras	51	27	24	-	126	79	37	10	151	104	37	10
Jamaica	12	8	-	4	15	8	-	7	21	8	-	13
Martinique	5	2	3	-	4	1	3	-	4	1	3	-
Mexico	481	433	48	-	590	510	26	54	668	558	28	82
Montserrat	1	1	-	-	3	3	-	-	3	3	-	-
Netherland Antilles	13	10	2	1	11	9	2	-	14	10	4	-
Nicaragua	90	...	...	...	...	...	...	...	137	67	11	59
Panama	86	63	4	19	114	73	4	37	117	76	1	40
Puerto Rico	55	55	-	-	75	75	-	-	95	95	-	-
St. Lucia	1	1	-	-	2	2	-	-	2	2	-	-
St. Pierre and Miquelon	2	2	-	-	2	2	-	-	2	2	-	-
St. Vincent	2	2	-	-	3	2	-	1	1	-	-	1
Trinidad and Tobago	6	3	-	3	17	5	-	12	9	5	-	4
United States of America	5 818	4 068	35	1 715	6 337	4 171	44	2 122	7 785	...	...	...
Virgin Islands (U. K.)	1	1	-	-	2	2	-	-	2	2	-	-
Virgin Islands (U. S.)	3	3	-	-	5	3	2	-	5	3	2	-
Turks and Caicos Islands	...	...	...	...	1	-	1	-	1	1	-	-
AMERICA, SOUTH												
Argentina	105	91	14	-	108	94	14	-	163	147	16	-
Bolivia	75	60	15	-	92	54	38	-	133	70	48	15
Brazil	922	821	76	25	994	866	79	49	999	915	49	35
Chile	193	132	29	32	217	176	41	-	229	188	41	-
Columbia	223	197	26	-	231	188	43	-	244	...	...	...
Ecuador	237	230	5	2	336	329	5	2	336	329	5	2
Falkland Islands	2	1	1	-	2	1	1	-	2	1	1	-
French Guiana	2	1	1	-	4	1	2	1	6	1	2	3
Guyana, Republic of	5	4	1	-	2	1	1	-	8	4	3	1
Paraguay	12	...	...	...	24	...	...	...	37	23	8	6
Peru	201	104	93	4	304	187	106	11	304	187	106	11
Surinam	4	4	-	-	5	4	1	-	5	4	1	-
Uruguay	72	57	13	2	99	79	16	4	101	79	18	4
Venezuela	164	99	55	15	235	132	87	16	235	139	78	18

| | CIRCA 1965 | | | | CIRCA 1970 | | | | CIRCA 1974 | | | |
COUNTRY	Total	LMW	SW	USW	Total	LMW	SW	USW	Total	LMW	SW	USW
ASIA												
Afghanistan	5	2	3	-	8	3	4	1	6	2	3	1
Bahrain	2	2	-	-	4	4	-	-	3	3	-	-
Bangladesh	...	...	...	...	...	...	...	...	16	7	4	5
Brunei	5	4	1	-	7	4	2	1	10	6	2	2
Burma	5	2	3	-	8	4	4	-	5	2	3	-
Cyprus	4	4	-	-	4	4	-	-	4	4	-	-
Hong Kong	8	5	1	2	13	11	-	2	20	16	-	4
India	103	74	29	-	128	98	30	-	146	114	32	-
Indonesia	71[2]	-	71	-	138	6	131	1	586	100	484	2
Iran	22	14	8	-	38	28	6	4	53	36	-	17
Iraq	16	4	12	-	19	5	14	-	12	10	2	-
Israel	29	14	4	11	28	11	4	13	39	16	5	18
Japan	540	442	17	81	735	426	19	96	911	474	7	430
Jordan	10	6	4	-	9	6	3	-	7	3	2	2
Korea, Rep. of	110	41	7	62	172	77	-	95	172	77	-	95
Korea, Democratic Rep.	...	...	...	...	19	7	12	-	19	7	12	-
Lao	5	1	4	-	6	3	3	-	9	4	5	-
Lebanon	3	2	1	-	5	2	1	2	6	2	1	3
Macau	5	3	2	-	4	2	-	2	5	3	2	-
Malaysia	55	32	21	2	66	32	26	8	97	66	31	-
Maldive Islands	3	-	-	3	5	1	4	-	5	1	4	-
Nepal	3	1	2	-	5	2	3	-	5	2	3	-
Pakistan	22	12	10	-	45	23	13	9	22	10	12	-
Philippines	219	181	25	13	192	...	...	...	327	289	38	...
Saudi Arabia	10	3	7	-	20	12	7	1	20	12	7	1
Singapore	12	5	7	-	16	5	7	4	16	5	7	4
Sri Lanka	27	7	14	6	29	9	12	8	24	11	7	6
Syria	22	11	4	7	30	25	5	-	11	8	3	-
Thailand	36	15	10	11	134	108	26	-	144	108	26	10
Turkey	15	10	5	-	52	19	32	1	21	16	2	3
Yemen, People's Dem.	4	3	1	-	4	3	1	-	4	3	1	-
Vietnam	49	33	11	5	22	14	6	2	27	18	7	2
EUROPE												
Andorra	2	2	-	-	2	2	-	-	4	1	1	2
Albania	12	...	...	...	16	...	...	...	19	11	8	-
Austria	207	134	9	64	348	158	5	185	399	142	5	252
Belgium	27	8	3	16	30	8	5	17	48	16	-	32
Bulgaria	14	9	2	3	26	12	4	10	32	13	4	15
Czechoslovakia	80	...	...	...	126	55	33	38	123	59	32	32
Denmark	9	8	1	...	39	8	1	30	19	5	1	13
Faeroe Islands	1	1	-	-	4	1	-	3	4	1	3	-
Finland	93	13	4	76	97	13	4	80	96	13	-	83
France	191	61	21	109	229	54	21	154	290	51	-	239
German, Dem. Rep.[3]	62	20	3	39	106	35	10	61	106	35	10	61
Germany, Federal Rep.[3]	290	58	14	218	309	52	17	240	346	46	29	271
Gibraltar	3	3	-	-	3	3	-	-	3	3	-	-
Greece	15	13	2	-	19	12	2	5	51	12	2	37
Holy See	15	...	...	...	16	3	12	1	17	3	12	2
Hungary	21	12	5	4	29	14	10	5	37	12	7	18
Iceland	27	20	-	7	21	14	-	7	29	14	-	15
Ireland	3	3	-	-	12	3	-	9	18	6	-	12
Italy	1 607	127	10	1 470	1 801	128	10	1 663	1 964	129	-	1 835
Luxembourg	7	2	2	3	7	2	2	3	7	2	2	3
Malta					1	...	...	...	1	...	...	...
Monaco	7	1	4	2	7	2	4	1	6	2	2	2
Netherlands	29	5	5	19	34	7	5	22	30	7	-	23
Norway	136	41	7	88	222	39	2	181	843	36	-	307
Poland	42	...	...	...	51	30	21	...	51	30	21	-
Portugal	84	39	29	16	95	46	33	16	180	60	35	85
Romania	30	15	9	6	46	20	18	8	62	23	20	19
Spain	462	435	6	21	468	186	11	271	406	180	13	213
Sweden	209	62	2	145	311	58	2	251	282	8	-	274

COUNTRY	CIRCA 1965				CIRCA 1970				CIRCA 1974			
	Total	LMW	SW	USW	Total	LMW	SW	USW	Total	LMW	SW	USW
EUROPE (cont'd.)												
Switzerland	107	7	8	92	163	6	9	148	211	5	10	196
United Kingdom	233	57	34	142	404	78	62	264	397	79	66	252
Yugoslavia	146	78	4	64	167	149	1	17	487	326	7	154
OCEANIA												
American Samoa	1	1	-	-	1	1	-	-	1	1	-	-
Australia	198	180	18	-	211	188	23	-	219	198	21	-
British Solomon Islands	3	1	2	-	3	1	2	-	...	...	...	...
Cook Islands	4	1	3	-	3	1	2	-	1	1	-	-
Fiji Islands	10	...	...	...	12	...	...	...	11	...	...	...
French Polynesia	1	-	1	-	3	1	2	-	5	1	4	-
Gilbert & Ellice Islands	3	1	2	-	1	1	-	-	1	1	-	-
Guam	3	3	-	-	1	1	-	-	2	2	-	-
Nauru	...	...	...	...	1	1	-	-	1	1	-	-
New Caledonia	4	2	2	-	4	2	2	-	3	1	2	-
New Hebrides	1	-	1	-	2	1	1	-	4	2	2	-
New Zealand	48	46	2	-	49	47	2	-	58	56	2	-
Norfolk Islands	1	1	-	-	1	1	-	-	1	1	-	-
Niue	...	...	...	...	1	1	-	-	1	1	-	-
Pacific Islands	6	6	-	-	6	6	-	-	10	10	-	-
Papua-New Guinea	4	1	3	-	5	1	4	-	22	2	20	-
Tonga	1	1	-	-	2	2	-	-	2	2	-	-
Western Samoa	2	2	-	-	2	2	-	-	1	1	-	-

1. Not including very high and super high frequency and relay transmitters. 2. Including West Iranian. 3. The data which relate to the Federal Republic of Germany and the German Democratic Republic include the relevant data relating to Berlin for which separate data have not been supplied. This is without prejudice to any question of status which may be involved.

Table 2 — Number of radio receivers and receivers per 1,000 inhabitants
Number of countries and territories presented in this table: 185
R = Estimated number of receivers in use
L = Number of licenses issued or sets declared

Country	Code	1960	1961	1962	1963	1964	1965	1966	1967	1968	1969	1970	1971	1972	1973	1974	1975	1976
AFRICA																		
Algeria	R						480^L	550^L	650^L	*750^L	850^L	870^L	927^L	992^L	3 000	3 000	3 000	3 000
							40.3	*43.4*	*49.7*	*55.6*	*61.1*	*60.7*	*62.6*	*64.8*	*190.2*	*184.4*	*178.7*	*173.0*
Angola	R	53	58	64	68	73	79	81	*86	90	*93	95	100	110	115	116	116	116
		11.2	*12.1*	*13.1*	*13.7*	*14.4*	*15.3*	*15.4*	*16.1*	*16.5*	*16.7*	*16.8*	*17.3*	*18.6*	*19.0*	*18.7*	*18.3*	*17.8*
Benin	R	25	30	35	*35	35	35	36	45	60	75	85	97	150	*150	*150	150	150
		11.8	*13.9*	*15.9*	*15.5*	*15.2*	*14.8*	*14.9*	*18.1*	*23.5*	*28.7*	*31.7*	*35.2*	*53.0*	*51.6*	*50.2*	*48.8*	*47.8*
Botswana	R	2.1^L	2.1^L	2.8^L	4.0^L	*4.0^L	4.0	4.0	5.2	5.8	6.5	20	*30	*40	50	55	57	60
		4.2	*4.1*	*5.3*	*7.5*	*7.4*	*7.2*	*7.1*	*9.0*	*9.8*	*10.8*	*32.4*	*47.5*	*62.1*	*75.9*	*81.6*	*82.5*	*84.6*
Burundi	R										60	65	75	100	100	100	100	105
											18.1	*19.4*	*22.0*	*28.7*	*28.0*	*27.3*	*26.6*	*27.2*
Cape Verde, Rep. of	R	1.8	2.3	2.8	3.0	3.5	3.7	*3.9	4.0	4.4	4.4	4.6	4.9	5.2	25	30	31	36
		8.9	*11.1*	*13.1*	*13.6*	*15.5*	*15.9*	*16.3*	*16.2*	*17.3*	*16.8*	*17.2*	*17.9*	*18.6*	*87.7*	*103.5*	*105.1*	*120.0*
Central African Empire	R	12	*13	15	20	25	30	33	*37	*41	45	46	50	60	65	70	70	75
		9.1	*9.6*	*10.9*	*14.3*	*17.6*	*20.7*	*22.3*	*24.5*	*26.9*	*28.5*	*28.5*	*30.4*	*35.7*	*37.9*	*40.0*	*39.1*	*41.0*
Chad	R	6	8	16	20	22	25	30	35	50	50	60	60	70	70	70	75	76
		2.0	*2.6*	*5.2*	*6.3*	*6.8*	*7.6*	*8.9*	*10.2*	*14.3*	*14.0*	*16.5*	*16.2*	*18.5*	*18.1*	*17.8*	*18.6*	*18.5*
Comoro Islands	R	0.5	*1.5	2.5	3.0	3.6	5.0	8.0	8.0	10	*17	24	*27	30	35	36	36	36
		2.3	*6.7*	*11.0*	*12.9*	*15.2*	*20.7*	*32.4*	*31.6*	*38.8*	*64.4*	*88.9*	*97.5*	*106.0*	*120.3*	*120.8*	*117.7*	*114.7*
Congo	R	11	*15	20	25	47	47	60	60	62	62	65	65	70	75	80	81	83
		11.4	*15.2*	*19.9*	*24.3*	*44.9*	*44.0*	*55.0*	*53.9*	*54.4*	*53.3*	*54.6*	*53.3*	*56.0*	*58.6*	*61.0*	*60.2*	*60.1*
Djibouti	R											7	7	10	10	12	13	15
												73.7	*72.2*	*101.0*	*99.0*	*115.4*	*122.3*	*138.9*
Egypt	R	1 500	1 750	1 800	1 980	2 178	*2 700	*3 227	*3 751	4 275	4 275	4 400	4 500	5 000	5 100	5 115	5 120	5 250
		57.9	*65.8*	*66.0*	*70.9*	*76.0*	*91.9*	*107.1*	*121.4*	*134.9*	*131.5*	*132.0*	*131.8*	*142.9*	*142.4*	*139.5*	*136.4*	*136.6*
Equatorial Guinea	R				15	19	*29	*39	*50	*60	70	71	72	75	76	*77	78	80
					57.7	*72.0*	*108.6*	*144.4*	*182.5*	*216.6*	*249.1*	*249.1*	*248.3*	*255.7*	*253.3*	*252.5*	*251.6*	*253.2*
Ethiopia	R		100	150	*150	*150	*150	*150	*150	150	155	160	163	170	175	200	200	210
			4.9	*7.2*	*7.0*	*6.9*	*6.8*	*6.6*	*6.5*	*6.3*	*6.4*	*6.4*	*6.4*	*6.5*	*6.6*	*7.3*	*7.2*	*7.3*
Gabon	R		25	25	30	35	36	40	50	50	50	62	65	90	90	90	92	93
			55.0	*54.6*	*65.1*	*75.3*	*76.8*	*84.2*	*104.0*	*102.7*	*101.2*	*124.0*	*128.5*	*176.1*	*174.4*	*172.7*	*174.9*	*175.5*
Gambie	R	2.0	2.5	22	30	35	44	*45	*46	*48	*49	50	60	60	60	60	61	61
		5.1	*6.3*	*54.6*	*73.4*	*84.1*	*104.3*	*104.7*	*105.0*	*107.6*	*107.9*	*108.0*	*127.1*	*124.7*	*122.5*	*120.0*	*119.8*	*117.3*
Ghana	R		300	403	504	555	555	555	*628	700	700	703	750	775	1 058	1 060	1 060	1 080
			43.0	*56.2*	*68.4*	*73.5*	*71.7*	*70.1*	*77.7*	*84.8*	*83.0*	*81.5*	*84.8*	*85.4*	*113.4*	*110.5*	*107.4*	*106.3*
Guinea	R		40	*43	*46	50	75	*78	*81	85	90	91	91	100	101	105	110	120
			12.3	*13.0*	*13.7*	*14.5*	*21.4*	*21.8*	*22.1*	*22.7*	*23.5*	*23.2*	*22.7*	*24.3*	*24.0*	*24.4*	*24.9*	*26.5*
Guinea Bissau	L	1.8	1.9	2.0	2.2	*2.7	3.3	3.2	3.4	3.5	*3.7	4.0	4.0	*6.5	9.0	9.0	10.0	11.0
		3.5	*3.7*	*3.9*	*4.4*	*5.4*	*6.7*	*6.6*	*7.0*	*7.2*	*7.6*	*8.2*	*8.1*	*13.1*	*17.8*	*17.4*	*19.1*	*20.6*
Ivory Coast	R	55	*55	*56	*57	58	60	*62	65	67	70	75	80	80	202	*204	300	600
		16.0	*15.7*	*15.6*	*15.6*	*15.5*	*15.7*	*15.8*	*16.2*	*16.3*	*16.6*	*17.4*	*18.1*	*17.7*	*43.5*	*42.9*	*61.4*	*119.7*
Kenya	R	57	55	60	200	300	350	*425	500	500	500	*500	*500	500	508	510	511	514
		7.0	*6.6*	*6.9*	*22.4*	*32.5*	*36.7*	*43.2*	*49.1*	*47.5*	*46.0*	*44.5*	*43.0*	*41.6*	*41.0*	*39.8*	*38.6*	*37.5*

Country	Code	1960	1961	1962	1963	1964	1965	1966	1967	1968	1969	1970	1971	1972	1973	1874	1975	1976
AFRICA (cont'd.)																		
Lesotho	L	4 4.5	4 4.5	4 4.4	5 5.4	*5 5.3	*5 5.2	*5 5.2	*5 5.1	*5 5.0	*5 4.9	5 4.8	10 9.4	10 9.2	11 10.0	11 9.8	22 19.2	23 19.6
Liberia	R	100 79.6	100 78.2	100 76.8	100 75.5	125 92.6	150 109.0	152 108.3	152 106.2	*152 104.1	152 102.0	155 107.8	155 99.6	250 157.0	260 159.6	261 156.6	264 154.6	265 151.4
Libyan Arab Jamehiriya	L				40 26.6	45 28.9	50 30.9	74 44.1	75 43.0	76 42.0	77 41.1	85 43.9	90 45.0	100 48.5	100 47.1	105 48.0	106 47.1	110 47.3
Madagascar	R	82 15.3	*159 28.9	235 41.7	285 49.3	*300 50.6	*315 51.8	330 52.9	380 59.4	400 60.9	500 74.1	541 78.0	592 83.0	600 81.8	600 79.4	606 77.8	608 75.8	609 73.7
Malawi	R			3 0.8	3 0.8	11 2.9	80 20.6	85 21.4	*92 22.6	100 24.0	105 24.7	106 24.3	107 24.0	110 24.1	112 23.9	125 26.1	127 25.8	130 25.8
Mali	R	8 2.0	10 2.4	15 3.5	*15 3.5	15 3.4	20 4.4	30 6.5	40 8.5	45 9.3	60 12.2	60 11.9	60 11.6	75 14.2	75 13.8	75 13.5	81 14.2	82 14.0
Mauritania	R	12 12.6	20 20.6	*25 25.3	30 29.8	*33 32.1	*36 34.3	*40 37.4	*43 39.3	*46 41.2	50 43.9	55 47.3	75 63.3	80 66.2	81 65.8	82 65.2	82 83.9	95 72.5
Mauritius	L	40 60.4	45 66.0	51 72.6	57 78.7	*59 79.3	62 81.5	66 84.6	70 88.6	78 96.3	79 96.3	85 103.2	85 101.4	107 125.4	*116 133.6	125 141.4	*162 180.2	200 218.8
Morocco	L	532 45.7	543 45.5	575 47.1	615 49.2	650 50.7	700 53.3	748 55.4	800 57.7	826 57.9	884 60.2	935 61.8	1 002 64.4	1 100 68.6	1 200 72.7	1 300 76.5	1 400 80.0	1 500 83.2
Mozambique	L	37 5.6	37 5.5	*42 6.1	*47 6.7	*53 7.4	60 8.2	75 10.0	78 10.2	85 10.8	85 10.6	90 10.9	160 19.0	*168 19.5	176 20.0	180 19.9	200 21.7	225 23.8
Niger	R		10 3.3	15 4.8	20 6.1	40 11.8	45 12.8	70 19.3	75 20.2	75 19.6	100 25.5	145 36.1	150 36.4	150 35.4	---	---	---	---
Nigeria	L	143 3.3	*229 5.2	*314 7.0	400 8.6	600 21.8	*765 15.7	*930 18.6	*1 095 21.4	1 260 24.1	1 265 23.6	1 275 23.2	1 500 26.5	1 550 26.7	3 500 58.7	5 000 81.7	5 000 79.5	5 100 78.8
Reunion	L	14 41.4	18 51.6	22 61.1	25 67.4	36 94.2	46 117.1	54 133.7	59 142.2	67 157.3	79 181.2	*79 176.7	80 174.7	90 191.9	90 187.5	91 185.3	91 181.6	95 185.9
Rwanda	R								25 7.4	30 8.6	*30 8.4	30 8.2	31 8.2	41 10.6	50 12.6	60 14.7	65 15.5	70 16.2
St. Helena	R										0.6 120.0	0.7 140.0	0.7 140.0	0.8 160.0	0.8 160.0	0.9 180.0	0.9 180.0	0.9 180.0
Sao Tome and Principe	L		0.7 10.8	0.9 13.6	1.2 17.9	1.5 22.1	1.9 27.5	2.2 31.4	2.6 36.6	*4.3 59.7	6.0 82.2	6.2 83.8	*6.6 88.0	7.0 92.1	*7.2 92.3	7.5 94.9	10.0 125.0	20.0 246.9
Senegal	R	125 40.2	*133 41.9	*142 43.7	150 45.1	200 58.7	*230 65.9	260 72.8	262 71.6	265 70.8	265 69.1	268 68.3	275 68.4	280 68.1	285 67.7	286 66.3	287 65.0	290 64.1
Seychelles	R	0.5 11.9	0.6 14.0	0.8 18.2	1.2 26.7	1.5 32.6	6.0 127.7	*6.2 129.2	*6.4 130.6	*6.6 132.0	*6.8 133.3	7.0 134.6	7.5 141.5	7.5 136.4	9.0 160.7	15.0 258.6	16.0 271.2	17.0 283.3
Sierra Leone	R	9.2 4.3	*9.2 4.2	9.2 4.1	20 8.8	25 10.8	*27 11.4	*29 12.0	*32 13.0	35 13.9	35 13.5	40 15.1	50 18.5	51 18.4	60 21.1	61 21.0	62 20.8	---
Somalia	R	24 10.8	24 10.5	25 10.7	26 10.9	30 12.3	35 14.0	36 14.1	40 15.3	*42 15.8	45 16.5	50 17.9	50 17.5	60 20.5	65 21.6	67 21.7	68 21.5	69 21.2
South Africa	R	996 54.8	1 068 57.3	1 151 60.2	1 500 76.4	*1 500 74.3	*1 500 72.2	*1 500 70.0	*1 500 67.9	*1 500 65.8	1 500 63.8	2 000 82.6	*2 083 83.7	*2 166 84.8	2 250 85.8	2 335 86.7	2 337 84.4	2 500 87.8
Southern Rhodesia	R								55 11.5	135 27.3	135 26.3	145 27.3	212 38.6	215 37.9	225 38.4	225 37.1	250 39.8	255 39.3
Sudan	L				221 17.3	225 17.1	*373 27.6	*521 37.4	*669 46.6	*817 55.3	*965 63.4	*1 113 70.9	1 261 78.0	*1 300 78.0	*1 300 75.7	*1 300 73.4	---	---
Swaziland	R	1.8 5.6	2.2 6.7	*2.4 7.2	2.6 7.6	3.6 10.3	8 22.2	10 27.1	11 29.1	12 30.9	13 32.7	30 73.4	35 83.5	50 116.0	51 115.1	53 116.5	55 117.5	60 124.5
Togo	R	5.3 3.6	6.3 4.2	*7.1 4.6	8 5.0	8 4.9	30 17.7	31 17.7	31 17.2	35 18.9	40 21.0	45 23.0	45 22.3	46 22.2	50 23.5	50 22.9	51 22.7	52 22.5
Tunisia	R	170 40.3	270 62.9	*285 65.2	300 67.4	306 67.5	*338 73.2	370 78.5	370 76.8	370 75.2	374 74.4	380 74.0	388 73.9	388 72.3	401 73.1	805 143.5	*808 140.6	810 137.5
Uganda	R	90 11.9	90 11.6	92 11.6	100 12.3	200 23.9	200 23.3	*206 23.4	*212 23.5	*218 23.5	*224 23.5	*230 23.5	*236 23.4	*242 23.3	250 23.4	250 22.7	250 22.0	250 21.4
United Republic of Cameroon	R						115 21.5	200 36.8	205 37.0	210 37.3	210 36.6	212 36.3	214 36.0	216 35.7	225 36.5	603 96.1	---	---

Country	Code	1960	1961	1962	1963	1964	1965	1966	1967	1968	1969	1970	1971	1972	1973	1974	1975	1976
AFRICA (cont'd.)																		
United Republic of Tanzania	R	20L 2.0	36L 3.5	36L 3.4	*75 6.9	114 10.2	115 10.0	120 10.1	*128 10.5	135 10.8	135 10.5	150 11.3	200 14.6	225 16.0	230 15.8	231 15.4	232 15.0	300 18.8
Upper Volta	R	3 0.7	12 2.7	15 3.3	45 9.7	50 10.5	50 10.3	50 10.1	70 13.8	80 15.5	80 15.2	87 16.2	88 16.0	90 16.0	100 17.4	100 17.0	100 16.6	105 17.0
Western Sahara	R									8 140.4	10 156.3	14 194.9	*15 205.5	*15 205.5	*16 216.2	16 213.3	16 213.3	--- ---
Zaire	R										60 2.9	*68 3.1	75 3.4	100 4.4	100 4.3	1 000 41.9	1 000 40.8	1 000 39.8
Zambia	R			16 4.7	16 4.6	42 11.7	43 11.6	*45 11.8	*48 12.2	51 12.6	55 13.2	75 17.5	80 18.1	100 21.9	100 21.2	100 20.6	100 19.9	110 21.2
AMERICA, NORTH																		
Antigua	R	2.8 50.9	2.9 51.8	2.9 50.9	3.0 50.9	3.8 63.3	*4.8 78.7	*5.8 92.1	*6.9 106.2	*7.9 119.7	*8.9 130.9	9.9 141.4	*10.9 155.7	*12 169.0	13 183.1	14 194.4	15 205.5	16 219.2
Bahama	R	16 141.6	18 151.3	*24 193.6	30 230.8	30 219.0	40 279.7	47 315.4	*56 359.0	*65 398.8	75 441.2	80 452.0	*82 450.6	84 449.2	85 442.7	90 454.6	95 456.7	96 461.5
Barbados	R	35 151.5	38 163.8	39 180.3	39 179.5	39 178.7	40 178.7	45 190.7	55 232.1	57 240.5	57 239.5	89 372.4	94 391.7	110 456.4	116 479.3	116 475.4	130 530.6	130 526.3
Belize	L	2.2L 23.9	2.4L 25.5	5.0L 51.6	6.0L 60.0	6.0L 58.3	30 283.0	32 293.6	37 333.3	43 377.2	48 410.3	57 475.0	60 483.9	62 484.4	68 515.2	68 500.0	68 485.7	70 486.1
Bermuda	R	19 431.8	21 466.7	*21 456.5	22 468.1	23 479.2	*23 479.2	23 469.4	28 560.0	29 568.6	29 568.6	38 730.8	38 717.0	40 740.7	49 890.9	50 909.1	50 892.9	51 894.7
Canada	R	8 050 449.5	9 200 503.5	9 200 494.3	*9 600 506.2	10 000 517.5	*11 000 560.0	12 000 598.5	12 050 589.5	14 100 678.8	14 740 698.9	15 890 742.3	16 850 780.3	17 932 820.8	19 133 864.8	20 252 900.9	21 900 960.5	23 400 999.1
Cayman Island	R						1.5 166.7	*1.6 177.8	1.8 180.0	*2.1 210.0	*2.4 240.0	*2.6 236.4	*2.9 263.6	*3.2 290.9	*3.5 318.2	*3.8 345.5	4.0 363.6	6.0 545.5
Costa Rica	R	77 61.6	81 62.4	*95 70.6	*109 78.1	123 85.1	*130 87.0	130 84.3	130 81.7	130 79.3	130 77.0	130 74.8	130 72.8	135 73.5	140 74.2	142 73.2	145 72.7	150 73.2
Cuba	R	1 100 156.7	1 300 181.3	*1 303 177.8	*1 307 174.6	*1 310 171.3	*1 313 168.3	*1 316 165.5	*1 320 162.9	*1 323 160.3	1 326 157.8	1 330 155.3	1 338 153.2	1 500 168.3	1 790 196.8	1 805 194.4	2 100 221.5	2 100 216.9
Dominica	R				5.0 79.4	5.4 84.4	*5.4 83.1	*5.5 83.3	5.5 80.9	5.6 81.2	5.6 80.0	5.6 78.9	5.7 79.2	5.7 79.2	5.8 79.5	5.8 78.4	5.8 77.3	17 223.7
Dominican Republic	R	102 32.3	*112 34.3	123 36.5	139 40.0	*142 39.6	*146 39.4	150 39.3	150 38.0	155 38.1	160 38.1	164 37.8	165 36.8	170 36.7	180 37.6	*185 37.4	190 37.1	200 37.8
El Salvador	R	225 89.0	353 135.6	358 133.4	*376 135.9	395 138.3	396 134.1	396 129.5	396 125.0	398 121.2	400 117.7	405 115.2	500 137.7	932 248.7	939 243.1	940 236.0	1 400 340.8	1 400 330.3
Greenland	R			4.5 72.6	5.0 135.1	6.0 157.9	*6.2 155.0	*6.4 156.1	*6.6 157.1	6.8 154.6	7.0 155.6	7.1 151.1	7.1 147.9	7.3 149.0	10 196.1	11 211.5	13 240.7	13 236.4
Grenada	R			2.7L 29.7	2.8L 30.8	3.3L 35.9	10 108.7	11 119.6	*12 129.0	*13 139.8	*14 148.9	15 159.6	*16 170.2	*18 189.5	20 210.5	21 218.8	22 229.2	22 229.2
Guatemala	L	210 52.6	210 51.2	*211 50.0	212 48.9	212 47.6	*213 46.5	*214 45.4	*214 44.1	*215 43.0	216 42.0	220 41.5	221 40.5	250 44.5	260 45.0	261 43.9	262 42.8	265 42.0
Haiti	R	21 5.8	21 5.7	50 13.3	55 14.4	60 15.4	63 16.0	64 16.0	75 18.5	80 19.4	81 19.4	83 19.6	85 19.8	86 19.8	90 20.4	91 20.3	93 20.4	95 20.5
Honduras	R	125 66.7	125 64.5	*126 62.9	*127 61.3	128 59.8	135 61.1	135 59.4	136 58.1	140 58.2	145 58.6	147 57.6	147 55.7	150 54.9	155 54.8	158 53.9	160 52.7	161 51.2
Jamaica	R	147 90.2	200 121.5	210 126.4	*226 133.1	242 138.9	350 198.9	365 204.5	400 221.1	425 232.0	450 242.5	500 265.7	550 288.0	550 283.7	550 279.3	550 275.1	550 271.1	555 269.7
Martinique	L	13 46.8	15 52.6	17 58.6	*20 67.6	*23 76.2	*26 84.7	*29 92.4	32 100.0	32 98.2	32 96.4	32 94.7	32 93.0	32 91.7	32 90.7	32 89.4	32 88.2	35 94.9
Mexico	R	3 300 90.7	3 500 93.1	5 830 151.1	6 506 162.1	7 281 175.5	8 593 200.5	9 897 223.6	10 840 237.2	12 049 255.3	12 990 266.6	14 005 278.4	14 923 287.2	15 841 295.2	16 870 304.3	17 514 305.7	--- ---	--- ---

Country	Code	1960	1961	1962	1963	1964	1965	1966	1967	1968	1969	1970	1971	1972	1973	1974	1975	1976
AMERICA, NORTH (cont'd.)																		
Netherlands Antilles	R	41	73	75	*83	*92	100	*103	*106	*109	112	115	120	125	130	131	132	150
		213.5	374.4	378.8	412.9	448.8	480.8	488.2	495.3	504.6	511.4	518.0	531.0	543.5	555.6	550.4	545.5	607.3
Nicaragua	R	75	100	100	100	100	100	105	105	105	107	109	110	115	125	126	363	---
		51.0	66.0	64.1	62.3	60.5	58.8	60.0	58.3	56.6	56.0	55.3	54.1	54.8	57.6	56.2	156.6	---
Panama	R	163	186	225	225	225	225	225	225	*226	226	230	230	250	255	260	265	270
		150.7	166.7	195.5	189.6	184.0	178.4	173.2	168.3	164.1	159.5	157.8	153.3	162.0	160.8	159.4	157.9	156.5
Puerto Rico	R										1 600	1 625	1 650	1 750	1 753	1 755	1 760	1 765
											588.0	592.4	594.6	624.8	618.6	611.9	606.5	601.2
St. Lucia	R	2.0L	2.2L	7.6	13.0	18.4	*23.8	29.2	34.6	40	*48	56	*64	*72	80	81	82	82
		21.3	23.4	80.0	136.8	191.7	247.9	301.0	353.1	404.0	480.0	554.5	621.4	692.3	761.9	757.0	759.3	745.5
St. Pierre & Miquelon	L					1.0	1.1	*1.2	*1.4	*1.5	1.6	1.6	2.0	2.0	2.1	2.1	2.1	2.2
						200.0	220.0	240.0	280.0	300.0	320.0	320.0	400.0	400.0	420.0	420.0	420.0	440.0
Trinidad & Tobago	R	71	97	124	150	163	165	200	*208	*216	224	*232	240	250	250	250	*260	270
		84.2	112.7	141.7	169.1	181.5	181.7	217.9	224.4	230.8	236.8	242.9	248.7	256.2	253.3	250.5	257.7	265.0
Turks & Caicos	R										1.2	1.3	2.8	2.9	3.0	3.0	3.0	3.0
											200.0	216.7	466.7	483.3	500.0	500.0	500.0	500.0
United States of America	R	170 000	177 000	184 000	192 000	225 000	240 000	262 700	285 000	*286 700	288 300	290 000	336 000	354 000	368 000	401 600	402 000	---
		940.9	963.6	986.4	1 014.6	1 172.6	1 235.2	1 336.5	1 434.2	1 428.5	1 422.5	1 415.5	1 622.8	1 695.1	1 749.1	1 895.2	1 879.2	---
Virgin Islands (U.S.)	R					20	25	30	*31	*32	*32	33	*41	*50	*58	*67	75	76
						425.5	480.8	555.6	553.6	551.7	533.3	523.8	650.8	781.3	892.0	1 031.0	1 136.4	1 151.5
AMERICA, SOUTH																		
Argentina	R	3 500	4 000	4 900	5 800	6 200	6 600	7 000	8 000	9 000	9 000	9 000	10 000	18 000	21 000	21 000	---	---
		169.8	191.1	230.6	269.0	283.5	297.6	311.3	350.9	389.4	384.1	379.0	415.5	737.9	849.5	838.3	---	---
Bolivia	R		255	350	360	*367	*373	*380	*387	*393	400	402	405	410	415	425	426	430
			65.9	88.4	88.8	88.5	87.9	87.4	87.0	86.3	85.7	84.1	82.7	81.7	80.7	80.6	78.7	77.5
Brazil	R	4 750	*4 850	*4 950	*5 050	*5 150	*5 250	*5 350	*5 450	5 550	5 575	11 800	*12 836	*13 872	*14 908	*15 944	16 980	---
		66.4	65.9	65.3	64.8	64.2	63.6	63.0	62.4	61.7	60.3	123.9	131.0	137.7	143.8	149.5	154.7	---
Chile	R		1 016	*1 061	*1 106	*1 151	*1 196	*1 240	*1 285	*1 330	1 375	1 400	1 400	1 500	1 500	1 600	1 700	1 800
			130.8	133.4	135.8	138.2	140.5	142.7	145.1	147.3	149.5	149.4	146.7	154.4	151.7	158.9	165.8	172.4
Columbia	R	1 971	2 159	*2 167	*2 175	*2 184	*2 192	2 200	2 200	2 210	2 214	2 217	2 250	2 255	2 793	2 805	2 808	2 850
		123.9	131.5	127.8	124.2	120.8	117.3	113.9	110.1	107.0	103.7	100.4	98.7	95.8	114.9	111.8	108.5	106.7
Ecuador	R	170	175	320	500	510	540	650	801	1 000	1 210	1 700	1 700	---	---	---	---	---
		39.3	39.2	69.3	104.8	103.5	106.0	123.3	147.0	177.3	207.4	281.9	272.8	---	---	---	---	---
Falkland Islands	L					0.6	1.0	1.0	1.0	1.0	1.1	1.1	1.1	---	---	---	---	---
						300.0	500.0	500.0	500.0	500.0	550.0	550.0	550.0	---	---	---	---	---
French Guiana	L	0.8	1.0	1.0	1.7	*2.0	2.5	*2.6	2.7	2.7	2.7	2.7	2.9	2.9	2.9	2.9	2.9	---
		24.2	28.6	27.8	44.7	51.3	56.1	60.5	65.9	63.0	60.4	56.9	55.8	53.7	51.8	50.0	48.3	---
Guyana, Republic of	L	37	42	44	66	70	80	80	80	80	80	80	90	100	150	268	272	275
		66.1	73.0	74.7	109.3	113.3	126.4	123.5	120.7	118.0	115.3	112.8	124.1	135.0	198.2	346.3	343.9	340.4
Paraguay	R		150	160	*161	*161	*162	*163	*164	*164	165	169	175	175	175	176	180	180
			82.4	85.7	84.1	81.9	80.4	78.8	77.2	75.2	73.7	73.5	74.0	72.0	70.0	68.4	68.0	66.1
Peru	R	1 100	*1 179	*1 259	*1 338	*1 418	*1 487	*1 577	*1 656	*1 736	1 815	1 819	1 825	2 000	2 001	2 010	2 050	2 068
		110.1	114.9	119.5	123.6	127.5	130.9	114.0	136.6	139.0	141.1	137.3	133.8	142.4	138.4	135.0	133.8	131.1
Surinam	R	40	40	45	*46	*48	*49	50	65	88	90	92	95	100	108	109	110	112
		137.9	134.2	146.6	145.6	148.2	147.6	147.1	187.3	247.9	247.9	248.0	250.0	257.1	270.7	265.9	260.7	258.1
Uruguay	R	800	850	900	*905	910	900	1 000	1 000	1 000	1 000	1 000	1 100	1 500	1 500	1 500	1 500	1 600
		305.0	319.2	333.2	330.8	328.5	321.2	352.9	349.0	371.3	369.2	388.4	368.5	497.4	492.5	487.5	482.6	509.7
Venezuela	R	1 250	1 300	*1 417	*1 534	1 651	*1 660	1 675	1 676	1 680	1 685	*1 700	1 750	2 000	2 000	*3 398	4 795	5 034
		163.7	163.7	171.9	179.8	187.2	182.3	178.4	173.2	168.6	164.3	161.0	161.0	178.7	173.6	286.5	392.6	400.3

Country	Code	1960	1961	1962	1963	1964	1965	1966	1967	1968	1969	1970	1971	1972	1973	1974	1975	1976
ASIA																		
Afghanistan	R	24 1.8	24 1.7	25 1.8	25 1.7	*34 2.3	*42 2.8	*51 3.3	*59 3.7	*68 4.2	76 4.6	100 5.9	105 6.0	108 6.1	110 6.0	111 5.9	113 5.9	115 5.8
Bahrain	R	12 74.1	15 90.4	46 269.0	*47 268.6	*49 272.2	*50 270.3	*51 271.3	*53 274.6	*54 270.0	55 263.2	56 260.5	57 256.8	75 327.5	80 339.0	100 411.5	100 398.4	100 386.1
Bhutan	L						2.1 2.2	*2.4 2.5	*2.7 2.8	3.0 3.0	*4.2 4.1	*5.3 5.1	*6.5 6.1	*7.7 7.0	*8.9 8.0	10 8.7	10 8.5	10 8.3
Brunei	R	6.0 66.7	7.0 74.5	7.3 73.7	7.8 75.0	9 82.6	10 87.7	12 101.7	12 99.2	13 104.0	14 108.5	15 112.8	16 117.7	16 115.1	16 113.5	20 138.9	24 163.3	26 174.5
Burma	L	115 5.2	117 5.2	147 6.3	203 8.6	259 10.7	335 13.5	367 14.5	370 14.3	388 14.7	399 14.7	400 14.4	423 15.1	600 21.2	627 21.5	659 21.7	*662 21.2	665 20.8
Cyprus	L	85 148.3	97 168.1	102 175.9	112 190.2	127 216.4	130 218.9	139 230.9	142 232.4	147 237.9	159 254.4	167 263.8	174 271.5	177 272.7	*178 270.9	*179 269.2	180 267.5	200 293.7
Democratic Kampuchea	R	32 6.0	*45 8.2	*58 10.3	*71 12.2	*84 14.1	97 15.8	*98 15.5	*99 15.3	*101 15.1	*102 14.9	103 14.6	*104 14.3	*106 14.2	*107 14.0	*109 13.8	110 13.6	--- ---
East Timor	L	0.7 1.4	0.8 1.6	1.0 1.9	1.1 2.1	1.3 2.4	1.4 2.6	1.8 3.2	1.9 3.3	2.3 4.0	2.5 4.2	2.7 4.5	3.1 5.0	3.4 5.4	--- ---	--- ---	--- ---	--- ---
Hong Kong	R	165 53.7	172 54.2	189 56.5	*302 86.2	*416 115.8	529 143.3	589 157.8	623 163.1	639 165.5	675 173.1	694 176.1	725 181.7	725 179.2	1 000 243.6	2 500 600.1	2 505 592.9	2 508 585.6
India	L	2 148 5.0	2 600 5.9	3 072 6.9	3 737 8.1	4 317 9.2	5 401 11.2	6 485 13.1	7 579 15.0	9 275 17.9	10 135 19.1	11 747 21.6	12 372 22.2	12 895 22.6	14 034 24.0	*14 055 23.5	14 075 23.0	14 848 23.6
Indonesia	L	678 7.3	1 250 13.2	1 250 15.9	1 250 12.5	1 250 12.2	*1 250 11.9	1 250 11.6	1 500 13.6	*2 000 17.6	2 500 21.5	2 550 21.3	3 300 26.9	3 500 27.8	5 000 38.7	5 000 37.7	5 010 36.8	5 100 36.5
Iran	L	935 43.4	1 350 61.0	1 400 61.6	1 600 68.5	*1 633 116.7	*1 666 67.6	1 700 67.1	*1 704 65.4	*1 708 63.8	1 712 62.1	1 800 63.5	1 810 62.0	1 825 60.7	1 900 61.3	*1 966 61.6	2 080 62.3	2 400 61.8
Iraq	R		100 14.2	500 68.8	700 93.4	*747 96.6	*793 99.4	*840 102.1	*886 104.3	*933 106.4	*979 108.1	*1 026 109.7	1 072 110.9	1 072 107.2	1 250 120.9	1 250 116.9	1 252 113.1	--- ---
Israel	L	400 189.2	*408 186.7	*415 181.0	*423 177.8	*431 174.1	*439 171.3	*446 170.0	*454 165.4	*462 164.8	*469 163.0	477 161.3	*501 164.6	*524 167.2	*548 169.8	*571 171.9	595 174.1	655 186.5
Japan	R	12 410 131.9	17 608 185.5	18 351 191.5	19 318 199.5	19 666 201.0	20 425 206.6	*21 069 211.1	*21 713 215.4	*22 356 219.3	23 000 222.9	*23 250 222.9	23 500 222.5	24 000 224.4	46 600 430.1	46 600 427.4	51 630 464.6	59 650 530.3
Jordan	R	64^L 37.8	65^L 37.3	102 56.8	139 75.3	215 113.2	*269 137.6	*289 143.6	*309 148.9	*330 154.2	*350 158.4	370 162.3	410 174.1	500 205.5	521 207.2	529 203.5	529 196.8	531 191.1
Korea, Rep. of	R	781 31.6	1 158 45.7	1 303 50.2	1 661 62.6	1 729 71.7	1 961 70.8	2 632 93.0	*2 725 94.3	*2 818 95.5	3 242 107.7	4 012 130.6	4 100 130.8	4 115 128.7	*4 464 136.8	4 812 144.6	*4 906 144.5	5 000 144.4
Kuwait	R	75 269.8	80 260.6	90 262.4	*92 240.2	*94 260.7	96 202.1	*98 187.4	*100 174.8	102 162.4	102 152.5	105 138.2	110 133.7	200 225.5	210 220.6	215 211.2	500 460.8	502 435.0
Laos	L		20 8.2	22 8.9	*36 14.2	50 19.3	50 18.9	50 18.4	50 18.0	50 17.6	50 17.3	50 16.9	51 16.9	100 32.3	102 32.3	125 38.7	*162 49.1	200 59.2
Lebanon	R	100 53.9	*144 75.3	*188 95.4	*231 113.7	275 131.5	*363 168.8	450 203.4	451 198.4	550 235.6	590 245.8	600 243.0	605 238.0	1 320 504.2	1 320 489.3	1 321 474.8	1 321 460.4	1 600 540.7
Macau	L	4.6 27.2	4.8 26.8	*4.9 25.0	*5.1 23.9	*5.2 23.9	5.3 23.8	5.9 25.9	6.5 27.9	8.0 33.6	8.0 32.9	9.0 36.3	12.0 47.4	*28 109.0	*44 167.9	60 255.6	61 255.1	70 253.6
Malaysia	L	303 38.3	345 42.5	*349 41.8	353 41.1	387 43.8	421 46.4	*423 45.3	*425 44.2	*426 43.1	*428 42.1	430 41.1	*458 42.5	*487 43.9	*515 45.1	*543 46.2	*572 47.3	600 48.2
Maldives	L							1.1 10.8	1.1 10.6	1.3 12.3	1.3 12.0	1.7 15.5	2.0 17.9	2.3 20.0	2.4 20.5	2.5 21.0	3.5 28.7	
Mongolia	R										91 75.2	*95 76.1	96 74.7	100 75.5	111 81.4	114 81.1	114 78.8	115 77.2
Nepal	R				30 3.1	31 3.1	*40 4.0	45 4.4	50 4.8	50 4.7	50 4.6	55 4.9	60 5.2	*67 5.7	75 6.2	76 6.2	*113 9.0	150 11.7
Pakistan	L	276[1] 6.0	281[1] 6.0	396[1] 8.2	459[1] 9.3	549[1] 10.8	972[1] 9.3	*985 10.8	*998 18.5	*1 010 18.3	*1 023 18.0	*1 036 17.7	*1 049 17.4	*1 062 17.1	*1 074 16.8	*1 087 16.5	1 100 16.2	1 200 15.9
Philippines	R	600 21.8	*604 21.3	*608 20.8	*611 20.3	*615 19.8	619 19.3	*1 059 32.0	1 499 43.9	1 633 46.4	*1 675 46.0	*1 717 45.7	1 758 45.2	1 800 44.8	1 800 43.3	1 825 42.5	1 850 41.6	1 875 40.8

Country	Code	1960	1961	1962	1963	1964	1965	1966	1967	1968	1969	1970	1971	1972	1973	1974	1975	1976
ASIA (cont'd.)																		
Qatar	R											25 316.5	30 370.4	35 416.7	*36 413.8	37 415.7	38 413.0	40 421.1
Saudi Arabia	R										78 10.4	85 11.0	87 10.9	250 30.5	250 29.6	*252 29.0	255 28.4	260 28.1
Singapore	L	142 86.9	*147 87.1	*153 87.4	*158 88.0	*164 89.0	*169 89.9	*175 90.5	*180 91.0	*186 92.5	191 93.5	274 132.1	*276 130.8	278 129.5	303 138.7	320 144.2	356 158.4	356 155.9
Sri Lanka	L	354 35.8	*376 37.1	397 32.2	406 38.1	417 38.3	438 39.2	*442 38.6	*446 38.1	450 37.5	500 40.8	500 40.0	*501 39.3	502 38.3	515 38.5	*523 38.2	530 37.9	540 37.8
Thailand	R	163 6.2	*525 19.3	*887 31.7	*1 248 43.3	1 610 54.2	*2 188 71.4	2 765 87.6	2 765 84.9	2 766 82.4	2 767 79.9	2 775 77.6	2 800 75.9	3 000 78.7	3 009 76.3	5 111 125.5	5 500 130.7	---
Turkey	L	1 352 49.2	1 503 53.2	1 504 52.0	1 633 55.1	2 165 71.2	2 443 78.4	2 637 82.6	2 721 83.1	2 933 87.3	3 030 88.0	3 136 89.0	3 856 106.8	3 941 106.5	4 033 106.3	4 096 105.3	4 154 104.2	4 228 103.4
United Arab Emirates	R										---				50 240.4	51 237.2	52 234.2	55 240.2
Yemen	R													85 13.9	86 13.7	86 13.3	87 13.1	90 13.1
Yemen, Democratic	R	60 54.1	60 52.9	60 51.6	62 52.1	64 52.5	*67 53.5	69 53.7	71 53.8	73 53.8	76 54.4	*78 54.3	80 54.1	*87 57.2	94 60.0	95 58.9	96 57.8	100 58.5
EUROPE																		
Albania	R	54 32.9	60 35.4	66 37.8	69 38.4	76 41.1	130 68.3	130 66.6	135 67.3	150 72.8	160 75.6	161 74.2	165 74.1	170 74.3	172 73.1	173 71.6	175 70.5	180 70.6
Andorra	R	1.0 125.0	1.5 166.7	3.0 300.0	4.0 363.6	4.2 323.1	4.6 328.6	5.0 333.3	5.5 343.8	5.9 347.1	6.0 333.3	6.0 315.8	6.0 300.0	6.0 300.0	6.1 290.5	6.5 295.5	6.6 287.0	6.6 287.0
Austria	L	1 977 280.5	2 040 287.9	2 079 291.8	2 110 294.6	2 134 296.4	2 154 296.9	2 171 298.3	2 215 302.7	2 261 443.3	2 306 311.8	2 012 270.2	2 396 321.3	2 440 325.9	2 485 330.2	2 530 336.3	2 164 287.1	2 185 289.2
Belgium	L	2 644 288.9	2 767 301.3	2 896 314.1	3 049 328.2	3 080 328.4	3 093 326.8	3 026 318.3	3 120 326.9	3 200 334.2	3 303 343.9	3 383 351.0	3 497 361.5	3 560 366.6	3 662 375.9	3 769 384.5	3 891 395.2	4 044 408.9
Bulgaria	L	1 431 181.9	1 601 201.6	1 733 216.3	1 843 228.2	1 959 240.6	2 055 250.6	2 144 259.5	2 218 266.9	2 245 268.2	2 271 269.3	2 291 269.9	2 305 270.0	2 356 274.7	2 409 279.5	2 460 281.7	2 512 285.7	2 750 310.7
Czechoslovakia	L	3 530 258.5	3 621 262.8	3 664 264.4	3 684 264.1	3 696 262.9	3 727 263.2	3 829 269.7	3 844 270.1	3 849 269.8	3 853 269.4	3 858 269.1	3 871 268.7	3 884 268.2	3 897 267.3	3 910 266.6	3 916 265.4	3 928 264.6
Denmark	L	1 523 332.5	1 529 331.7	1 536 330.5	1 542 329.2	1 548 328.0	1 587 333.5	1 561 325.4	1 564 323.2	1 566 321.8	1 582 323.5	1 597 324.0	1 628 328.0	1 636 327.7	1 671 334.1	1 693 338.0	1 785 355.2	1 851 367.1
Faeroe Islands	L	7.7 220.0	8.0 228.6	8.3 230.6	8.8 244.4	11 297.3	12 324.3	13 351.4	14 368.4	15 394.7	15 394.7	15 384.6	17 435.9	20 512.8	22 564.1	23 575.0	---	---
Finland	L	1 228 227.2	1 290 289.2	1 330 296.2	1 397 308.9	1 456 320.1	1 541 337.6	1 605 350.4	1 663 361.1	1 678 362.7	1 717 371.3	1 789 388.4	1 817 393.6	1 896 409.2	1 944 417.4	1 997 430.1	2 036 437.7	2 179 467.6
France	R	10 981 240.4	12 966 280.9	13 776 293.1	14 581 304.9	14 981 310.1	15 336 314.5	15 440 314.1	15 514 313.1	15 558 311.7	15 796 313.9	15 995 315.7	16 025 312.7	16 311 315.5	16 596 318.4	17 000 324.1	17 200 325.1	17 442 326.9
German Democratic Rep.[2]	L	5 574 323.3	5 602 327.1	5 670 331.5	5 739 334.5	5 741 338.0	5 743 337.5	5 812 340.7	5 881 344.3	5 942 347.8	5 983 350.4	5 985 350.9	6 016 352.6	6 050 355.0	6 082 358.2	6 114 356.2	6 141 357.2	6 167 358.0
Germany, Federal Republic[2]	L	15 892 286.7	16 270 289.6	16 696 293.2	17 099 296.9	17 471 299.9	17 843 302.4	18 215 306.1	18 587 310.4	18 978 315.3	19 368 320.4	19 400 319.6	19 431 318.9	19 463 318.2	19 495 317.6	19 526 317.2	19 558 317.1	20 224 327.4
Gibraltar	L	4.8L 200.0	4.8L 200.0	4.8L 200.0	4.8L 192.0	4.8L 192.0	4.9 196.0	5.4 216.0	5.9 226.9	6.5 250.0	7.0 269.2	9.9 380.8	9.9 366.7	9.9 366.7	9.9 366.7	9.9 366.7	9.9 366.7	---
Greece	R		713 84.9	740 87.6	800 94.3	832 97.8	893 104.4	936 108.7	985 113.0	985 112.7	985 112.3	990 112.6	1 000 113.2	1 300 146.8	1 900 213.9	2 500 280.7	2 750 308.0	2 750 307.0
Hungary	L	2 224 222.8	2 314 230.7	2 390 237.5	2 452 243.0	2 484 245.4	2 484 244.7	2 485 244.0	2 500 244.6	2 514 244.9	2 530 245.7	2 530 244.8	2 532 244.2	2 533 243.6	2 535 243.0	2 536 241.7	2 538 240.9	---
Iceland	L	50 284.1	50 279.3	51 280.2	51 275.7	51 269.8	54 281.3	57 290.8	59 296.5	60 298.5	62<
305.4	63 308.8	64 310.7	64 306.2	64 301.9	64 299.1	64 296.3	64 292.2
Ireland	R	494 174.3	496 176.0	516 182.3	538 188.8	552 192.7	610 212.1	610 210.9	610 209.6	610 208.4	610 207.1	611 206.8	611 205.0	630 209.0	825 272.4	860 278.0	907 289.7	949 299.8

Country	Code	1960	1961	1962	1963	1964	1965	1966	1967	1968	1969	1970	1971	1972	1973	1974	1975	1976
EUROPE (cont'd.)																		
Italy	L	8 005	8 488	9 039	9 564	10 209	10 724	10 808	10 892	10 976	11 333	11 702	12 068	12 204	12 448	12 641	12 818	13 024
		159.4	168.0	177.8	186.8	197.9	206.5	206.5	206.8	207.2	212.6	218.5	224.0	225.3	228.6	230.9	233.0	235.5
Liechetenstein	L	3.6	3.7	3.8	3.9	4.1	4.2	4.3	4.4	4.5	4.9	5.3	5.6	6.0	6.4	6.8	7.4	8.0
		225.0	217.7	223.5	216.7	227.8	221.1	226.3	220.0	225.0	233.3	252.4	266.7	272.7	290.9	309.1	336.4	363.6
Luxembourg	R	98	101	103	107	115	121	126	133	140	149	157	160	170	176	176	176	205
		312.1	318.6	320.9	329.2	349.5	364.5	377.3	395.8	415.4	440.8	463.1	470.6	498.5	516.1	514.6	514.6	597.7
Malta	L																63	63
																	191.5	190.9
Monaco	R		5.5	6.0	6.2	6.3	6.3	6.5	6.5	6.5	6.6	6.6	6.7	6.7	7.5	7.5	7.5	7.5
			239.1	260.9	269.6	273.9	273.9	282.6	282.6	282.6	287.0	287.0	291.3	279.2	312.5	312.5	312.5	312.5
Netherlands	L	3 126	3 127	3 128	3 129	3 130	3 132	3 134	3 154	3 174	3 395	3 616	3 719	3 776	3 811	3 846	3 909	4 017
		272.3	268.7	265.2	261.5	258.2	254.8	251.6	250.4	249.4	263.7	277.5	281.9	283.3	283.6	285.0	287.5	293.2
Norway	L	1 021	1 034	1 052	1 060	1 071	1 089	1 110	1 135	1 152	1 171	1 191	1 204	1 235	1 255	1 277	1 277	1 288
		285.1	286.4	289.1	289.1	289.9	292.5	295.7	299.8	301.7	304.1	307.2	308.5	314.0	316.8	320.7	318.7	319.5
Poland	L	5 268	5 487	5 620	5 629	5 637	5 646	5 647	5 648	5 649	5 649	5 658	5 709	5 795	5 872	7 000	8 127	8 228
		178.2	183.1	185.3	183.4	180.9	179.3	178.2	177.2	176.1	175.0	174.2	174.0	175.2	176.0	208.7	240.2	241.0
Portugal	L	848	902	1 005	1 068	1 127	1 173	1 240	1 345	1 353	1 360	1 368	1 411	1 449	1 506	1 516	1 519	1 525
		96.1	101.1	111.2	116.7	122.1	127.0	135.3	148.9	152.5	155.9	158.6	164.2	168.4	174.1	174.1	173.4	173.2
Romania	L	2 208	2 165	2 372	2 548	2 684	2 790	2 925	3 019	3 031	3 050	3 075	3 084	3 084	3 084	3 084	3 084	3 104
		120.0	116.6	127.0	135.4	141.8	146.6	152.8	156.6	153.7	152.4	151.9	150.7	149.3	148.1	146.8	145.6	145.4
San Marino	R		1.9	2.3	2.7	2.9	3.0	3.0	3.0	3.3	3.5	3.7	4.4	4.6	4.7	4.7	6.0	6.0
			126.7	143.8	168.8	170.6	176.5	176.5	166.7	183.3	184.2	194.7	231.6	230.0	235.0	235.0	300.0	300.0
Spain	R	2 717	3 174	3 491	4 000	4 000	4 550	6 010	6 475	6 951	7 042	7 105	7 174	8 100	9 100	9 200	9 250	9 300
		89.7	103.8	112.9	128.0	126.7	142.6	186.4	198.7	211.0	211.5	210.3	210.2	235.1	261.7	262.1	261.1	260.0
Sweden	L	2 744	2 843	2 938	2 950	2 952	2 954	2 958	2 963	2 967	2 972	*2 976	2 981	2 985	3 020	3 086	3 140	3 203
		366.8	378.1	388.5	388.0	385.3	382.0	378.8	376.6	375.0	373.0	353.9	368.1	367.5	371.1	374.4	378.7	384.0
Switzerland	L	1 445	1 490	1 539	1 590	1 619	1 654	1 685	1 725	1 752	1 800	1 852	1 900	1 958	2 003	2 036	2 076	2 108
		269.5	273.1	277.0	281.0	281.1	282.4	281.0	284.5	285.7	289.8	295.5	300.4	306.7	311.5	313.8	317.7	320.4
United Kingdom	L	15 163	15 316	15 580	15 882	16 015	16 194	16 432	17 493	17 650	18 008	34 706	36 000	37 500	39 000	39 000	39 100	39 500
		288.5	289.2	291.5	295.4	295.7	297.0	299.9	318.1	320.0	325.5	625.6	646.2	671.1	696.2	693.6	692.9	697.5
Yugoslavia	L	1 562	1 826	2 080	2 280	2 700	2 783	3 003	3 059	3 171	3 320	3 372	3 476	3 556	3 685	4 081	4 181	4 526
		84.9	98.1	110.5	119.8	140.5	143.2	152.9	154.2	158.3	164.3	165.5	169.1	171.4	176.0	193.2	196.1	210.4
USSR[3]	R	44 000	54 950	65 900	68 900	71 800	73 800	76 800	80 700	85 500	90 100	94 600	99 900	105 300	110 300	116 100	122 477	--
		205.3	251.9	297.2	306.1	314.7	319.6	328.9	342.0	358.8	374.6	389.7	407.6	425.5	441.6	460.6	480.2	---
OCEANIA																		
American Samoa	R						0.8	0.8	0.9	0.9	1.0	4.0	4.0	4.0	4.1	4.2	---	---
							33.3	33.3	36.0	34.6	37.0	148.2	142.9	137.9	136.7	135.5	---	---
Australia	L	2 283	2 287	2 292	2 296	2 300	2 524	2 526	2 580	2 650	4 950	7 250	7 625	8 000	8 000	8 500	9 500	10 500
		221.3	216.8	213.4	209.7	206.0	221.7	217.8	218.7	220.7	403.7	577.6	597.8	617.3	609.2	512.8	688.0	746.3
Cook Island	R	0.6	0.8	1.0	1.7	2.0	2.2	2.5	2.5	2.5	3.3	*4.0	4.8	5.5	6.3	7.0	7.0	7.0
		33.3	44.4	55.6	89.5	105.3	110.0	125.0	125.0	125.0	157.0	190.5	218.2	250.0	273.9	291.7	280.0	280.0
Fiji Island	R	24	30	30	30	30	*35	36	40	40	45	*50	52	53	250	300	300	300
		60.9	73.5	71.1	68.7	66.5	75.4	75.6	82.5	80.8	88.9	96.2	97.9	97.8	451.3	530.0	519.9	509.3
French Polynesia	R						30	35	35	40	40	41	41	42	65	70	---	---
							329.7	368.4	357.1	392.2	377.4	376.2	362.8	362.1	541.7	564.5	---	---
Guam	R						28	43	58	72	85	90	95	100	100	85	85	87
							378.4	558.4	734.2	878.1	1 000	1 022.7	1 055.6	1 087.0	1 063.8	876.3	858.6	852.9
Gilbert Island	R	0.2	0.2	0.5	0.8	1.0	1.5	2.0	2.7	3.4	4.1	*4.8	5.5	6.1	6.8	7.5	8.2	8.2
		4.4	4.3	10.4	16.7	20.4	30.0	39.2	51.9	63.0	74.6	85.7	94.8	101.7	109.7	117.2	124.2	120.6
Nauru	R							1.0	1.2	1.4	*1.8	2.3	2.7	3.2	3.6	3.6	3.6	
								142.9	171.4	200.0	257.0	328.6	385.7	457.1	514.3	450.0	450.0	
New Caledonia	R		10	11	12	13	14	15	15	16	17	25	31	34	36	45	60	60
			123.5	131.0	139.5	146.1	152.2	159.6	154.6	160.0	165.1	229.4	276.8	295.7	305.1	368.9	480.0	465.1
New Hebrides	R		0.9	0.8	1.4	1.9	*2.5	3.0	7.0	9.0	9.5	10	10	10	10.5	11	11	15
			13.4	11.8	20.0	26.4	33.8	40.0	90.9	113.9	117.3	119.1	116.3	112.4	115.4	117.0	114.6	151.5

Country	Code	1960	1961	1962	1963	1964	1965	1966	1967	1968	1969	1970	1971	1972	1973	1974	1975	1976
OCEANIA (cont'd.)																		
New Zealand	R	580L 244.5	605L 250.0	614L 247.4	616L 243.3	641L 248.0	*648L 246.6	646L 241.4	655L 240.3	657L 238.8	665L 239.5	678L 240.4	713L 249.9	2 325 800.3	2 700 911.2	2 700 892.0	2 704 892.1	2 715 882.6
Niue	R	0.2 50.0	0.2 50.0	0.3 60.0	0.3 60.0	0.3 60.0	0.3 60.0	0.3 60.0	0.6 120.0	0.6 120.0	0.6 120.0	*0.6 120.0	0.8 160.0	0.8 160.0	0.8 160.0	0.8 160.0	0.8 160.0	0.8 160.0
Norfolk Island	R					0.4 200.0	0.4 200.0	0.5 250.0	0.5 250.0	0.5 250.0	0.5 250.0	0.5 250.0	1.0 500.0	1.1 550.0	1.1 550.0	1.1 550.0	1.2 600.0	1.2 600.0
Pacific Islands	R					5 57.5	6 67.4	15 164.8	24 255.3	27 281.3	36 363.6	60 594.1	65 625.0	68 635.5	71 639.6	72 631.6	--- ---	--- ---
Solomon Islands	R	0.6L 4.8	0.8L 6.3	0.9L 6.8	1.0L 7.4	1.6L 11.4	2.4 16.9	3.2 21.8	4.0 26.5	5.0 32.3	6.0 37.7	8.4 51.5	10 59.5	10 57.5	10 56.5	10 55.0	10 53.5	11 57.0
Tonga	R	1.0 16.4	2.0 31.8	2.2 33.9	2.5 37.3	3.2 46.4	4.0 55.6	4.6 62.2	4.9 63.6	6.4 80.0	7.9 95.2	7.9 91.9	8.0 89.9	9.0 97.8	9.1 95.8	10 102.0	11 108.9	15 144.2
Western Samoa	R	3.0 28.0	4.4 40.0	5.8 51.3	12 103.5	12 100.0	14 113.8	15 119.1	30 230.8	31 233.1	31 226.3	32 227.0	50 344.8	50 333.3	50 324.7	50 314.5	--- ---	--- ---

1. Including Bangladesh. 2. The data which relate to the Federal Republic of Germany and the German Democratic Republic include the relevant data relating to Berlin for which separate data have not been supplied. This is without prejudice to any question of status which may be involved. 3. Figures relating to the Byelorussian SSR and the Ukrainian SSR are included with those of the USSR.

Table 3 — Number of television transmitters (circa 1960, 1965, 1970, 1974)
Number of countries and territories presented in this table: 130
A = total; B = auxiliary; Exp = experimental

Country		Date of first regular broadcoast	Circa 1960	Circa 1965	Circa 1970	Circa 1974
AFRICA						
Algeria	A	1956	6	6	13	75
	B		2	1	4	50
Congo	A		—	1	1	1
	B		—	—	—	—
Djibouti	A		—	—	1	1
	B		—	—	—	—
Egypt	A	1960	13	20	28	29
	B		8	10	---	---
Ethiopia	A	1964	—	1	1	8
	B		—	—	—	—
Gabon	A	1963	—	2	3	8
	B		—	—	—	6
Ghana	A		—	3	4	4
	B		—	—	1	1
Ivory Coast	A	1963	—	2	7	---
	B		—	—	3	---
Kenya	A	1962	—	2	3	4
	B		—	—	—	3
Liberia	A	1964	—	1	2	3
	B		—	—	1	2
Libyan Arab Jamahiriya	A		2	---	---	11
	B		—	---	---	2
Madagascar	A	1967	—	3	5	5
	B		—	—	2	3	3
Mauritius	A	1965	—	4	4	4
	B		—	3	3	3
Morocco	A	1962	—	12	---	23
	B		—	9		8
Mozambique	A	1972	—	—	—	1
	B		—	—	—	—
Niger	A		—	1	1	1
	B		—	—	—	—
Nigeria	A	1959	2	9	3	10
	B		—	—	2	---
Reunion	A		—	8	14	13
	B		—	7	13	12
Senegal	A	1972	—	—	1	2
	B		—	—	—	—
Sierra Leone	A	1963	—	1	1	---
	B		—	—	—	
Southern Rhodesia	A	1960	---	2	2	---
	B		---	—	—	
Sudan	A	1963	—	1	1	3
	B		—	—	—	—
Tunisia	A		—	1	8	10
	B		—	—	4	3
Uganda	A	1963	—	5	6	---
	B		—	—	—	
Upper Volta	A		—	1	1	---
	B		—	—	—	
Western Sahara	A		—	—	1	5
	B		—	—	—	—
Zaire	A		—	—	—	3
	B		—	—	—	—
Zambia	A	1961	—	1	4	---
	B		—	—	2	---
AMERICA, NORTH						
Antigua	A		—	1	2	3
	B		—	—	1	1
Barbados	A	1964	—	1	1	2
	B		—	—	—	—
Bermuda	A	1958	---	2	2	2
	B		---	—	1	1

Country		Date of first regular broadcoast	Circa 1960	Circa 1965	Circa 1970	Circa 1974	Country		Date of first regular broadcoast	Circa 1960	Circa 1965	Circa 1970	Circa 1974
Canada	A	1952	98	262	360	661	Virgin Islands (US)	A			1	3	3
	B		24	---	---	---		B			—	1	1
Costa Rica	A	1960	2	3	8	12	**AMERICA, SOUTH**						
	B		—	—	5	6	Argentine	A	1951	4	16	55	82
Cuba	A	1950	27	25	---	---		B		—	3	24	---
	B		20	8			Bolivia	A	1969		---	---	2
Dominican Republic	A	1952	4	4	6	10		B					—
	B		2	2	2	2	Brazil	A	1950	42	41	50	78
El Salvador	A	1956	3	3	3	7		B		14	5	5	20
	B		—	—	—	—	Chile	A	1959	—	3	4	76
Guadeloupe	A			1	3	--		B		—	1	---	46
	B			—	—		Columbia	A	1954	13	15	15	74
Guatemala	A	1956	2	3	3	12		B		11	—	—	49
	B		—	—	1	3	Ecuador	A	1959	1	4	14	19
Haiti	A	1959	1	1	1	2		B		—	—	—	—
	B		—	—	—	—	French Guiana	A			2	3	3
Honduras	A	1959	1	3	5	6		B			1	---	---
	B		—	—	—	5	Guyana	A			4	---	---
Jamaica	A	1963		7	12	13		B			—		
	B			—	3	4	Paraguay	A	1965		1	1	1
Martinique	A			1	6	---		B			—	—	—
	B			—	.		Peru	A	1958	5	16	18	52
Mexico	A	1950	29	33	78	83		B		—	7	9	11
	B		4	2	4	---	Surinam	A	1968		1	3	6
Netherlands Antilles	A	1960		2	3	--		B			—	2	3
	B			—	—		Uruguay	A	1956	1	4	17	17
Nicaragua	A	1956		2	7	---		B		—	—	—	—
	B			—	—		Venezuela	A	1952	14	27	30	49
Panama	A	1959	1	10	13	13		B		9	21	21	45
	B		—	5	9	---	**ASIA**						
Panama Canal Zone	A			4	2	2	Bahrain	A			16	55	82
	B			2	—	—		B		—	3	24	---
Puerto Rico	A	1954		10	17	17	Bangladesh	A	1964	—	—	1	---
	B			—	5	5		B		—	—	—	---
St. Pierre and Miquelon	A	1967		1	3	---	Cyprus	A	1957	1	2	2	5
	B			—	2			B		—	—	—	3
St. Vincent	A			---	---	2	Democratic Kampuchea	A	1962 (exp.)	—	1	1	2
	B							B		—	—	—	—
Trinidad and Tobago	A	1962		2	---	3	Hong Kong	A	1957	1	1	9	26
	B			1		1		B		—	—	7	---
United States	A	1920 (exp.)	579	2 555	2 703	3 695	India	A	1959	—	1	1	5
	B		—	1 855	1 958	---		B		—	—	—	—

Country		Date of first regular broadcast	Circa 1960	Circa 1965	Circa 1970	Circa 1974	Country		Date of first regular broadcast	Circa 1960	Circa 1965	Circa 1970	Circa 1974
Indonesia	A			2	5	21	**EUROPE**						
	B			—	1	9	Albania	A	1960	1	147	---	---
Iran	A	1958	2	3	10	157		B	(exp.)	—	45	---	---
	B		—	1	---	---	Austria	A	1956	10	77	239	461
Iraq	A	1956	1	1	4	6		B		7	---	---	---
	B		—	—	—	—	Belgium	A	1953	10	15	19	28
Israel	A	1969		---	16	33		B		5	10	10	12
	B				3	19	Bulgaria	A	1959	1	27	92	154
Japan	A	1953	127	785	3 582	6 117		B		—	25	85	143
	B		12	613	3 434	5 952	Czechoslovakia	A	1954	15	331	601	788
Jordan	A	1968		3	6	6		B		4	310	588	764
	B			1	4	4	Denmark	A	1954	11	16	25	30
Korea Republic of	A	1956	1	4	28	59		B		3	8	17	22
	B		—	—	6	---	Finland	A		16	98	68	83
Kuwait	A		—	3	7	7		B		7	55	35	36
	B		—	—	2	---	France	A	1935	91	287	2 156	3 001
Lebanon	A	1959	2	4	8	---		B		59	252	2 024	2 771
	B		—	1	3	---	German, Democratic	A	1952	41	257	333	461
Malaysia	A	1963		10	18	38		B		28	242	308	440
	B			4	8	12	Germany, Federal	A	1963	325	589	824	1 153
Mongolia	A	1967	—	—		1		B		28	530	760	1 087
	B		—	—		—	Gibraltar	A			2	2	2
Pakistan	A	1964		2	4	15		B			1	1	1
	B			—	—	10	Greece	A			—	4	54
Philippines	A	1953	4	16	15	22		B					37
	B		—	—	—	—	Hungary	A	1958	6	12	12	22
Qatar	A	1970		—	2	3		B		1	11	3	9
	B				1	1	Iceland	A	1966	—	—	32	80
Saudi Arabia	A	1965	1	2	8	10		B		—	—	25	71
	B		—	—	4	---	Ireland	A	1961	---	11	23	28
Singapore	A	1963	—	2	2	2		B		---	3	16	21
	B		—	1	—	—	Italy	A	1954	425	783	1 153	1 199
Syrian Arab	A	1960	1	---	5	8		B		397	719	1 079	1 106
	B		—	—	—	—	Luxembourg	A	1955	1	6	4	—
Thailand	A	1955	5	8	30	48		B		—	5	3	—
	B		—	4	21	---	Malta	A	1962	—	1	1	1
Turkey	A	1968	—	---	1	38		B		—	—	—	—
	B	(exp.)	—		—	30	Monaco	A	1955	1	2	1	3
Viet-Nam Socialist Republic	A			2	4	5		B			—	—	1
	B			—	—	—	Netherlands	A	1953	6	8	16	21
Yemen, Peoples' Democratic Rep.	A	1964	—	1	6	5		B		1	1	10	---
	B		—	—	—	2	Norway	A	1960	12	87	373	665
								B		9	68	333	621

Country		Date of first regular broadcoast	Circa 1960	Circa 1965	Circa 1970	Circa 1974	Country		Date of first regular broadcoast	Circa 1960	Circa 1965	Circa 1970	Circa 1974
Poland	A	1954	17	53	56	69	**OCEANIA**						
	B		8	35	21	---							
Portugal	A	1956	7	17	23	41	American Samoa	A			6	6	6
	B		3	12	---	29		B			—	—	—
Romania	A	1957	6	26	95	194	Australia	A	1956	16	53	181	198
	B			4	16	78	174		B		—	—	87	98
Spain	A	1951	9	256	593	741	French Polynesia	A			4	4	---
	B		5	240	566	706		B			3	3	
Sweden	A	1956	45	118	247	358	Guam	A			1	5	---
	B		—	70	150	206		B			—	1	
Switzerland	A	1958	26	67	318	583	New Caledonia	A			3	6	7
	B		---	54	269	505		B			3	4	6
United Kingdom	A	1936	50	150	291	596	New Zealand	A	1960	1	10	24	144
	B		8	72	162	423		B		—	6	20	137
Yugoslavia	A	1958	12	160	296	430	Pacific Islands	A				3	3
	B		8	131	256	371		B				2	2
USSR	A	1938-1948	169	502	1 089	1 749							
	B		76	---	---	---							

Table 4 — Total number of television receivers (thousands) and receivers per 1,000 inhabitants (in italics)

Number of countries and territories presented in this table: 139
L = Number of licenses issued or sets declared
R = Estimated number of receivers in use

Country	Code	1960	1961	1962	1963	1964	1965	1966	1967	1968	1969	1970	1971	1972	1973	1974	1975	1976
AFRICA																		
Algeria	R	60 5.6	67 6.1	68 6.2	68 6.1	*70 6.0	72 6.7	85 7.7	100 7.4	100 7.2	100 7.7	110 10.8	160 13.7	210 16.5	260 25.2	410 29.8	500 30.3	525
Benin	L															0.3 0.1	0.3 0.1	0.3 0.1
Central African Republic	L															0.1 0.1	0.1 0.1	0.1 0.1
Congo	R				0.1 0.1	0.4 0.4	0.4 0.4	0.5 0.5	*0.8 0.7	*1.2 1.1	*1.5 1.3	1.8 1.5	1.9 1.6	2.5 2.0	2.6 2.0	3.0 2.3	*3.1 2.3	3.3 2.4
Djibouti	R										0.8 8.6	1.0 10.5	2.0 20.6	2.2 22.2	2.3 22.8	2.8 26.9	3.1 29.3	3.5 32.4
Egypt	R	50 1.9	47 1.8	128 4.7	197 7.1	273 9.5	323 11.0	361 12.0	399 12.9	418 13.2	475 14.6	529 15.9	584 17.1	584 16.7	600 16.8	610 16.6	620 16.5	--- ---
Ethiopia	R	— —	— ---	— ---	— —	— —	2.5 0.1	5.0 0.2	5.6 0.2	6 0.3	8 0.3	8 0.3	16 0.6	17 0.7	20 0.8	20 0.7	20 0.7	21 0.7
Gabon	R	— —	— —	— —	1.0 2.2	1.2 2.6	1.2 2.6	1.2 2.5	1.2 2.5	1.2 2.5	1.2 2.4	1.2 2.4	1.3 2.6	*3.2 6.3	5.0 9.7	5.1 9.8	8.0 15.2	8.5 16.0
Ghana	R					0.5 0.07	0.9 0.1	4.0 0.5	5.0 0.6	*8.5 1.0	12 1.4	16 1.9	20 2.3	21 2.3	30 3.7	33 3.4	33 3.3	35 3.4
Ivory Coast	R	— —	— —	— —	1.5 0.4	1.6 0.4	6.0 1.6	*6.2 1.6	*6.3 1.6	6.7 1.6	10 2.0	*23 5.3	35 8.0	40 9.0	100 21.5	108 22.6	115 23.5	257 51.3
Kenya	R	— —	— —	2.2 0.3	8.2 0.9	8.5 0.9	9.9 1.1	10.5 1.1	14 1.4	15 1.5	16 1.5	16 1.4	27 2.3	37 3.0	*37 3.0	37 3.0	38 3.0	50 3.7
Liberia	R	— —	— —	— —	0.1 0.0	2.0 1.5	2.7 2.0	4.0 2.9	4.6 3.2	*5.3 3.6	6.0 4.0	6.5 4.3	7.0 4.5	8.0 5.0	8.5 5.2	*8.7 5.2	8.8 5.2	8.9 5.1
Lybian Arab Jamahiriya	L											1.0 0.5	2.0 1.0	2.5 1.2	5 2.4	6 2.7	10 4.4	--- ---
Madagascar	R	— —	— —	— —	— —	— —	— —	— —	0.1 0.0	0.7 0.1	1.7 0.3	3.5 0.5	4.6 0.7	6.0 0.8	7.2 1.0	7.5 1.0	7.5 0.9	8.0 1.0
Mauritius	L	— —	— —	— —	— —	— —	3.6 4.7	6.2 8.0	10 12.7	13 16.1	15 18.3	19 23.1	22 26.3	27 31.7	31 35.7	38 43.0	40 44.5	41 44.9
Morocco	R	5 0.4	5 0.4	5 0.4	15 1.2	20 1.6	33 2.5	36 2.7	61 4.4	100 7.0	145 9.9	174 11.5	223 14.3	286 17.9	331 20.1	382 22.5	448 25.6	522 28.9
Mozambique	L	— —	— —	— —	— —	— —	— —	— —	— —	— —	— —	— —	— —	— —	--- ---	1.0 0.1	*1.1 0.1	1.2 0.1
Niger	L															0.3 0.1	*0.4 0.1	0.5 0.1
Nigeria	R	1 0.02	6 0.14	10 0.22	10 0.22	15 0.3	30 0.6	40 0.8	42 0.8	*48 0.9	53 1.0	75 1.4	*75 1.3	75 1.3	85 1.4	90 1.5	100 1.6	105 1.6
Reunion	L						2.7 6.9	7 17	10 24	14 32.9	18 41.3	21 47	26 56.8	28 59.7	30 62.5	30 61.1	37 73.9	37 72.4
Senegal	R	— —	— —	— —	— —	— —	— —	— —	— —	— —	1.0 0.3	1.4 0.4	1.5 0.4	1.6 0.4	1.7 0.4	1.7 0.4	1.8 0.4	2.0 0.4
Sierra Leone	R	— —	— —	— —	0.4 0.2	0.6 0.3	1.1 0.5	2.0 0.8	2.5 1.0	*2.7 1.1	*2.8 1.1	3.0 1.1	3.1 1.2	5.0 1.8	6.0 2.1	6.0 2.1	6.1 2.0	8.5 2.8
Southern Rhodesia	R	6 1.6	18 4.9	29[1] 7.5	35[1] 8.6	39 9.2	43 9.7	45 9.8	45 9.4	45 9.1	48 9.4	50 9.4	51 9.3	57 10.0	*61 10.4	65 10.7	69 11.0	72 11.1

Country	Code	1960	1961	1962	1963	1964	1965	1966	1967	1968	1969	1970	1971	1972	1973	1974	1975	1976
AFRICA (cont'd.)																		
Sudan	R	—	—	—	—	10	10	11	11	15	30	45	65	70	100	100	100	*100
		—	—	—	—	0.8	0.7	0.8	0.8	1.0	2.0	2.9	4.0	4.2	5.8	5.7	5.5	5.3
Togo	L															1.0	*1.3	1.5
																0.5	0.6	0.7
Tunisia	R	0.4	2.0	2.0	3.1	3.5	5.5	20	35	35	37	51	75	131	147	169	191	208
		0.1	0.5	0.5	0.7	0.8	1.2	4.2	7.3	7.1	7.4	9.9	14.3	24.4	26.8	30.1	33.2	35.3
Uganda	L	—	—	—	1.0	3.9	5.8	*6.7	7.5	9	12	*14	15	15	*33	*52	70	71
		—	—	—	0.1	0.5	0.7	0.8	0.8	1.0	1.3	1.4	1.5	1.4	3.1	4.7	6.2	6.1
United Rep. of Tanzania	L										4.0	*4.0	*4.1	*4.1	*4.2	4.2	*4.3	45
											0.3	0.3	0.3	0.3	0.3	0.3	0.3	0.3
Upper Volta	R					0.1	0.3	0.3	0.5	0.5	2.2	5	5.5	6	*6	*6	6	*6	...
						0.02	0.06	0.1	0.1	0.1	0.4	1.0	1.0	1.1	1.1	1.0	1.0	1.0	...
Western Sahara	R								1.8	2.0	*2	*2	*2	*2	2	2	2	2
									35.0	35.1	31.3	27.8	27.4	27.4	27.0	26.7	26.7	26.3
Zaire	R										6.5	7.0	7.0	7.0	7.0	7.0	7.0	7.0
											0.3	0.3	0.3	0.3	0.3	0.3	0.3	0.3
Zambia	R	—	—	...	...	7.5	8.6	10	11	11	*14	17	19	20	21	22	23	25
		—	—	...	...	2.1	2.3	2.6	2.8	2.7	3.4	4.0	4.3	4.4	4.5	4.5	4.6	4.8
AMERICA, NORTH																		
Antigua	L						1.5	2.0	2.5	3.0	4.5	*6.7	8.8	8.8	12	12	15	15
							24.6	31.8	38.5	45.5	66.2	95.7	125.7	123.9	169.0	166.7	205.5	205.5
Barbados	R	—	—	—	—	—	6	9	9.1	15	15	16	18	32	35	40	40	48
		—	—	—	—	—	25.5	38.1	38.4	63.3	63.0	67.0	75.0	132.8	144.6	163.9	163.3	194.3
Bermuda	R	8.3	9.4	10	11	11	*11.5	12	14	15	16	17	17	19	20	20	20	21
		188.6	208.9	217.4	234.0	229.2	239.6	244.9	280.0	294.1	313.7	326.9	320.8	351.9	363.6	363.6	357.1	368.4
Canada	R	3 930	4 100	4 375	4 655	4 950	5 310	5 700	*5 900	6 100	*6 600	7 100	*7 198	7 296	7 705	8 232	9 390	9 895
		219.4	224.4	235.0	245.5	256.1	270.3	284.3	288.6	293.7	313.0	331.7	333.3	333.9	348.3	366.2	411.8	428.0
Costa Rica	R	3.0	7.2	12	15	35	50	65	66	*83	100	100	120	120	122	131	150	155
		2.4	5.6	8.9	10.7	24.2	33.4	42.1	41.5	50.6	59.2	57.6	67.2	65.3	64.6	67.5	75.2	75.7
Cuba	R	500	500	520	525	550	*552	555	575	575	*578	*582	*585	*588	*592	595	600	650
		71.2	69.7	68.2	70.1	71.9	70.8	70	71	69.7	68.8	68.0	67	66	65.1	64.1	63.3	67.1
Dominican Republic	R	...	10	11	19	35	50	65	75	75	100	100	*125	150	155	156	158	160
		...	3.1	3.3	5.5	9.8	13.5	17.0	19.0	18.4	23.8	23.0	27.9	32.4	32.4	31.5	30.9	30.2
El Salvador	R	20	20	25	30	30	35	40	45	*60	75	92	*100	108	110	111	135	136
		7.9	7.7	9.3	10.8	10.5	11.9	13.1	14.2	18.3	22.1	26.2	27.5	28.8	28.5	27.9	32.9	32.1
Greenland															2.7	2.7	...	...
															52.9	51.9	...	...
Guadeloupe	L						0.7	2.6	4.0	5.2	5.8	*6.9	7.9	9	10	13	13	15
							2.3	8.5	12.8	16.4	18.4	21.0	23.7	26.6	29.1	37.3	36.7	41.7
Guatemala	R	32	35	40	50	50	55	60	*62	65	72	72	82	85	105	106	110	120
		8.0	8.5	9.5	11.5	11.2	12.0	12.7	12.8	13.0	14.0	13.6	15.0	15.1	18.2	17.8	18.0	19.0
Haiti	R	1.8	2.0	2.5	3.5	4	*7	10	11	11	11	11	11	12	13	13	13.2	13.5
		0.5	0.5	0.7	0.9	1.0	1.8	2.5	2.7	2.7	2.6	2.6	2.6	2.8	2.9	2.9	2.9	2.9
Honduras	R	1.3	4	4.5	6.5	7.2	2.2	10	11	11	17	22	25	*36	46	46	47	48
		0.7	2.1	2.3	3.1	3.4	1.0	4.4	4.7	4.6	6.9	8.6	9.5	13.2	16.3	15.7	15.5	15.3
Jamaica	R	—	—	—	11	20	25	40	47	56	56	70	73	89	100	100	110	111
		—	—	—	6.5	11.5	14.2	22.4	26.0	30.6	30.2	37.2	38.2	45.9	50.8	50.0	54.2	53.9
Martinique	L						1.5	3.5	4.9	5.9	7.4	9.5	10	12	14	16	20	20.1
							4.9	11.2	15.3	18.1	22.3	28.1	29.1	34.4	39.7	44.7	55.1	54.5
Mexico	R	650	900	930	1 040	*1 129	1 218	1 517	1 790	2 150	2 563	2 993	3 385	3 821	4 339	4 885	...	...
		17.9	23.4	23.9	25.9	27.2	28.4	34.3	39.2	45.6	52.6	59.5	65.2	71.2	78.3	85.3	...	...
Netherlands Antilles	R	3	8	10	22	24	25	25	*27	29	30	32	32	33	34	34	35	36
		15.6	41.0	50.5	109.5	117.1	120.2	118.5	126.2	134.3	137.0	144.1	141.6	143.5	145.3	142.9	144.6	145.8
Nicaragua	R	5	5	6.5	10	*13	16	19	25	35	45	55	56	60	63	75	*83	90
		3.4	3.3	4.2	6.2	7.9	9.4	10.9	13.9	18.9	23.6	27.9	27.6	28.6	29.0	33.4	35.8	37.6
Panama	R	11	30	30	48	65	70	77	77	*101	125	142	158	*167	175	183	185	186
		10.2	26.9	26.1	40.4	53.2	55.5	59.3	57.6	73.4	88.2	97.4	105.3	108.2	110.3	112.2	110.3	107.8

Country	Code	1960	1961	1962	1963	1964	1965	1966	1967	1968	1969	1970	1971	1972	1973	1974	1975	1976
AMERICA, NORTH (cont'd.)																		
Panama Canal Zone	R						20 571.4	20 540.5	20 540.5	20 526.3	20 526.3	20 512.8	20 500.0	20 487.8	20 476.2	20 476.2	20 465.1	20 454.6
Puerto Rico	R											410 149.5	505 182.0	600 214.2	605 213.5	625 217.9	630 217.1	631 214.9
St. Lucia	R								0.3 2	0.6 5	1.5 14	1.5 14.9	1.6 15.5	1.6 15.4	1.7 16.2	1.7 16	1.7 16	1.7 16
St Pierre & Miquelon	R	—	—	—	—	—	—	—	0.8 160.0	0.9 180.0	1.2 240.0	1.3 260.0	1.4 280.0	1.5 300.0	1.6 320.0	1.7 340.0	1.7 340.0	2.0 400.0
St. Vincent																0.6 6.5	---	---
Trinidad & Tobago	R	0.02 0.02	0.02 0.02	3.5 4.0	7.7 8.7	*14 15.6	20 22.0	20 21.8	36* 38.8	40 42.7	43 45.5	60 62.8	70 72.5	82 84.0	93 94.2	100 100.2	*105 104.1	110 108.0
United States of America	R	55 600[2] 307.7	57 000 310.3	59 000[2] 316.3	61 850 326.8	67 100 349.7	70 350 326.1	74 100 377.0	78 000 392.5	*79 500 396.1	81 000 399.7	84 600 412.9	93 000 449.2	99 000 474.0	117 000 556.1	121 000 571.0	---	---
Virgin Islands (U.S.)	R					8 170.2	9 173.1	9 166.7	15 267.9	16 275.9	*18 300.0	21 333.3	*23 365.1	*25 390.6	*28 430.8	30 461.5	30 455.6	32 484.9
AMERICA, SOUTH																		
Argentina	R	450 21.8	700 33.4	850 40.0	1 200 55.7	1 500 68.6	1 600 72.1	1 850 82.3	1 900 83.3	2 500 108.2	3 100 132.3	3 500 147.4	*3 606 149.8	3 711 152.1	3 731 150.9	3 950 157.7	4 500 177.3	---
Brazil	R	1 200 16.8	1 356 18.4	1 430 18.9	1 800 23.1	2 300 28.7	*2 400 29.1	2 500 29.4	*3 400 38.9	*4 300 47.8	*5 200 56.2	6 100 64.1	6 500 66.4	6 600 65.5	*7 625 73.6	8 650 81.1	*9 588 87.4	10 525 93.2
Bolivia		—	---	—	—	—	—	—	—	—	—	---	---	---	---	---	43.5 8.0	48.0 8.7
Chile	R	0.5 0.07	3 0.4	4 0.5	35 4.3	50 6.0	*52 6.1	55 6.3	*170 19.2	*285 31.6	400 43.5	500 53.4	*500 52.4	500 51.5	525 53.1	558 55.4	700 68.3	710 68.0
Columbia	R	150 9.4	200 12.2	205 12.1	210 12.0	300 16.6	350 18.7	400 20.7	*450 22.5	500 24.2	622 29.1	810 36.7	891 39.1	971 41.2	*1 181 48.6	*1 390 55.4	1 600 61.8	1 700 63.6
Ecuador	R	2 0.5	5 1.1	16 3.5	17 3.6	32 6.5	42 8.2	55 10.4	71 13.0	*97 17.2	*124 21.3	150 24.9	*164 26.3	178 27.6	*214 32.2	250 36.4	252 35.5	300 41.0
French Guiana	L								0.1 2.3	0.9 19.6	1.3 27.1	1.9 37.3	2.5 48.1	2.5 46.3	2.5 44.6	2.5 51.7	3.0 51.7	5.0 80.7
Paraguay	R	—	—	—	—	—	—	---	---	13 5.0	17 7.6	*34 14.8	50 21.1	*51 21.0	53 21.2	53 20.6	54 20.4	55 20.2
Peru	R	33 3.3	82 8.0	120 11.4	150 13.9	175 15.7	210 18.4	275 23.4	275 22.7	300 24.0	390 30.3	395 29.8	400 29.3	410 29.2	411 28.4	425 28.6	500 32.6	600 38.0
Surinam	R	—	—	—	—	—	6.8 20.5	16 47.1	*19 54.8	*22 62.0	25 68.9	28 75.5	31 81.6	*31 80.0	31 77.7	33 80.5	34 80.6	38 87.6
Uruguay	R	25 9.5	60 22.5	70 25.9	158 57.8	175 63.2	200 71.4	*205 72.3	*210 73.3	215 74.3	*236 80.7	*258 87.3	*279 93.5	300 99.5	305 100.1	350 113.8	351 112.9	355 113.1
Venezuela			250 32.7	263 33.1	549 66.6	573 67.2	591 67.0	650 71.4	*667 71.0	*683 70.6	700 70.3	700 68.2	*794 75.2	887 81.6	980 87.6	1 095 95.0	1 200 101.2	1 284 105.1	1 431 113.8
ASIA																		
Bahrain	R				5.5 32.2	8.0 45.7	10.5 58.3	*13 70.3	15 79.8	18 93.3	21 105	*23 110.1	*24 111.6	*26 117.1	*27 117.9	*29 112.9	30 123.5	30 119.5	31 119.7
Bangladesh																10 0.1	*15 *0.2	20 0.3
Brunei																	14 95.2	20 134.2
Cyprus	L	1.6 2.8	3.5 6.1	5.6 9.7	7.2 12.2	9.2 15.7	14 23.6	21 34.9	28 45.8	32 51.8	42 67.2	49 77.4	50 78.0	51 78.6	52 79.2	53 79.7	54 80.2	57 83.7
Democratic Kampuchea		—	0.3 0.1	0.4 0.1	1.0 0.2	1.1 0.2	7.0 0.2	*16 1.1	25 2.5	*25.2 3.9	*25.3 3.8	*25.5 3.7	*25.7 3.6	*25.9 3.5	26 3.5	26 3.4	30 3.3	35 4.2
Hong Kong	R	6.8 2.2	9.5 3.0	16 4.8	25 7.1	36 10.0	50 13.5	58' 15.5	78 20.4	90 23.3	158 40.5	444 112.6	570 142.8	670 165.6	748 182.8	785 188.4	*812 192.2	839 195.9
India	L	0.4 0.0	*0.4 0.0	0.4 0.0	0.5 0.0	0.7 0.0	0.8 0.0	4.0 0.0	6.2 0.01	7.8 0.02	12 0.02	25 0.05	49 0.09	86 0.2	163 0.3	275 0.5	*277 0.5	280 0.5
Indonesia	R					10 0.1	35 0.3	45 0.4	46 0.4	54 0.5	72 0.6	75 0.6	90 0.8	95 0.8	*166 1.3	237 1.8	290 2.2	300 2.2	325 2.3

Country	Code	1960	1961	1962	1963	1964	1965	1966	1967	1968	1969	1970	1971	1972	1973	1974	1975	1976
ASIA (cont'd.)																		
Iran	R	38 / 1.8	40 / 1.8	78 / 3.4	100 / 4.3	*105 / 4.4	110 / 4.5	130 / 5.1	131 / 5.0	200 / 7.5	250 / 9.1	533 / 18.8*	800 / 27.4	1 000 / 33.3	1 200 / 38.7	1 500 / 47.0	1 700 / 51.6	1 720 / 50.7
Iraq	R	35 / 5.1	50 / 7.1	50 / 6.9	107 / 14.3	163 / 21.1	171 / 21.4	180 / 21.9	190 / 22.4	200 / 22.8	220 / 24.3	350 / 37.4	363 / 37.5	375 / 37.5	388 / 37.5	400 / 37.4	410 / 37.1	425 / 37.1
Israel	L	— / —	— / —	— / —	1.8 / —	3 / 0.8	14 / 1.2	20 / 5.5	26 / 7.6	*92 / 9.5	210 / 32.8	356 / 73.0	345 / 120.4	370 / 113.3	440 / 118.1	460 / 136.4	475 / 138.5	475 / 139.0 / 135.3
Japan	L	6 860 / 72.9	9 249 / 97.4	12 612 / 131.6	15 153 / 156.5	16 716 / 170.9	18 080 / 182.9	19 002 / 190.4	20 016 / 198.5	21 027 / 206.2	22 070 / 213.9	22 883 / 219.3	23 511 / 222.7	24 194 / 226.2	24 797 / 228.9	25 753 / 236.2	26 545 / 238.9	--- / ---
Jordan	R	—	—	—	—	—	—	4 / 2.0	5 / 2.4	17 / 7.9	25 / 11.3	46³ / 20.2	85 / 36.1	95 / 39.1	95 / 37.8	120 / 46.2	120 / 44.6	125 / 45.0
Korea, Republic of	L	8 / 0.3	20 / 0.8	32 / 1.2	33 / 1.2	33 / 1.2	45 / 1.6	47 / 1.7	82 / 2.8	152 / 5.2	246 / 8.2	418 / 13.6	678 / 21.6	956 / 29.9	1 282 / 39.3	1 619 / 48.6	*1 960 / 57.7	2 300 / 66.4
Kuwait	R	0.7 / 2.5	2 / 6.5	8 / 23.3	35 / 91.4	60 / 140.9	*70 / 147.4	80 / 153	80 / 139.9	*80 / 127.4	80 / 119.6	100 / 131.6	120 / 145.8	160 / 180.4	180 / 189.1	182 / 178.8	---	---
Lebanon	R	8 / 4.3	25 / 13.1	55 / 27.9	100 / 49.2	120 / 57.4	135 / 62.8	140 / 63.3	150 / 66.0	215 / 92.1	250 / 104.2	260 / 105.3	300 / 118.0	320 / 122.2	321 / 119.0	375 / 134.8	410 / 142.9	425 / 143.6
Malaysia	R	—	—	—	—	28 / 3.2	53 / 5.8	80 / 8.6	107 / 11.1	121 / 12.2	151 / 14.9	*184 / 17.6	217 / 20.2	274 / 24.7	326 / 28.6	390 / 33.2	452 / 37.4	555 / 44.6
Mongolia		—	—	—	—	—	—	—	—	—	---	---	1.0 / 0.8	*1.5 / 1.2	2.0 / 1.5	3.0 / 2.2	3.0 / 2.1	3.5 / 2.4	3.6 / 2.4
Oman																2.0 / 2.7	*2.3 / 3.0	2.3 / 3.2
Pakistan	R	—	—	—	—	1 / 0.02	10 / 0.2	16 / 0.3	20 / 0.4	32 / 0.6	80 / 1.4	99 / 1.6	116 / 1.9	129 / 2.0	*132 / 2.0	135 / 2.0	250 / 3.5	350 / 4.8
Philippines	R	38 / 1.4	45 / 1.6	55 / 1.9	70 / 2.3	75 / 2.4	120 / 3.8	160 / 4.8	190 / 5.6	*270 / 7.7	350 / 9.6	400 / 10.6	421 / 10.8	430 / 10.7	645 / 15.5	711 / 16.5	*756 / 17.0	800 / 17.4
Qatar		—	—	—	—	—	—	—	—	—	—	---	---	---	---	---	20 / 217.4	40 / 421.1
Saudi Arabia	R	6.5 / 1.1	8.7 / 1.4	14 / 2.2	19 / 3.0	30 / 4.6	*40 / 5.9	*50 / 7.2	*61 / 8.6	*71 / 9.7	*81 / 10.8	*91 / 11.8	*102 / 12.8	*112 / 13.7	122 / 14.4	122 / 14.0	124 / 13.8	130 / 14.1
Singapore	L	—	—	—	31 / 17.3	55 / 29.9	63 / 33.5	84 / 43.4	98 / 49.5	113 / 56.2	131 / 64.1	157 / 75.7	179 / 84.8	205 / 95.5	231 / 105.7	252 / 113.6	269 / 119.7	294 / 128.7
Syrian Arab Republic	R	—	1.0 / 0.2	1.5 / 0.3	30 / 6.0	45 / 8.7	65 / 12.2	100 / 18.2	*100 / 17.6	100 / 17.1	106 / 17.5	116 / 18.6	125 / 19.4	150 / 22.6	*187 / 27.4	224 / 31.8	224 / 30.9	230 / 30.7
Thailand	R	60 / 2.3	80 / 2.9	87 / 3.1	115 / 4.0	200 / 6.7	200 / 6.5	210 / 6.7	210 / 6.5	210 / 6.3	241 / 7.0	*241 / 6.7	241 / 6.5	*296 / 7.8	350 / 8.9	715 / 17.6	738 / 17.5	761 / 17.5
Turkey	L	1 / 0.04	1 / 0.04	1.5 / 0.05	*1.5 / 0.05	*1.6 / 0.05	1.6 / 0.05	2.5 / 0.08	*10 / 0.3	*17.5 / 0.5	25 / 0.7	*64 / 1.8	102 / 2.8	133 / 3.6	227 / 6.0	458 / 11.8	1 000 / 25.1	1 769 / 43.2
United Arab Emirates																17 / 79.1	*17.5 / 78.8	18 / 78.6
Viet-nam, Socialist Rep.											373 / 21.2	450 / 25.1	*475 / 26.0	500 / 26.9	500 / 26.4	500 / 25.9	---	---
Yemen, People's Demo. Rep.	R	—	—	—	3 / 2.5	*8 / 6.6	13 / 10.4	20 / 15.6	*20 / 15.1	*20 / 14.7	20 / 14.3	21 / 14.6	*23 / 15.6	25 / 16.4	26 / 16.6	30 / 18.6	31 / 18.7	32 / 18.7
EUROPE																		
Albania						1.0 / 0.5	1.0 / 0.5	1.0 / 0.5	1.0 / 0.5	1.0 / 0.5	1.6 / 0.8	2.1 / 1.0	2.5 / 1.1	3.0 / 1.3	4.0 / 1.7	4.0 / 1.7	4.5 / 1.8	4.5 / 1.8
Andorra						0.7 / 50.0	1.0 / 66.7	1.4 / 87.5	1.6 / 94.1	1.7 / 94.4	*1.8 / 94.7	*1.8 / 90.0	*1.9 / 95.0	*1.9 / 90.5	2 / 90.9	*2.5 / 108.7	3 / 130.4
Austria	L	193 / 27.4	291 / 41.1	377 / 52.9	465 / 64.9	586 / 81.4	711 / 98.0	853 / 117.2	978 / 133.7	1 129 / 153.5	1 277 / 172.7	1 426 / 191.5	1 586 / 212.7	1 695 / 226.4	1 739 / 231.1	1 739 / 231.2	1 739 / 230.7	1 772 / 230.7
Belgium	L	618 / 67.5	820 / 89.3	1 018 / 110.4	1 206 / 129.8	1 382 / 147.4	1 543 / 163.0	1 660 / 174.6	1 801 / 188.7	1 894 / 197.8	2 000 / 208.3	2 004 / 207.9	2 203 / 227.8	2 289 / 235.7	2 376 / 243.9	2 464 / 251.4	2 548 / 258.9	2 646 / 267.6
Bulgaria	L	5 / 0.6	11 / 1.4	31 / 3.9	66 / 8.2	122 / 15.0	185 / 22.6	288 / 34.9	420 / 50.5	621 / 74.2	829 / 98.3	1 028 / 121.1	1 181 / 138.4	1 286 / 150.0	1 383 / 160.5	1 457 / 166.8	1 508 / 171.5	1 546 / 174.7
Czechoslovakia	L	795 / 58.2	1 089 / 79.0	1 356 / 97.8	1 630 / 116.8	1 899 / 135.1	2 113 / 149.2	2 375 / 167.3	2 600 / 182.7	2 864 / 200.7	2 996 / 209.5	3 091 / 215.6	3 187 / 221.2	3 305 / 228.2	3 404 / 233.5	3 602 / 245.6	3 689 / 250.0	3 793 / 255.5
Denmark	L	542 / 118.3	707 / 153.4	851 / 183.1	927 / 197.9	1 020 / 216.1	1 084 / 227.8	1 140 / 237.7	1 145 / 236.6	1 210 / 248.6	1 228 / 251.1	1 131 / 266.0	1 375 / 277.1	1 442 / 288.9	1 527 / 304.1	1 556 / 310.6	1 557 / 309.8	1 637 / 324.7

Country	Code	1960	1961	1962	1963	1964	1965	1966	1967	1968	1969	1970	1971	1972	1973	1974	1975	1976
EUROPE (cont'd.)																		
Finland	L	93	190	336	476	622	776	822	899	958	987	1 036	1 099	1 183	1 224	1 261	1 440	1 714
		21	42.6	74.8	105.2	136.7	170.0	179.4	195.2	207.1	213.5	224.9	238.1	255.3	262.8	271.6	309.5	367.8
France	L	1 902	2 555	3 427	4 400	5 414	6 489	7 471	8 316	9 252	10 153	10 968	11 655	12 279	12 332	12 335	14 197	14 500
		41.6	55.4	72.9	92.0	112.1	133.1	152.0	167.8	185.4	201.8	216.5	227.4	237.5	236.6	235.2	268.3	271.7
German, Democratic Republic [4]	L	1 035	1 459	1 892	2 379	2 801	3 216	3 559	3 933	4 173	4 262	4 499	4 649	4 820	4 966	5 096	5 177	5 180
		60.0	85.2	110.6	138.7	164.9	189.0	208.6	230.2	244.3	249.6	263.8	272.5	282.8	292.5	296.9	301.1	300.7
Germany, Federal Republic [4]	L	4 635	5 888	7 213	8 539	10 024	11 379	12 720	13 806	14 958	15 970	16 750	17 430	18 064	18 468	18 920	19 226	---
		83.6	104.8	126.7	142.3	172.0	192.8	213.8	230.5	248.5	264.2	276.0	280.0	295.3	300.9	307.4	311.7	---
Gibraltar	L			1	2.9	4.9	5.0	5.1	5.2	5.3	5.4	5.5	5.6	5.7	5.8	5.9	6.0	6.6
				41.7	116.0	196.0	200.0	204.0	200.0	203.9	207.7	211.5	207.4	211.1	214.8	218.5	222.2	235.7
Greece	R							3	15	40	86	*183	280	520	950	950	1 140	1 165
								0.4	1.7	4.6	9.8	20.8	31.7	58.7	107.0	106.7	127.7	130.1
Hungary	L	104	206	325	471	675	831	996	1 169	1 397	1 596	1 769	1 943	2 085	2 199	2 296	2 352	2 495
		10.4	20.5	32.3	46.7	66.7	81.9	97.8	114.4	136.1	154.9	171.1	187.4	200.5	210.8	218.8	223.3	236.0
Iceland	R	–	–	–	–	–	–	–	...	30	31	41	44	46	46	50	51	53
		–	–	–	–	–	–	–	...	149.3	152.7	201.0	213.6	220.1	217.0	233.6	236.1	242.0
Ireland	R	50	60	127	201	264	329	288	394	412	446	447	486	524	532	550	600	655
		17.6	21.3	44.9	70.5	92.2	114.4	99.6	135.4	140.8	151.4	151.3	163.1	173.9	175.6	177.8	191.6	206.9
Italy	L	2 124	2 762	3 457	4 285	5 216	6 045	6 855	7 666	8 347	9 016	9 717	10 344	10 951	11 426	11 817	12 103	12 377
		42.3	54.7	68.0	83.4	101.4	116.4	131.0	145.6	157.5	169.1	181.4	192.0	202.2	209.8	215.9	220.0	223.8
Luxembourg	L	7.2	10	13	17	25	31	38	44	52	62	71	75	82	85	88	97	105
		22.9	31.6	40.5	52.3	76.0	93.4	113.8	131.0	154.3	183.4	209.4	220.6	240.5	249.3	257.3	283.6	306.1
Malta	L	14	16	16	21	24	26	31	35	39	44	47	53	57	57	57	58	63
		42.6	48.6	48.6	64.0	74.1	81.3	97.8	110.1	122.3	136.2	144.2	163.1	178.7	177.0	174.9	176.3	190.9
Monaco	R	---	12	12	12	13	*14	15	15	*15	*15	*15	*16	*16	16	16	16	16
		---	521.7	521.7	521.7	565.2	608.7	652.2	652.2	652.2	652.2	652.2	695.7	666.7	666.7	666.7	666.7	666.7
Netherlands	L	801	1 040	1 275	1 574	1 836	2 113	2 370	2 559	2 658	2 869	3 086	3 211	3 353	3 462	3 510	3 646	3 774
		69.8	89.4	108.1	131.5	151.4	171.9	190.3	203.1	208.9	208.9	236.7	243.4	251.5	257.6	260.1	268.1	275.4
Norway	L	49	107	204	292	406	488	574	662	739	796	854	895	951	986	1 021	1 051	1 087
		13.7	29.6	56.1	79.6	109.9	131.1	152.9	174.9	193.5	206.7	220.3	229.3	241.8	248.9	256.4	262.3	269.7
Poland	L	426	648	959	1 295	1 698	2 078	2 540	2 934	3 389	3 828	4 215	4 709	5 200	5 687	6 100	6 472	6 820
		14.4	21.6	31.6	41.8	54.8	66.0	80.1	92.0	105.7	118.6	129.8	143.6	157.3	170.5	181.8	191.3	199.8
Portugal	L	46	68	90	119	151	180	214	271	293	347	387	472	542	569	572	575	723
		5.2	7.6	10.0	13.0	16.4	19.5	23.3	30.0	33.0	39.8	44.9	54.9	63.0	65.8	65.7	65.6	82.1
Romania	L	55	88	110	245	357	501	712	916	1 115	1 288	1 484	1 703	1 944	2 145	2 405	2 692	2 963
		3.0	4.7	5.9	13.0	18.9	26.3	37.2	47.5	56.5	64.4	73.3	83.2	94.1	103.0	114.5	127.1	138.8
San Marino	L	0.2	*0.5	*0.8	*1.1	1.3	1.5	1.8	1.9	2.1	2.2	2.4	3.1	3.1	3.2	3.3	*3.7	4
		13.3	33.3	50.0	68.8	76.5	88.2	105.9	105.6	116.7	115.8	126.3	163.2	155.0	160.0	165.0	185.0	200.0
Spain	R	250	325	375	850	1 100	*1 713	2 325	2 685	*3 265	3 845	4 115	4 520	5 200	5 719	6 125	6 525	6 640
		8.3	10.6	12.1	27.2	34.8	53.7	72.1	82.4	99.1	115.5	121.8	132.5	150.9	164.5	174.5	184.2	185.6
Sweden	L	1 167	1 357	1 626	1 821	1 964	2 085	2 160	2 268	2 345	2 420	2 513	2 619	2 701	2 758	2 841	2 909	2 988
		156.0	180.5	215.0	239.5	256.4	269.6	276.6	288.3	296.4	303.7	312.5	323.4	332.6	339.0	344.7	350.9	358.2
Switzerland	L	129	194	274	367	492	621	752	868	1 011	1 144	1 274	1 403	1 536	1 627	1 714	1 759	1 809
		24.1	35.6	49.3	64.9	85.4	106.0	125.4	143.2	164.9	184.2	203.3	221.9	240.6	253.0	264.1	269.2	275.0
United Kingdom	L	11 076	11 657	12 231	12 789	13 155	13 516	13 919	14 910	15 434	15 792	16 316	16 569	16 999	17 294	17 325	17 701	17 729
		210.7	220.1	228.8	237.8	242.9	247.9	254.1	271.1	279.8	285.5	294.1	297.4	304.2	308.7	308.1	313.7	313.1
Yugoslavia	L	25	62	126	205	393	577	777	1 002	1 298	1 546	1 796	2 061	2 354	2 544	2 784	3 076	3 463
		1.4	3.3	6.7	10.8	20.5	29.7	39.6	50.5	64.8	76.5	88.2	100.3	113.5	121.5	131.8	144.3	160.9
USSR [5]	R	4 800	4 800	8 300	10 400	12 900	15 700	19 000	22 700	26 800	30 700	34 800	39 300	45 400	49 200	52 500	55 181	---
		22.4	22.0	37.4	46.2	56.5	68.0	142.3	96.2	112.5	127.6	143.4	160.4	183.5	197.0	208.3	216.4	---

Country	Code	1960	1961	1962	1963	1964	1965	1966	1967	1968	1969	1970	1971	1972	1973	1974	1975	1976
OCEANIA																		
American Samoa	R									2.0	2.0	2.8	3.5	3.5	3.5	5.0	5.0	5.7
										76.9	74.1	103.7	125	120.7	116.7	161.3	156.3	172.7
Australia	L	1 122	1 500	1 568	1 695	1 789	1 954	2 081	2 234	2 519	2 649	2 758	2 845	2 939	3 013	3 500	4 549	4 785
		108.8	142.2	146.0	154.8	160.2	171.6	179.4	189.3	209.8	216.0	219.7	223.0	226.8	229.4	258.3	329.4	340.1
French Polynesia	R							2.5	3.2	5.5	7.7	9.8	12.0	12.3	12.6	13.0	---	---
								26.3	32.7	53.9	72.6	89.9	106.2	106.0	105.0	104.8	...	...
Guam	R						28	30	32	40	40	40	42	43	45	46	100	101
							378.4	389.6	405.1	487.8	470.6	454.6	466.7	467.4	478.7	474.2	1 010.1	990.2
New Caledonia	R						0.4	3.0	5.2	6.0	6.0	8	9	12	13	14	15	15.1
							4.4	31.9	53.6	60.0	58.3	78.4	80.4	104.4	110.2	114.8	120.0	117.1
New Zealand	R	3.5	19	66	144	287	413	515	569	604	617	661	698	726	755	791	799	813
		1.5	7.9	26.6	56.9	111.0	157.2	192.5	208.7	219.6	222.2	234.4	244.7	249.9	254.8	261.3	263.6	264.3

1. Includes data for Zambia for 1962 and 1063. 2. Data include figures for Guam and Puerto Rico. 3. The data which relate to the German Democratic Republic include the relevant data relating to Berlin for which separate data have not been supplied. This is without prejudice to any question of status which may be involved. 4. Figures relating to the Byelorussian S.S.R. and the Ukrainian S.S.R. are included with those of the U.S.S.R.

Table 5 — Composition of domestic radio broadcasting programmes, according to national classifications during a typical week in 1959 (or 1960)

Country, type of programme and total broadcasting time per week	Approximate percentage of total programme time per week
ARGENTINA - 135 hours	100
Popular music	26
News and informations	16
Theatre, complete features	6
Humour	5
Theatre, serial features	4
Entertainment	4
Light music	4
Miscellaneous	35
AUSTRALIA	
Commercial programme - 248 hours	100
Popular music	41
Drama	12
Advertising	12
Light music	11
News, weather, etc.	6
Religion	4
Sports	4
Talks, interviews	2
Women's	2
Children's	2
Variety, talent	1
Serious music	1
Quiz game panel	1
Hill-billy music	1
National programme (ABC) - 133 hours. (Metropolitan transmitters)	100
Classical music	24
Popular music	20
Light music	12
News	7
Sports	6
Talks, discussions, comments	4
Announcements, films, etc.	4
Religion	3
Parliamentary	3
Drama	3
Magazine (women's)	3
Children's	2
Schools	2
Rural	2
Services (including weather)	1
AUSTRALIA (cont'd.)	
Variety	1
Kindergarten	1
Features	2
New Australian sessions	
AUSTRIA[1] - 277 hours	100
Music :	
Serious music	
Symphonic music	6
Opera concerts	2
Operas	1
Chamber music	1
Instrumental concerts	1
Instrumental soloist concerts	1
Soloist singers concerts	1
Light music	
Dance and popular music	17
Other light music	16
Requested concerts	6
Light music mixed with spoken word	5
Light music of a higher level	3
Folk music	3
Operettas	1
Jazz	1
Interval music	1
Spoken word :	
Current news	12
Advertisements	4
Science	3
Literary	3
School broadcasts	2
Women	2
Conferences on music	1
Civism and folklore	1
Literary for children	1
Religion	1
Sport	1
Politics	1
Agriculture	1

Country, type of programme and total broadcasting time per week	Approximate percentage of total programme time per week
AUSTRIA (cont'd.)	
Practical advice	
Announcements	1
Youth	
Other	
BAHAMA ISLANDS - 125 hours	100
Music	70
News and weather reports	10
Drama	8
Religious	7
Variety	2
Remote broadcasts	1
Educational	1
Talks	1
BELGIUM	
Flemish programme - 178 hours	100
Light music	
Light music (commercial records)	37
Popular music (live programme)	5
Miscellaneous	3
Welfare transmissions	2
Serious music	
Classical music (commercial records)	14
Symphonic music (orchestras)	3
Popular music (commercial records)	2
Chamber music (orchestras)	2
Recitals (vocals and instrumental music)	2
Choirs	2
Welfare transmissions	1
Spoken Word	
News, comments, actualities, and other	16
School and other youth education	7
Sport (reports and commentaries)	2
Religious	1
Literature and drama	1
French programme - 203 hours	100
Light music (records)	29
Relayed programmes	14
News	13
Variety	11

Country, type of programme and total broadcasting time per week	Approximate percentage of total programme time per week
BELGIUM (cont'd.)	
Special Broadcasts	10
Serious music (records)	7
Music (orchestra and instrumental)	5
Theatre and quizzes	4
Lyric	2
Music (soloist)	2
Chamber music	1
Cabaret	1
School broadcasts	1
BRAZIL	100
Folk and popular music	39
Advertising	21
Light music	10
Classical music	5
Sport	4
News	4
Games and quizzes	2
Educational	2
Politics and public affairs	2
Theatre	1
Children and youth	1
Humour	1
Interviews	1
Lectures	1
Civic and religious	1
Women	
Gymnastic	
Classes	1
Others	
BULGARIA - 215 hours (Programmes Radio Sofia I, II.)	100
Spoken word	
News	10
Children	3
Literature	2
Youth	2
Theatre	1
Others	7
Music	
Music for Radio Sofia	55
Music for Turkish population	6
Regional programme - music for Radio Varna and Stara Zapora	14

Table 6 — Composition of television broadcasting programmes, according to national classifications, during a typical week in 1960 (or 1961)

Country, type of programme and total broadcasting time per week	Approximate percentage of total programme time per week
AUSTRALIA	
National programme (ABC)	100
Drama (including films)	17
Sport	13
Light entertainment (including popular music, variety)	12
Children's	10
News and newsreels	9
Documentaries	8
Talks, interviews	6
Services	5
Schools broadcasts	4
Women's programmes	4
Religious	4
Rural	3
Classical and light music	2
Kindergarten	2
Actualities and outdoor broadcasts	1
Commercial programme	100
Drama	53
Children's	9
Advertising	8
Variety and talent	6
Sport	4
News and weather	4
Cartoons	4
Women's	3
Light and popular music	2
Talks, interviews	2
Religious	2
Documentaries	2
Quiz, game and panel	1
AUSTRIA - 25 hours	100
Films	24
Actualities	20
Transmissions from abroad	14
Youth and family	12
Entertainment	9
Plays	8
Sport	3
Culture and popular education	2
Other	1

Country, type of programme and total broadcasting time per week	Approximate percentage of total programme time per week
BELGIUM	
French programme - 31 hours	100
Films (fiction and short films)	24
News	18
Variety, games	11
Youth programmes	10
Theatre	8
Documentaries	6
Sport	6
Scientific programmes	6
Music	3
Literary programmes	2
Women's	2
Religion	2
Political	2
Flemish programmes - 42 hours	100
News	23
Films (fiction and short films)	19
Culture	18
Sport	12
Scientific programmes	7
Theatre, literary, music	7
Variety, games	6
Youth programmes	6
Announcements	1
BRAZIL[1]...	100
Advertisements	20
Sport	10
Theatre	10
News	8
Children's programmes	8
Popular and folk music	6
Games and quizzes	5
Humour	4
Interviews	4
Women's programmes	3
Instructive programmes	3
Light music	3
Lectures	3
Civic and religious solemnities	1

Country, type of programme and total broadcasting time per week	Approximate percentage of total programme time per week
BRAZIL (cont'd.)	
Classes	
Political	
Classical music	2
Gymnastics	
Miscellaneous	10
CANADA[2] **-130 hours**	100
Predominantly Entertainment :	
"General" entertainment	45
Sport	10
Creative arts	5
Predominantly Information :	
News and weather	5
Household and its activities	5
Sciences, nature	3
Foreign information	3
Farm, fisheries	1
Other	9
Predominantly Idea or Opinion :	
Political, other controversial public affairs	4
Religious	3
Canadian activities and heritage	2
School, other youth education	2
Social, human relations	2
Other	1
COSTA RICA - 32 hours	100
Entertainment	65
News	20
Cultural	5
Science	5
Religious	3
Economics	2
CZECHOSLOVAKIA[1] **-37 hours**	100
Films (TV and cinema)	33
News	17
Sport	16
Entertainment	8
Drama	7
Operas and ballets	5
Scientific and cultural programmes	5
Quiz programmes	4
Concerts	1
Operetta	1
Marionettes	1
Announcements	1
Other	1
DENMARK - 23 hours	100
Spoken word, actualities	51
Sport	15
Theatre, literature	15

Country, type of programme and total broadcasting time per week	Approximate percentage of total programme time per week
DENMARK (cont'd.)	
Entertainment	13
Classical music	6
FINLAND - 54 hours	100
Test card and tuning music	38
Advertisements	17
Films	13
Actualities	8
Programmes of social content	6
International programme exchange	5
Entertainment	4
News	4
Youth and children's	3
Drama	2
Music	1
FRANCE - 55 hours	100
News	25
Variety	22
Documentaries	20
Youth programmes	9
Sport	8
Drama	5
Films ("production R.T.F.")	5
Other films	4
Music	1
Outside broadcasts	0,5
Regional broadcasts	0,5
GERMANY, Federal Republic	100
Children's, youth, women's	15
Theatre	14
Entertainment	12
Sport	11
Documentaries	11
Broadcasts from aboard	10
Films	7
News	7
Actualities	7
Intervals, advertisements, etc.	5
Religion	1

Tableau 7 — Domestic radio classified by main type of programmes, in hours of broadcasting
(latest data available for the period 1968-1971)
Number of countries and territories covered: 119
A = total; B = of which: nationally produced

Data refer either to a week that is considered typical or to an average week of a given year. Broadcasting time to foreign countries is not included in this table.

In the questionnaires used for the collection of the data the seven main categories of programmes shown in this table were subdivided as follows:

Information: News bulletins and commentaries, community and special events, public affairs and sports.
Advertising: Commercial and publicity.
Education: (a) formal — in school; (b) informal — child and youth, adult.
Light entertainment: Music and comedy, drama and serials, contest, quizzes, games.
Arts, letters and sciences: Music and dance, drama, poem and story, critical evaluation in arts and letters, sciences.
Broadcasts for ethnic minorities: Language courses, others.
Broadcasts for special audiences: Religious, for women, for children and youth, others.

In certain cases the total broadcasting time is shown with an asterisk due mainly to the fact that the replies to the questionnaires were incomplete or because of discrepancies between the total for each chapter heading and the figures given for the total broadcasting time.

Type of programme		Algeria		Benin		Botswana	
		A	B	A	B	A	B
		(1968)		(1970)		(1971)	
Total		302 h 30	286 h 40	70 h 30	60 h 52	98 h 40	97 h 10
1. Information		33 h 56	33 h 56	27 h 40	27 h 40	37 h 58	37 h 58
2. Advertising		—	—	0 h 20	0 h 02	—	—
3. Education	Africa	33 h 40	29 h 10	7 h 35	6 h 05	30 h 25	28 h 55
4. Light entertainment		121 h 14	111 h 24	4 h 45	—	25 h 30	25 h 30
5. Arts, letters and sciences		74 h 35	73 h 05	24 h 35	22 h 30	2 h 00	2 h 00
6. Broadcasts for ethnic minorities		4 h 00	4 h 00	—	—	—	—
7. Broadcasts for special audiences		35 h 05	35 h 05	5 h 35	4 h 35	2 h 47	2 h 47

Type of programme		Burundi		Congo, People's Republic of the		Egypt, Arab Republic of
		A	B	A	B	A
		(1971)		(1971)		(1970)
Total		88 h 30	67 h 35	90 h 45	87 h 15	907 h 26
1. Information		34 h 30	32 h 45	31 h 00	31 h 00	115 h 16
2. Advertising		—	—	3 h 30	3 h 30	8 h 10
3. Education		12 h 50	9 h 05	10 h 30	10 h 30	5 h 43
4. Light entertainment		29 h 15	19 h 55	19 h 00	18 h 00	417 h 12
5. Arts, letters and sciences		9 h 10	3 h 35	19 h 30	19 h 30	85 h 24
6. Broadcasts for ethnic minorities		—	—	0 h 30	0 h 30	23 h 55
7. Broadcasts for special audiences		2 h 45	2 h 15	6 h 45	4 h 15	251 h 46

Table 8 — Television classified by main type of programmes, in hours of broadcasting
(latest data available for the period 1968-1971)
Number of countries and territories covered: 80
A = total; B = of which: nationally produced

Data refer either to a week that is considered typical or to an average week of a given year.

In the questionnaires used for the collection of the data the seven main categories of programmes shown in this table were subdivided as follows :

Information : News bulletins and commentaries, community and special events, public affairs and sports.
Advertising : Commercial and publicity.
Education : (a) formal—in school; (b) informal—child and youth, adult.
Light entertainment : Music and comedy, drama and serials, contest, quizzes, games.
Arts, letters and sciences : Music and dance, drama, poem and story, critical evaluation in arts and letters, sciences.
Broadcasts for ethnic minorities : Language courses, others.
Broadcasts for special audiences : Religious, for women, for children and youth, others.

In certain cases the total broadcasting time is shown with an asterisk due mainly to the fact that the replies to the questionnaires were incomplete or because of discrepancies between the total for each chapter heading and the figures given for the total broadcasting time.

Type of programme		Algeria		Congo, People's Republic of the		Egypt, Arab Republic of	
		A	B	A	A	A	B
		(1968)		(1971)		(1970)	
Total		40 h 00	19 h 30	25 h 00	*16 h 30	113 h 03	
1. Information		9 h 30	8 h 15	16 h 00	10 h 00	12 h 57	
2. Advertising	Africa	—	—	—	—	[1]...	
3. Education		5 h 30	2 h 00	1 h 00	1 h 00	[2]...	
4. Light entertainment		8 h 00	3 h 00	2 h 00	1 h 30	[1,3] 52 h 44	
5. Arts, letters and sciences		8 h 30	3 h 45	5 h 30	3 h 30	[2,3] 40 h 43	
6. Braodcasts for ethnic minorities		0 h 30	0 h 30	—	—	—	
7. Broadcasts for special audiences		8 h 00	2 h 00	0 h 30	0 h 30	[3] 6 h 39	

Type of programme		Mauritius and deps		Nigeria	Réunion	
		A	B	A	A	B
		(1970)		(1969)	(1971)	
Total		57 h 32	19 h 17	*30 h 55	25 h 32	22 h 32
1. Information		13 h 40	6 h 40	4 h 30	6 h 10	6 h 10
2. Advertising		2 h 37	*2 h 37	2 h 55	—	—
3. Education		9 h 45	6 h 30	4 h 00	1 h 30	1 h 30
4. Light entertainment		17 h 45	1 h 00	13 h 00	12 h 17	9 h 17
5. Arts, letters and sciences		4 h 00	0 h 30	—	3 h 00	3 h 00
6. Broadcasts for ethnic minorities		—	—	—	—	—
7. Broadcasts for special audiences		9 h 45	2 h 00	6 h 30	2 h 35	2 h 35

Table 9 — Radio broadcasting: programmes by type
Number of countries and territories covered: 85
A = Total hours and percentage distribution by type of programme
B = of which: nationally produces

Data refer either to a week that is considered typical or to an average week of a given year. Broadcasting time to foreign countries is not included in this table.

In the questionnaires used for the collection of the data the eight main categories of programmes shown in this table were subdivided as follows:

Information (political, economic and social news, national and foreign): news bulletins and commentaries, special events, public affairs (political speeches, debates, magazines etc.) sports news (special programmes), other (weather, road conditions, etc.).

Education: school and university education, out of-school, education for children and youth, out-of-school education for adults, professional training, language courses.

Culture (the following items also include critical evaluations): theatre, literature, music, other.

Sciences: sciences and popularization of science.

Entertainment: music, contests, quizzes and various games, sports (transmission of sporting events), other.

Programmes for special audiences: for women, for children and youth, religious, other.

Advertising: commercial and non-commercial announcements.

Other programmes not elsewhere classified.

In certain cases the total broadcasting time is shown with an asterisk due mainly to the fact that the replies to the questionnaires were incomplete or because of discrepancies between the total for each chapter heading and the figures given for the total broadcasting time.

Type of programme		Algeria		Botswana		Comoro Islands
		A	B	A	B	A
		(1973)		(1974)		(1973)
Total	Africa	44 h 34	44 h 34	115 h 00	115 h 00	68 h 47
1. Information		41.4	41.4	27.0	27.0	19.1
2. Education		21.5	21.5	29.8	29.8	80.9
3. Culture		4.9	4.9	24.4	24.4	—
4. Sciences		—	—	—	—	—
5. Entertainment		32.2	32.2	4.4	4.4	—
6. Programmes for special audiences		—	—	8.3	8.3	—
7. Advertising		—	—	5.5	5.5	—
8. Other programmes not elsewhere classified		—	—	—	—	—

Type of programme	Djibouti		Ethiopia		Ghana	
	A	B	A	B	A	B
	(1973)		(1974)		(1972)	
Total	189 h 00	143 h 00	122 h 30	122 h 30	179 h 48	119 h 13
1. Information	11.1	13.3	18.3	18.3	32.6	28.5
2. Education	2.1	—	20.8	20.8	9.0	7.0
3. Culture	15.9	2.1	—	—	1.1	1.3
4. Sciences	1.6	—	—	—	—	—
5. Entertainment	67.7	83.9	50.3	50.3	44.7	63.2
6. Programmes for special audiences	1.6	0.7	0.8	0.8	12.5	—
7. Advertising	—	—	9.2	9.2	—	—
8. Other programmes not elsewhere classified	—	—	—	—	—	—

Table 10 — Television broadcasting: programmes by type
Number of countries and territories covered: 64
A = total hours and percentage distribution by type of programme
B = of which: nationnaly produced

Data refer either to a week that is considered typical or to an average week of a given year.

In the questionnaires used for the collection of the data the eight main categories of programmes shown in this table were subdivided as follows :

Information (political, economic and social news, national and foreign) : news bulletins and commentaries, special events, public affairs (political speeches, debates, magazines, etc.), sports news (special programmes), documentary, other (weather, road conditions, etc.).

Education : school and university education, out-of-school education for children and youth, out-of-school education for adults, professional training, language courses.

Culture (the following items also includes critical evaluations) : theatre, literature, music and dance, films : (a) long films, (b) serials and series production, (c) other (plastic arts, town planning, festivals, travel, cultural tourism, etc.).

Sciences : sciences and popularization of science.

Entertainment : Music, dance, contests, quizzes and various games, sports (transmission of sporting events), other.

Programmes for special audiences : for women, for children and youth, religious, other.

Advertising : commercial and non-commercial announcements.

Other programmes not elsewhere classified.

In certain cases the total broadcasting time is shown with an asterisk due mainly to the fact that the replies to the questionnaires were incomplete or because of discrepancies between the total for each chapter heading and the figures given for the total broadcasting time.

Type of programme		Algeria		Egypt	Ethiopia	
		A	B	A	A	B
		(1973)		(1973)	(1973)	
Total	Africa	472 h 59	291 h 10	118 h 53	61 h 22	41 h 02
1. Information		26.0	40.2	17.4	12.2	14.6
2. Education		13.0	10.1	10.2	58.9	73.5
3. Culture		34.1	18.0	34.3	14.8	1.4
4. Sciences		3.4	4.2	—	—	—
5. Entertainment		15.1	14.6	23.2	7.3	5.7
6. Programmes for special audiences		8.3	13.0	14.6	5.8	3.9
7. Advertising		—	—	0.4	0.9	0.9
8. Other programmes not elsewhere classified		—	—	—	—	—

Type of programme		Réunion	Sudan		Tunisia	
		A	A	B	A	B
		(1973)	(1973)		(1973)	
Total		37 h 02	50 h 00	35 h 00	242 h 30	198 h 12
1. Information		18.2	12.0	14.3	19.9	22.3
2. Education		5.4	8.0	5.7	12.4	13.9
3. Culture		42.5	26.0	2.9	25.4	12.1
4. Sciences		4.9	—	—	5.2	6.3
5. Entertainment		19.8	18.0	25.7	24.7	30.3
6. Programmes for special audiences		9.2	22.0	31.4	12.4	15.1
7. Advertising		—	4.0	5.7	—	—
8. Other programmes not elsewhere classified		—	10.0	14.3	—	—

Table 11 — Radio broadcasting: programme by type
Number of countries and territories covered: 109
A = total hours and percentage distribution by type of programme
B = of which: nationally produced

Country	Year	Hours per year	PERCENTAGE DISTRIBUTION BY TYPE OF PROGRAMME							
			Information	Education	Culture	Sciences	Entertainment	Programmes for special audiences	Advertising	Other programmes not elsewhere classified
		(1)	(2)	(3)	(4)	(5)	(6)	(7)	(8)	(9)
AFRICA										
Algeria	1974 A	5 940	17.5	21.9	23.9	—	28.8	7.9	0.0	—
	B	5 940	17.5	21.9	23.9	—	28.8	7.9	0.0	—
Benin	1972 A	*4 351	33.0	24.0	1.8	—	32.0	6.8	2.4	—
	B	*3 878	37.1	20.8	1.3	—	31.8	6.3	2.7	—
Botswana	1974 A	*5 980	27.0	29.8	24.4	—	4.4	8.3	5.5	—
	B	*5 980	27.0	29.8	24.4	—	4.4	8.3	5.5	—
Burundi	1974 A	5 104	22.6	8.5	1.0	—	65.4	2.5	—	—
	B	5 000	23.0	8.7	—	—	65.7	2.6	—	—
Comoro Islands	1973 A	*3 577	19.1	80.9	—	—	—	—	—	—
Congo	1974 A	*6 794	49.4	24.4	2.5	0.3	16.8	4.0	1.2	1.4
	B	*6 500	50.5	25.5	1.2	—	16.6	4.0	0.9	1.3
Djibouti	1974 A	10 894	10.5	—	12.3	1.7	77.2	1.9	—	11.9
Egypt	1974 A	47 029	10.5	1.0	18.6	0.8	44.7	23.7	0.7	—
Ethiopia	1975 A	5 361	19.0	33.9	—	—	37.3	—	9.7	—
	B	4 121	—	44.2	—	—	45.4	—	10.4	—
Ghana	1974 A	5 330	35.3	3.9	7.3	8.3	20.4	9.4	15.3	—
	B	5 315	35.4	4.0	7.1	8.3	20.4	9.4	15.4	—
Madagascar	1974 A	2 520	14.3	15.2	4.2	1.1	46.6	15.0	3.6	—
	B	1 929	8.1	19.9	4.1	1.4	43.7	18.2	4.6	—
Malawi	1974 A	*7 965	17.6	26.1	33.3	—	10.1	5.0	7.8	—
	B	*7 939	17.7	26.2	33.5	—	9.8	4.9	7.9	—
Mauritius	1975 A	6 036	50.7	14.1	14.4	6.1	9.2	3.8	—	1.6
	B	3 780	60.0	15.4	7.5	3.1	7.4	5.1	—	1.5

Table 12— Television broadcasting: programmes by type
Number of countries and territories covered: 76
A = total hours and percentage distribution by type of programme
B = of which: nationally produced

Country	Year	Hours per year	PERCENTAGE DISTRIBUTION BY TYPE OF PROGRAMME							
			Information	Education	Culture	Sciences	Entertainment	Programmes for special audiences	Advertising	Other programmes not elsewhere classified
		(1)	(2)	(3)	(4)	(5)	(6)	(7)	(8)	(9)
AFRICA										
Algeria	1974 A	2 863	22.3	14.5	36.5	—	17.0	9.6	0.1	—
	B	1 513	29.7	27.4	13.7	—	16.6	12.3	0.2	—
Djibouti	1973 A	2 184	23.8	7.1	21.4	4.8	42.9	—	—	—
Egypt	1974 A	6 483	12.4	9.3	38.0	—	19.6	18.0	2.7	—
Ethiopia	1975 A	1 750	21.3	31.4	23.7	—	4.2	3.0	1.8	14.6
	B	1 318	28.2	41.7	2.7	—	1.7	4.0	2.4	19.3
Ghana	1974 A	2 838	17.0	34.5	23.8	1.8	8.2	7.3	7.3	—
	B	2 448	19.6	40.0	14.9	2.1	6.4	8.5	8.5	—
Madagascar	1974 A	949	30.1	—	50.7	5.5	11.0	2.7	—	—
	B	260	70.0	—	—	—	20.0	10.0	—	—
Mauritius	1975 A	2 694	32.8	8.4	35.0	—	22.7	1.1	—	—
	B	810	64.0	28.0	1.2	—	3.1	3.7	—	—
Nigeria	1973 A	2 782	15.4	26.2	29.5	—	11.2	14.0	3.7	—
	B	1 430	5.5	50.9	21.8	—	21.8	—	—	—
Reunion	1973 A	*1 926	18.2	5.4	42.5	4.9	19.8	9.2	—	—
Senegal	1974 A	1 300	22.0	2.0	54.0	—	12.0	10.0	—	—
Sudan	1973 A	*2 600	12.0	8.0	26.0	—	18.0	22.0	4.0	10.0
	B	1 820	14.3	5.7	2.9	—	25.7	31.4	5.7	14.3
Tunisia	1973 A	12 610	19.9	12.4	25.4	5.2	24.7	12.4	—	—
	B	*10 306	22.3	13.9	12.1	6.3	30.3	15.1	—	—
Zaire	1974 A	3 160	27.3	22.9	36.3	3.0	7.1	3.3	—	—

Table 13 — Radio broadcasting: programmes by type (1971-1974)
Number of countries and territories presented in this table: 101

Country	Year	Hours per year	Information	Education	Culture	Sciences	Entertainment	Programmes for special audiences	Advertising	Other programmes not elsewhere classified
AFRICA										
Algeria	1973	2 318	41.4	21.5	4.9	—	30.2	—	—	—
	1974	5 940	17.5	21.9	23.9	—	28.8	7.9	0.0	—
Benin	1971	*4 009	35.8	18.0	17.0	—	20.4	7.3	1.5	—
	1972	4 351	33.0	24.0	1.8	—	32.0	6.8	2.4	—
Botswana	1971	5 131	38.5	30.8	1.5	0.5	25.7	2.8	—	—
	1972	5 317	39.0	28.8	2.9	0.7	24.9	3.7	—	—
	1973	*5 649	32.7	29.4	14.3	0.3	14.1	6.2	3.0	—
	1974	5 980	27.0	30.0	24.4	—	4.4	8.5	5.7	—
Burundi	1971	4 602	39.0	14.5	6.2	4.1	33.1	3.1	—	—
	1972	*4 769	23.9	15.2	5.5	1.3	35.1	6.8	1.0	11.2
	1973	*4 937	23.2	11.7	3.2	0.6	50.8	4.6	0.5	5.4
	1974	5 104	22.6	8.5	1.0	—	65.4	2.5	—	—
Comoro Islands	1971	680	15.3	2.5	1.9	—	57.3	23.0	—	—
	1972	*2 129	18.5	68.4	0.3	—	9.1	3.7	—	—
	1973	3 577	19.1	80.9	—	—	—	—	—	—
Congo	1971	3 965	40.6	13.8	2.0	—	26.2	12.1	4.6	0.7
	1972	4 719	34.1	11.7	21.5	—	20.9	8.0	3.8	—
	1973	*5 757	43.1	19.2	10.3	0.2	18.5	5.6	3.8	—
	1974	6 794	49.4	24.4	2.5	0.3	16.8	4.0	1.2	1.4
Djibouti	1971	*8 099	10.7	7.4	19.0	1.0	59.8	2.1	—	—
	1972	*8 964	10.9	4.5	17.3	1.3	64.2	1.8	—	—
	1973	9 828	11.1	2.1	15.9	1.6	67.7	1.6	—	—
	1974	10 894	10.5	—	12.3	—	77.2	—	—	—
Egypt	1971	47 344	12.1	0.3	7.1	0.4	52.9	18.6	0.8	7.8
	1972	50 026	11.8	0.7	16.5	0.6	50.9	19.0	0.5	—
	1973	50 636	13.0	1.3	14.3	0.7	50.8	19.5	0.4	—
	1974	47 029	10.5	1.0	18.6	0.8	44.7	23.7	0.7	—
Ethiopia	1972	5 361	19.0	34.0	—	—	37.3	—	9.7	—
	1973	6 447	20.8	20.2	—	—	49.8	—	9.2	—
	1974	6 370	18.4	21.1	—	—	50.4	0.8	9.3	—
Gambia	1971	4 034	29.0	2.3	0.9	—	32.0	10.1	19.3	6.4
	1972	4 561	44.1	20.2	1.7	—	13.7	10.1	—	10.2

Country	Year	Hours per year	Information	Education	Culture	Sciences	Entertainment	Programmes for special audiences	Advertising	Other programmes not elsewhere classified
AFRICA (cont'd.)										
Madagascar	1971	6 006[1]	13.1	20.0	10.0	—	42.4	11.0	2.6	0.9
	1972	9 997	26.3	6.5	5.1	0.5	38.9	14.2	8.3	0.2
	1973	8 294	18.5	—	5.0	0.6	62.1	12.5	1.3	—
	1974	2 520[2]	14.3	15.2	4.2	1.1	46.6	15.0	3.6	—
Malawi	1971	6 084	22.2	17.8	4.9	—	49.4	3.6	1.7	0.4
	1972	6 517	18.8	19.8	37.5	—	6.9	7.5	9.5	—
	1973	6 673	18.3	19.3	36.6	—	6.7	7.4	9.4	2.3
	1974	7 965	17.6	26.1	33.3	—	10.1	5.0	7.9	—
Mauritius	1971	6 032	14.2	6.4	16.2	0.7	44.5	11.1	2.2	4.7
	1972	*6 032	15.3	5.9	19.6	0.6	48.3	6.8	1.1	2.4
	1973	6 032	16.4	5.3	23.1	0.4	52.2	2.6	—	—
	1974	6 015	15.1	7.9	7.1	0.9	62.7	6.3	—	—
Niger	1971	7 956	25.2	22.7	1.3	0.3	46.2	4.1	0.2	—
	1972	8 329	17.2	15.2	2.0	0.3	40.0	22.2	2.8	0.3
Nigeria	1973	8 284	20.8	9.3	26.8	—	30.2	6.7	6.2	—
	1974	8 284	20.8	9.3	26.8	—	30.2	6.7	6.2	—
Rwanda	1971	*5 086	18.5	8.9	7.6	0.2	54.1	7.3	3.4	—
	1972	*5 160	18.5	9.1	6.8	0.3	55.7	7.1	2.5	—
	1973	*5 233	18.5	9.3	6.1	0.3	57.2	6.9	2.5	—
	1974	*5 306	18.5	9.4	5.4	0.4	58.7	6.8	0.8	—
Seychelles	1971	2 028	8.9	25.5	10.2	—	49.7	2.5	3.2	—
	1972	2 340	15.0	22.2	8.9	—	42.8	3.3	3.3	4.5
	1973	3 133	14.9	28.2	3.3	0.4	45.6	4.2	3.3	—
	1974	3 121	19.7	27.0	4.3	—	36.7	10.4	1.9	—
Sudan	1971	6 307	32.6	—	4.3	0.2	36.9	15.6	0.9	9.5
	1972	*7 678	26.3	1.0	10.5	0.8	35.1	21.0	1.4	3.9
	1973	9 048	21.9	1.7	14.9	1.2	33.9	24.7	1.7	
Swaziland	1971	3 228	18.9	29.0	0.3	—	44.3	6.7	0.8	—
	1972	4 476	—	—	—	—	97.9	1.2	0.9	—
	1973	4 477	...	...	...	...	...	...	...	...
	1974	4 916	16.8	8.6	4.8	—	63.9	3.7	2.2	—
Tunisia	1972	6 192	12.3	15.1	16.0	0.8	52.9	2.9	—	—
	1973	6 192	12.3	15.1	16.0	0.8	52.9	2.9	—	—
	1974	6 744	25.9	10.3	7.2	—	47.5	9.1	—	—
United Rep. of Cameroon	1971	11 466	17.3	3.2	7.5	0.5	49.1	17.2	5.2	—
	1972	9 386	21.2	3.8	60.0	0.6	8.0	—	6.4	—
	1973	9 386	21.2	3.8	60.0	0.6	8.0	—	6.4	—
	1974	9 386	21.2	3.8	60.0	0.6	8.0	—	6.4	—
Western Sahara	1971	3 607	26.8	—	2.0	—	50.6	18.9	1.7	—
	1972	6 240	9.8	12.5	7.5	3.3	44.4	14.2	—	8.3
	1973	8 502	22.3	2.4	7.9	—	30.4	35.9	1.1	—
Zaire	1973	5 668	54.1	6.4	4.6	1.0	22.0	6.4	5.5	—
	1974	8 736	25.7	8.9	1.2	—	61.4	1.8	1.0	—
AMERICA, NORTH										
Barbados	1971	6 593	21.5	6.7	4.7	1.2	44.1	17.1	4.7	—
	1972	6 909	20.4	6.4	4.5	1.0	42.0	16.3	9.2	—
	1973	7 020	18.7	3.0	2.2	0.5	55.1	11.4	7.2	1.9
	1974	7 510	17.1	—	0.2	—	66.9	6.9	5.3	3.6

Country	Year	Hours per year	Information	Education	Culture	Sciences	Entertainment	Programmes for special audiences	Advertising	Other programmes not elsewhere classified
AMERICA, NORTH (cont'd.)										
Belize	1971	6 188	18.3	5.9	63.6	—	1.7	10.5	—	—
	1972	*6 018	18.8	4.6	43.6	1.6	15.6	12.3	3.5	—
	1973	*5 847	19.3	3.3	22.4	3.2	30.4	14.3	7.1	—
	1974	5 677	19.9	1.8	—	5.0	46.0	16.3	11.0	—
Bermuda	1971	*23 862	24.9	2.5	7.9	0.3	24.9	14.5	7.9	17.1
	1972	27 053	33.7	2.3	7.7	0.5	2.5	13.6	9.5	30.2
	1973	40 560	12.0	—	1.0	—	73.0	3.0	10.0	1.0
Canada [3]	1971	2 689 809	21.5	1.7	8.7	0.1	64.5	3.4	0.1	—
	1972	3 211 584	21.9	1.7	8.0	0.1	64.5	3.5	0.1	0.2
	1973	3 278 236	21.4	1.7	7.9	0.1	63.2	3.4	2.1	0.2
Cuba	1971	*145 173	27.6	12.1	32.9	—	23.7	1.3	2.3	0.1
	1972	*203 392	28.7	10.6	46.9	—	8.5	1.9	3.2	0.2
	1973	261 612	29.4	9.7	54.7	—	—	2.2	3.8	0.2
	1974	266 638	27.9	8.9	54.2	—	2.2	2.6	4.2	—
El Salvador	1972	7 280	37.1	2.2	—	—	30.0	5.7	25.0	—
	1973	*108 165	5.4	1.4	2.9	—	81.1	4.4	0.8	4.0
	1974	209 049	4.3	1.4	3.0	—	82.9	4.3	—	4.1
Greenland	1971	*3 556	34.6	5.1	10.6	0.4	36.3	12.2	—	0.8
	1972	3 293	42.1	—	12.4	0.8	38.0	5.1	—	1.6
	1973	*4 072	27.5	0.6	20.3	1.4	30.6	6.7	—	12.9
	1974	4 850	17.6	1.0	25.7	1.7	25.6	7.8	—	20.6
Guadeloupe	1971	6 162	13.9	—	25.0	3.1	51.5	4.9	1.6	—
	1972	6 852	24.9	4.3	4.9	—	53.7	8.6	3.6	—
Jamaica	1972	5 018	28.0	3.1	16.6	0.5	20.7	31.1	—	—
	1973	*6 104	30.6	1.3	9.2	0.2	41.7	17.0	—	—
	1974	7 189	32.4	—	4.0	—	56.4	7.2	—	—
Panama Canal Zone	1971	9 152	21.5	—	2.8	—	66.1	1.9	6.8	0.9
	1972	9 152	21.5	—	2.8	—	66.1	1.9	6.8	0.9
	1973	8 736	17.8	—	3.0	—	73.7	2.0	3.5	—
	1974	8 760	17.8	—	3.0	—	73.6	2.1	3.5	—
St Pierre et Miquelon	1971	3 623	17.5	2.2	15.4	1.4	56.9	5.9	—	0.7
	1972	3 202	20.1	3.2	9.2	0.8	62.4	4.3	—	—
	1973	3 380	18.3	—	13.5	—	63.2	5.0	—	—
	1974	5 824	21.5	2.0	23.8	—	50.7	2.0	—	—
AMERICA, SOUTH										
Argentina	1971	822 640	19.9	1.4	0.7	0.4	61.9	0.5	15.2	—
	1972	6 304 948	24.7	0.5	24.0	—	—	34.1	16.7	—
	1973	8 555 404	24.7	0.5	24.0	—	—	34.1	16.7	—
	1974	16 494 816	23.0	0.1	14.6	—	43.0	2.8	16.5	—
Brazil	1971	5 120 388	11.2	4.5	1.8	0.1	54.0	4.0	20.7	3.7
	1972	5 288 910	11.3	4.1	2.3	0.1	55.6	3.5	20.1	3.0
	1973	5 298 748	15.9	4.6	1.6	0.1	52.1	3.7	19.8	2.2
Falkland Islands	1971	1 976	23.7	5.3	—	1.3	59.2	9.2	1.3	—
	1972	1 976	23.7	5.3	—	1.3	59.2	9.2	1.3	—
	1973	1 976	23.7	5.3	55.3	1.3	3.9	9.2	1.3	—
	1974	1 957	33.8	0.9	9.3	—	16.1	37.2	2.7	

Country	Year	Hours per year	Information	Education	Culture	Sciences	Entertainment	Programmes for special audiences	Advertising	Other programmes not elsewhere classified
AMERICA, SOUTH (cont'd.)										
French Guyana	1971	3 666	19.3	—	17.0	—	55.5	8.2	—	—
	1972	4 134	23.8	7.0	5.9	—	57.3	3.2	2.8	—
Guyana	1973	5 832	37.8	3.3	—	—	48.4	10.5	—	—
	1974	7 072	19.9	1.8	1.1	—	61.9	15.3	—	—
Uruguay	1971	*512 791	17.4	11.2	9.9	1.4	43.4	1.4	13.9	4.4
	1972	*520 879	13.5	7.4	8.8	0.9	58.5	0.9	9.1	0.9
	1973	*528 968	9.7	3.8	7.5	0.4	73.1	0.5	4.5	0.5
	1974	537 056	6.0	0.3	6.4	—	87.3	—	—	—
ASIA										
Bahrain	1971	2 860	19.6	1.8	8.2	0.9	67.7	1.8	—	—
	1972	*3 471	21.9	1.1	6.0	0.7	63.5	3.4	—	3.4
	1973	4 082	23.5	0.6	4.5	0.6	60.6	4.5	—	5.7
	1974	4 082	23.6	0.6	4.5	0.6	60.5	4.5	—	5.7
Brunei	1971	7 280	20.6	2.2	2.9	0.7	65.9	7.7	—	—
	1972	7 163	21.0	0.5	3.0	0.7	67.0	7.8	—	—
	1973	9 984	18.9	0.4	3.4	0.5	61.7	14.3	—	0.8
	1974	12 211	20.1	1.2	4.7	0.6	58.9	10.2	—	4.3
Burma	1971	*4 102	25.4	4.8	7.5	0.3	52.8	9.2	—	—
	1972	*4 509	25.3	4.4	6.9	0.4	58.1	4.9	—	—
	1973	4 917	25.2	4.0	6.4	0.5	62.6	1.3	—	—
	1974	6 512	15.7	5.3	27.7	0.4	27.6	4.7	2.0	16.6
Cyprus	1971	12 588	9.6	4.1	14.1	0.3	62.8	5.9	1.0	2.2
	1972	20 315	11.2	2.2	16.8	0.3	59.7	8.3	1.5	—
Hong Kong	1971	50 467	15.7	8.4	8.8	0.4	60.1	2.8	2.7	1.1
	1972	50 176	14.6	7.8	11.6	0.2	59.9	1.6	2.5	1.8
	1973	33 970	16.8	3.0	16.7	0.3	58.8	2.0	0.8	1.6
	1974	33 970	16.8	3.0	16.7	0.3	58.8	2.0	0.8	1.6
India	1971	279 621	22.6	1.4	31.6	—	23.2	19.4	1.8	—
	1972	282 740	23.4	2.9	31.2	—	23.0	3.3	1.8	14.4
	1973	357 550	17.0	6.5	16.6	—	14.4	8.2	37.3	—
	1974	249 798	29.7	9.6	27.5	—	23.4	9.2	—	0.6
Indonesia	1971	73 889	26.9	11.6	7.7	0.1	45.6	2.0	0.3	5.8
	1972	141 288	27.3	11.9	7.5	0.1	46.5	0.5	0.1	6.1
	1973	208 687	27.5	12.0[4]	7.4	0.0[4]	46.9	0.0[4]	0.0[5]	6.2[5]
Iran	1971	*85 934	9.5	5.3	16.2	5.7	41.1	7.8	5.9	8.5
	1972	112 382	6.5	5.3	14.6	6.6	46.8	3.9	6.6	9.7
	1973	9 901	22.3	—	41.4	5.9	12.7	9.0	5.6	3.1
	1974	7 600	17.8	16.0	31.7	2.1	7.8	22.2	2.4	—
Israel	1971	19 387	11.7	2.0	11.3	0.3	17.7	48.5	2.1	6.4
	1972	20 696	11.2	1.3	13.2	0.3	19.6	24.9	2.1	27.4
	1973	26 208	9.6	0.6	16.1	0.2	29.2	20.0	1.7	22.6
Iraq	1971	7 453	11.6	1.2	6.1	—	72.6	7.3	1.2	—
	1972	7 826	22.2	14.3	16.3	7.0	11.0	25.2	—	4.0
	1973	*15 196	22.9	3.7	9.2	2.0	39.3	15.2	3.8	3.9
	1974	22 565	23.2	—	6.7	0.2	49.1	11.8	5.1	3.9

Country	Year	Hours per year	Information	Education	Culture	Sciences	Entertainment	Programmes for special audiences	Advertising	Other programmes not elsewhere classified
ASIA (cont'd.)										
Japan	1971	27 721	18.8	23.3	27.5	—	30.0	—	0.3	0.1
	1972	27 440	19.1	24.4	27.1	—	29.1	—	0.2	0.1
	1973	27 493	19.3	22.9	28.9	16.2	12.0	0.3	0.3	0.1
	1974	27 613	19.4	22.7	29.1	—	28.5	—	0.2	0.1
Jordan	1971	9 464	20.3	22.9	0.3	0.3	39.1	10.2	1.4	5.5
	1972	3 614	47.4	4.4	14.2	—	6.8	26.5	—	0.7
	1973	8 762	21.9	2.5	7.1	0.5	50.2	16.0	1.8	—
Korea, Rep. of	1971	7 280	18.1	42.7	28.3	—	2.1	3.8	—	5.0
	1972	9 490	20.7	37.3	6.0	—	28.5	2.9	—	4.6
	1973	9 551	29.6	10.9	32.1	—	20.6	0.1	—	6.7
	1974	45 762	18.4	11.0	22.5	0.9	29.8	10.1	4.4	2.9
Kuwait	1971	6 578	6.3	2.9	2.1	0.8	70.8	17.1	—	—
	1972	6 722	10.0	1.1	3.1	—	74.9	10.5	—	0.4
	1973	17 472	5.3	4.7	0.2	1.9	46.2	41.7	—	—
	1974	18 447	5.9	3.2	0.4	2.0	46.4	42.1	—	—
Lebanon	1971	29 475	6.2	0.5	85.2	0.2	3.3	4.2	—	0.4
	1972	*32 994	5.4	0.4	38.8	0.2	49.1	2.6	—	3.5
	1973	36 513	4.8	0.3	1.4	0.1	86.1	1.3	—	6.0
Malaysia	1971	27 794	24.9	11.4	3.6	0.5	49.5	7.1	0.6	2.4
	1972	8 736[6]	20.1	9.5	7.1	0.1	50.7	10.1	2.4	—
	1973	8 736[6]	19.3	0.6	11.4	0.1	49.0	15.6	4.0	—
	1974	24 446	21.7	5.5	2.0	2.1	59.1	8.7	0.9	—
Pakistan	1971	43 316	27.0	6.6	1.2	0.5	34.5	9.3	20.9	—
	1972	41 699	19.8	10.3	4.3	0.3	18.7	8.4	10.9	27.3
	1973	44 720	...	...	...	...	...	...	...	...
Philippines[7]	1971	252 053	17.3	1.0	2.7	—	65.5	11.6	1.9	—
	1972	358 434	17.3	1.0	2.8	—	66.1	11.8	1.0	—
	1973	464 815	17.2	1.1	2.9	—	66.4	11.9	0.5	—
	1974	571 197	17.2	1.1	3.0	—	66.6	11.9	0.2	—
Qatar	1971	3 952	14.8	1.3	5.9	0.7	59.4	17.9	—	—
	1972	5 434	14.4	1.2	5.7	0.7	57.9	12.9	—	7.2
	1973	*6 162	13.9	1.3	16.0	0.8	43.1	13.1	—	11.8
Saudi Arabia	1971	*6 762	30.8	5.9	15.5	—	32.2	12.3	—	3.3
	1972	7 024	37.0	9.1	21.5	—	16.9	9.2	—	6.3
	1973	6 105	22.8	—	22.8	—	23.9	30.5	—	—
Singapore	1971	27 300	14.3	—	10.3	—	59.1	15.0	1.3	—
	1972	27 295	15.0	0.1	10.5	0.5	58.0	13.6	1.3	1.0
	1973	26 572	21.6	0.6	19.1	0.5	49.9	8.3	—	—
	1974	25 498	19.5	0.7	10.0	0.9	58.3	9.7	0.1	0.8
Sri Lanka	1971	11 548	10.6	6.8	16.3	0.7	34.5	28.1	2.9	0.1
	1972	22 802	9.2	6.6	1.9	—	13.0	5.7	—	63.6
	1973	22 984	13.7	6.2	—	—	12.9	5.7	—	61.5
	1974	24 390	9.6	6.4	14.5	1.2	45.1	11.9	—	11.3
Thailand	1971	6 535	20.0	12.1	2.4	0.4	58.9	6.2	—	—
	1972	6 708	15.5	10.8	10.1	0.8	48.1	4.6	9.3	0.8
	1973	*7 800	24.1	14.5	6.9	0.5	44.3	5.3	4.0	0.4
	1974	8 892	30.6	17.3	4.5	0.3	41.5	5.8	—	—

Country	Year	Hours per year	Information	Education	Culture	Sciences	Entertainment	Programmes for special audiences	Advertising	Other programmes not elsewhere classified
ASIA (cont'd.)										
Turkey	1971	74 771	11.9	11.5	1.8	—	66.7	3.4	4.7	—
	1972	81 064	10.1	10.9	66.8	0.2	0.6	3.4	1.5	6.5
	1973	75 673	11.7	11.4	69.0	—	—	3.3	4.6	—
	1974	83 986	9.6	11.2	10.6	0.2	48.2	3.3	4.5	12.4
S. Vietnam	1971	8 563[8]	24.8	5.8	10.0	1.9	43.1	3.6	—	10.8
	1972	8 736[8]	24.3	4.2	11.7	1.9	42.3	15.6	—	—
	1973	56 628	25.7	15.0	2.4	0.9	36.2	19.5	—	0.3
	1974	73 460	34.3	15.9	12.5	0.8	21.8	4.5	5.4	4.8
EUROPE										
Austria	1971	35 622	21.0	2.9	15.7	4.3	40.2	5.7	9.8	0.4
	1972	34 713	20.6	3.2	15.0	3.7	44.0	3.9	9.3	0.3
	1973	35 799	20.0	2.3	16.3	3.1	40.7	5.6	9.6	2.4
	1974	35 297	20.9	2.3	17.4	2.0	42.4	5.0	9.3	0.7
Belgium[2]	1971	22 161	24.0	0.9	25.2	0.9	22.1	19.5	0.3	7.1
	1972	18 628	15.9	5.1	28.3	0.4	35.8	14.8	0.1	—
	1973	23 130	20.7	1.9	24.5	0.1	41.0	11.5	0.2	0.1
Czechoslovakia	1971	27 118	14.4	10.7	23.9	0.7	31.4	10.0	0.9	8.0
	1972	39 806	10.5	12.5	19.7	0.7	28.7	6.4	0.5	21.0
	1973	40 326	11.5	4.8	22.7	0.6	43.6	2.0	0.5	14.3
	1974	40 456	11.9	4.4	22.0	0.7	44.1	3.5	0.5	12.9
Denmark	1971	12 272	25.9	2.1	4.2	—	56.4	11.4	—	—
	1972	12 310	22.6	2.5	18.6	—	43.5	4.8	—	8.0
	1973	13 355	21.4	2.3	16.2	—	48.7	4.3	7.1	—
Faeroe Island	1971	1 704	23.4	—	—	—	55.9	20.7	—	—
	1972	1 800	17.8	—	24.4	—	35.8	21.0	—	1.0
	1973	*1 800	18.1	—	24.8	—	35.2	21.4	—	0.5
	1974	1 800	18.4	—	25.2	—	34.7	21.7	—	—
Finland	1971	15 786	34.9	2.2	2.3	2.5	49.4	8.1	—	0.6
	1972	16 857	37.8	2.3	17.7	2.3	31.0	8.9	—	—
	1973	17 294	29.1	0.9	3.2	3.0	47.6	2.2	—	14.0
France	1971	31 053	13.6	18.6	36.1	—	30.5	1.1	0.1	—
	1972	28 016	10.4	—	48.7	0.6	39.0	1.1	0.2	—
	1973	28 202	9.7	—	8.5	—	81.3	0.5	—	—
German, Demo.[10]	1973	44 997	34.0	0.7	55.0	0.9	5.7	3.7	—	—
	1974	44 677	33.5	0.8	54.4	0.9	6.3	4.1	—	—
Gibraltar	1971	5 824	21.4	—	—	—	67.9	6.2	4.5	—
	1972	5 824	28.5	0.9	12.5	0.9	47.3	5.4	2.7	1.8
	1973	5 831	28.5	—	13.3	0.9	47.4	5.4	2.7	1.8
	1974	5 967	28.4	0.1	14.4	0.9	47.3	4.5	2.7	1.7
Hungary	1971	*15 128	17.7	1.3	58.3	2.0	10.9	9.2	0.6	—
	1972	16 488	18.3	1.6	58.6	1.7	9.9	9.1	0.8	—
	1973	17 112	18.4	1.6	70.3	1.3	—	7.8	0.6	—
	1974	17 108	18.5	0.9	66.6	4.0	0.3	9.1	0.6	—
Iceland[11]	1971	5 905	13.1	3.5	31.2	7.1	28.4	9.6	5.9	1.2
	1972	5 981	14.5	0.9	29.4	5.9	30.3	8.7	5.5	4.8
	1973	6 036	25.0	0.4	23.5	—	33.0	4.5	7.2	6.4
	1974	6 062	24.4	0.4	25.0	—	30.4	4.7	9.1	6.1

Country	Year	Hours per year	Information	Education	Culture	Sciences	Entertainment	Programmes for special audiences	Advertising	Other programmes not elsewhere classified
EUROPE (cont'd.)										
Ireland	1971	5 889	27.4	0.6	16.9	—	36.5	7.2	11.4	—
	1972	6 005	38.2	0.5	7.0	—	40.2	4.1	—	10.0
	1973	6 254	21.4	1.3	19.3	—	35.3	7.6	15.0	0.1
	1974	6 348	22.0	0.5	26.4	—	29.6	6.7	14.8	—
Italy [12]	1971	17 628	15.4	0.3	4.7	—	69.6	6.2	3.8	—
	1972	17 836	15.5	0.6	4.1	—	70.5	5.8	3.5	—
	1973	17 933	14.6	0.6	4.0	—	71.7	5.0	3.6	0.5
	1974	17 775	13.7	0.6	4.3	—	72.8	5.0	2.9	0.7
Malta	1972	6 134	22.7	6.8	12.5	—	45.0	13.0	—	—
	1973	*6 161	25.8	5.9	12.2	0.2	45.5	7.7	—	2.7
	1974	6 188	28.8	5.0	11.8	0.4	46.1	2.5	—	5.4
Monaco	1971	*12 458	7.2	—	0.1	—	38.3	42.1	12.2	0.1
	1972	*14 671	6.5	—	0.3	—	46.6	39.6	6.9	0.1
	1973	*16 885	6.1	—	0.3	—	52.8	37.7	3.0	0.1
	1974	19 098	5.7	—	0.4	—	57.5	36.3	—	0.1
Norway [13]	1971	6 245	36.7	2.1	32.6	—	11.3	13.6	3.7	—
	1972	6 276	28.2	2.5	4.9	0.2	41.4	15.2	3.6	4.0
	1973	6 224	28.1	2.3	19.3	0.2	25.0	15.5	3.8	5.8
	1974	6 282	29.5	2.3	22.0	0.2	25.0	16.0	3.9	1.1
Poland	1971	22 463	23.7	1.8	13.0	—	48.8	6.0	2.5	4.2
	1972	22 714	20.2	2.0	13.8	—	51.0	8.0	2.5	2.5
	1973	26 026	20.7	1.9	7.3	—	51.0	6.7	2.2	10.2
	1974	40 217	...	...	...	...	...	...	...	...
Romania	1971	*26 876	14.4	4.2	40.1	0.7	30.7	4.3	0.7	4.9
	1972	27 205	13.7	1.7	32.4	0.3	42.0	8.4	0.4	1.1
Spain	1971	9 267[14]	23.9	2.5	19.5	0.2	46.6	5.4	1.7	0.2
	1972	9 618[14]	25.2	1.8	19.1	0.1	41.7	8.8	1.7	1.6
	1973	1 696 756	16.4	6.6	16.0	0.2	45.2	8.0	7.6	—
	1974	1 772 572	16.3	6.4	16.4	0.3	43.2	8.2	9.2	—
Sweden	1971	*18 200	18.2	4.8	20.1	2.1	41.6	10.9	—	2.3
	1972	18 356	16.2	4.2	21.6	2.3	41.7	11.6	—	2.4
	1973	18 541	17.4	4.8	22.2	2.3	37.8	12.3	1.9	1.3
	1974	18 566	16.5	4.4	22.9	2.4	38.7	12.2	—	2.9
Switzerland	1971	31 824	18.5	0.6	26.3	4.4	41.3	8.9	—	—
	1972	32 172	16.2	0.6	26.9	5.0	42.8	8.5	—	—
	1973	32 915	16.6	0.7	29.7	5.5	43.2	4.3	—	—
	1974	33 450	14.8	0.9	39.3	4.9	36.1	4.0	—	—
United Kingdom	1971	23 615	21.5	3.6	4.8	—	64.1	4.9	—	1.1
	1972	25 082	18.8	5.1	19.0	—	49.6	5.6	—	1.9
	1973	44 184	33.8	3.4	3.4	—	54.4	3.1	1.9	—
	1974	70 781	23.9	2.5	5.7	0.4	55.1	7.0	4.1	1.3
Yugoslavia	1971	232 908	14.9	2.0	38.6	—	30.8	3.0	8.7	2.0
	1972	280 332	11.6	1.9	9.5	—	61.8	4.5	7.8	2.9
	1973	286 543	14.8	5.5	9.4	—	63.4	—	6.9	—
	1974	298 413	14.4	5.1	9.1	—	64.1	—	7.3	—
OCEANIA										
American Samoa	1971	5 835	15.5	—	23.6	1.6	55.7	3.6	—	—
	1972	5 876	15.0	0.1	4.9	0.3	75.9	3.6	—	0.2
	1973	6 552	23.8	—	—	—	63.5	2.4	—	10.3
	1974	8 760	13.1	—	0.9	—	68.2	0.7	17.1	—

Country	Year	Hours per year	Information	Education	Culture	Sciences	Entertainment	Programmes for special audiences	Advertising	Other programmes not elsewhere classified
OCEANIA (cont'd.)										
Cook Islands	1971	*3 312	20.2	4.5	1.9	0.3	29.5	34.4	9.2	—
	1972	4 108	10.1	5.1	3.5	0.6	2.8	60.8	17.1	—
Gilbert Islands	1971	2 132	20.5	2.0	37.6	1.2	30.5	5.3	2.9	—
	1972	2 115	25.4	1.9	18.4	—	38.1	11.5	4.7	—
	1973	*2 471	28.8	4.3	14.3	—	37.6	12.8	2.2	—
	1974	2 826	31.3	6.1	11.2	—	37.3	13.7	0.4	—
Guam	1971	6 500	4.4	—	2.2	—	79.9	7.2	4.3	2.0
	1972	6 550	28.6	—	—	—	71.4	—	—	—
	1973	*7 656	20.6	—	—	—	65.1	—	14.3	—
	1974	8 760	14.6	—	—	—	60.4	—	25.0	—
New Caledonia	1971	3 484	14.9	1.5	26.9	1.5	25.3	3.0	26.9	—
	1972	5 824	12.5	2.2	11.6	0.9	60.7	5.8	5.4	0.9
	1973	5 840	13.4	2.2	19.4	1.0	53.3	4.4	6.3	—
	1974	6 194	8.2	—	30.4	—	61.2	0.2	—	—
New Hebrides (Eng.)	1971	708	44.4	—	4.5	—	44.4	6.7	—	—
	1972	1 170	32.2	6.7	—	—	57.8	2.2	1.1	—
	1973	2 340	35.0	4.4	1.1	—	55.6	2.8	1.1	—
New Hebrides (Fr.)	1971	780	26.6	5.0	—	—	35.0	6.7	—	26.7
	1972	1 170	32.2	6.7	—	—	57.8	2.2	1.1	—
	1973	1 170	62.2	—	2.2	—	26.7	2.2	2.2	4.5
New Zealand	1971	323 241	12.4	3.4	7.1	0.2	61.0	8.6	6.8	0.5
	1972	348 004	11.9	3.3	5.7	0.2	65.2	7.2	6.5	—
	1973	371 540	12.2	3.1	7.1	0.2	64.4	6.7	6.3	—
	1974	371 540	12.2	3.1	7.1	0.2	64.4	6.7	6.3	—
Niue	1971	1 300	25.7	2.0	—	—	70.4	1.2	0.7	—
	1972	*1 313	22.1	2.3	2.0	1.0	48.7	2.6	0.3	21.0
	1973	1 326	18.6	2.6	3.9	2.0	27.5	3.9	—	41.5
	1974	*1 472	18.5	4.9	1.8	0.9	51.3	3.9	—	18.7
Norfolk Islands	1971	*1 405	10.0	6.2	7.3	—	69.0	7.2	0.3	—
	1972	*1 898	8.5	2.3	7.3	—	77.6	3.8	0.5	—
	1973	2 392	7.6	—	7.4	—	82.6	1.8	0.6	—
	1974	2 288	11.2	4.6	14.7	1.1	52.5	13.6	2.3	—
Pacific Islands	1971	2 184	4.8	—	—	—	61.9	33.3	—	—
	1972	6 448[15]	22.7	4.4	—	1.4	57.4	8.9	1.5	3.7
	1973	6 734[15]	23.4	6.8	0.8	1.4	55.0	7.7	1.4	3.5
	1974	6 691	28.9	14.2	1.2	1.4	40.4	12.4	1.5	—
Tonga	1971	3 798	19.2	11.0	—	0.4	52.4	7.5	9.5	—
	1972	*4 220	17.7	8.0	—	0.2	52.6	6.0	15.5	—
	1973	4 641	16.4	5.6	—	—	52.8	4.8	20.4	—
	1974	3 484	17.2	9.7	2.2	—	54.5	13.4	3.0	—
Western Samoa	1971	5 486	33.9	13.3	5.7	—	24.6	13.0	9.5	—
	1972	5 798	18.4	4.5	—	—	47.3	2.5	27.3	—
	1973	5 798	13.9	4.5	4.5	0.4	59.2	4.9	12.6	—
	1974	5 789	10.8	2.9	0.1	—	77.3	4.6	4.3	—

1. One channel only. 2. Broadcasting in the Malagasy language only. 3. These data cover only 55% of all Canadian stations. 4. Data on sciences and programmes for special audiences are included with education. 5. Data on advertising are included with other programmes not elsewhere classified. 6. The figures refer to Nationsl Network only. 7. Data refer to radio stations located in the city of Manila and suburbs only. 8. Data refer to the central transmitting station in Saigon of the Système National de Radiodiffusion which also comprises 8 regional stations. 9. French Broadcasting only. 10. The data which relate to the German Democratic Republic include the relevant data relating to Berlin for which separate data have not been supplied. This is without prejudice to any question of status which may be involved. 11. National station Networks I and II. 12. National programmes only. 13. Regional programmes only. 14. Average established for each station of the national network. 15. Average broadcasting time of 6 district stations.

Table 14 — Radio broadcasting: programmes by type
total hours of broadcasting per year and percentage distribution by type of programme
Number of countries and territories presented in this table: 134

Country	Year	Code	Hours per year Total	Information	Education	Culture	Sciences	Entertainment	Programmes for special audiences	Advertising	Other programmes not elsewhere classified
AFRICA											
Algeria	1974	A	5 940	17.5	21.9	23.9	—	28.8	7.9	0.0	—
		B	5 940	17.5	21.9	23.9	—	28.8	7.9	0.0	—
Benin	1972	A	4 351	33.0	24.0	1.8	—	32.0	6.8	2.4	—
		B	3 878	37.1	20.8	1.3	—	31.8	6.3	2.7	—
Botswana	1974	A	5 980	27.0	30.0	24.4	—	4.4	8.5	5.7	—
		B	5 980	27.0	30.0	24.4	—	4.4	8.5	5.7	—
Burundi	1974	A	5 104	22.6	8.5	1.0	—	65.4	2.5	—	—
		B	5 000	23.0	8.7	—	—	65.7	2.6	—	—
Central African Rep.	1972	A	6 734	45.1	2.3	3.3	0.4	23.9	8.4	3.3	13.3
		B	6 605	45.4	2.4	3.4	—	23.6	8.5	3.2	13.5
Comoro Islands	1973	A	3 577	19.1	80.9	—	—	—	—	—	—
Congo	1974	A	6 794	49.4	24.4	2.5	0.3	16.8	4.0	1.2	1.4
		B	6 500	50.5	25.5	1.2	—	16.6	4.0	0.9	1.3
Djibouti	1974	A	10 894	10.5	—	12.3	—	77.2	—	—	—
Egypt	1974	A	47 029	10.5	1.0	18.6	0.8	44.7	23.7	0.7	—
Ethiopia	1974	A	6 370	18.4	21.1	—	—	50.4	0.8	9.3	—
		B	6 370	18.4	21.1	—	—	50.4	0.8	9.3	—
Gambia	1972	A	4 561	44.1	20.2	1.7	—	13.7	10.1	—	10.2
		B	3 948	44.7	18.5	1.3	—	13.8	11.3	—	10.4
Ghana	1975	A	5 330	35.3	3.9	7.3	8.3	20.4	9.4	15.3	—
		B	5 315	35.4	4.0	7.1	8.3	20.4	9.4	15.4	—
Ivory Coast	1973	A	7 001	2.1	67.5	4.4	—	2.2	1.5	1.5	20.8
Liberia	1972	A	14 681	32.6	2.6	2.5	—	38.2	19.5	4.4	0.2
		B	11 270	34.6	1.8	2.3	—	40.6	17.0	3.7	—
Madagascar	1973	A	8 294	18.5	—	5.0	0.6	62.1	12.5	1.3	—
		B	7 878	19.5	—	3.3	0.7	62.0	13.2	1.3	—
Malawi	1975	A	7 965	17.6	26.1	33.3	—	10.1	5.0	7.9	—
		B	7 939	17.7	26.2	33.5	—	9.8	4.9	7.9	—
Mauritania	1972	A	3 172	36.3	31.7	—	—	26.2	4.7	1.0	—

RADIO PROGRAMMES

Country	Year	Code	Hours per year Total	Information	Education	Culture	Sciences	Entertainment	Programmes for special audiences	Advertising	Other programmes not elsewhere classified
AFRICA (cont'd.)											
Mauritius	1975	A	6 036	50.7	14.1	14.4	6.1	9.2	3.8	—	1.7
		B	3 780	60.0	15.4	7.5	3.1	7.4	5.1	—	1.5
Morocco	1973	A	8 031	15.9	4.5	2.3	—	71.8	4.9	—	0.6
		B	8 031	15.9	4.5	2.3	—	71.8	4.9	—	0.6
Niger	1972	A	8 329	17.2	15.2	2.0	0.3	40.0	22.2	2.8	0.3
		B	5 781	24.7	20.8	0.9	—	17.1	32.0	4.0	0.5
Nigeria	1974	A	8 284	20.8	9.3	26.8	—	30.2	6.7	6.2	—
		B	7 786	22.1	9.9	28.2	—	32.1	6.7	1.0	—
Reunion	1973	A	5 954	15.4	0.6	8.7	1.7	63.8	6.7	3.1	—
		B	3 120	...	...	...	...	...	...	...	...
Rwanda	1975	A	5 379	18.5	9.6	4.7	0.5	60.1	6.6	—	—
		B	4 877	20.4	10.5	3.2	—	62.7	3.2	—	—
Senegal	1974	A	5 304	...	...	...	...	...	...	...	...
Seychelles	1974	A	3 121	19.7	27.0	4.3	—	36.7	10.4	1.9	—
		B	2 700	11.9	31.3	3.4	—	40.1	11.1	2.2	—
St. Helena	1974	A	1 100	...	...	...	...	...	...	...	...
Sudan	1973	A	9 048	21.9	1.7	14.9	1.2	33.9	24.7	1.7	—
		B	9 048	21.9	1.7	14.9	1.2	33.9	24.7	1.7	—
Somalia	1971	A	2 695	36.8	8.5	35.8	—	7.6	6.8	4.5	—
Swaziland	1975	A	4 916	16.8	8.6	4.8	—	63.9	3.7	2.2	—
		B	4 600	11.7	9.0	4.8	—	68.2	4.0	2.3	—
Togo	1971	A	4 625	30.9	4.4	18.3	0.3	34.9	11.2	—	—
		B	3 507	39.0	4.3	4.0	0.4	37.5	14.8	—	—
Tunisia	1974	A	6 744	25.9	10.3	7.2	—	47.5	9.1	—	—
		B	5 886	29.7	11.8	7.8	—	40.3	10.4	—	—
United Rep. of Cameroon	1974	A	9 386	21.2	3.9	60.0	0.6	8.0	—	6.4	—
		B	7 124	27.2	5.1	54.6	—	5.8	—	7.3	—
Western Sahara	1973	A	8 502	22.3	2.4	7.9	—	30.4	35.9	1.1	—
		B	5 678	7.9	—	2.3	—	34.5	53.7	1.6	—
Zaire	1974	A	8 736	25.7	8.9	1.2	—	6.4	1.8	1.0	—
NORTH AMERICA											
Antigua	1972	A	5 954	17.5	0.5	—	—	61.1	12.2	8.7	—
Bahamas	1971	A	14 517	18.1	0.5	6.6	0.1	54.5	9.8	9.8	0.6
		B	4 714	55.3	1.4	17.1	—	1.7	22.6	—	1.9
Barbados	1975	A	8 232	15.3	—	0.8	0.2	72.1	11.6	—	—
		B	7 465	12.1	—	—	—	76.0	11.9	—	—
Belize	1975	A	5 677	19.9	1.8	—	5.0	46.0	16.3	11.0	—
		B	4 845	22.0	2.2	—	5.4	53.9	10.1	6.4	—

RADIO PROGRAMMES

Country	Year	Code	Hours per year Total	Information	Education	Culture	Sciences	Entertainment	Programmes for special audiences	Advertising	Other programmes not elsewhere classified
AMERICA NORTH (cont'd.)											
Bermuda	1973	A	40 560	12.0	—	1.0	—	73.0	3.0	10.0	1.0
		B	24 336	...	...	...	...	...	...	...	...
Canada [1]	1973	A	3 278 236	21.4	1.7	7.9	0.1	63.2	3.4	2.1	0.2
Cayman Islands	1974	A	2 196	5.9	4.5	32.8	—	42.6	14.2	—	—
		B	1 664	4.2	4.7	31.5	—	44.0	15.6	—	—
Cuba	1974	A	266 638	27.9	8.9	54.2	—	2.2	2.6	4.2	—
El Salvador	1974	A	209 049	4.3	1.4	3.0	—	82.9	4.3	—	4.1
Greenland	1974	A	4 850	17.6	1.0	25.7	1.7	25.6	7.8	—	20.6
		B	4 390	19.5	1.1	24.2	0.9	25.6	7.6	—	21.1
Guadeloupe	1972	A	6 852	24.9	4.3	4.9	—	53.7	8.6	3.6	—
		B	3 960	30.9	7.6	—	—	45.6	13.6	2.3	—
Jamaica	1974	A	7 189	32.4	—	4.0	—	56.4	7.2	—	—
		B	6 782	33.3	—	1.9	—	59.8	5.0	—	—
Martinique	1972	A	4 970	9.1	7.0	6.0	—	70.4	7.5	—	—
		B	1 530	10.2	5.1	5.1	—	56.9	22.7	—	—
Panama	1971	A	438 831	9.0	0.8	1.6	0.4	66.0	2.3	19.7	0.2
		B	422 017	8.7	0.7	1.4	0.1	67.6	1.5	19.8	0.2
Panama Canal Zone	1974	A	8 760	17.8	—	3.0	—	73.6	2.1	3.5	—
		B	8 760	17.8	—	3.0	—	73.6	2.1	3.5	—
St. Lucia	1971	A	10 920	31.8	0.7	3.3	—	59.3	1.1	3.8	—
		B	7 501	35.5	1.0	—	—	58.9	1.6	3.0	—
St Pierre et Miquelon	1974	A	5 824	21.5	2.0	23.8	—	50.7	2.0	—	—
St Vincent	1974	A	3 564	29.7	—	4.4	—	62.7	2.5	0.7	—
		B	1 182	63.3	—	8.8	—	18.5	7.7	1.7	—
Trinidad & Tobago	1974	A	9 026	24.6	2.3	4.3	0.1	44.2	14.1	10.4	—
		B	5 703	30.0	2.3	3.2	—	31.2	19.6	13.7	—
Turks & Caicos	1974	A	1 684	12.2	1.2	—	—	66.8	19.8	—	—
		B	1 613	12.1	—	—	—	68.5	19.4	—	—
AMERICA, SOUTH											
Argentina	1974	A	16 494 816	23.0	0.1	14.6	—	43.0	2.8	16.5	—
Brazil	1973	A	5 298 748	15.9	4.6	1.6	0.1	52.1	3.7	19.8	2.2
		B	5 251 844	16.0	4.7	1.6	0.1	51.8	3.7	19.9	2.2
Ecuador	1974	A	5 804	9.6	1.2	1.7	3.8	48.8	4.2	30.7	—
Falkland Island	1974	A	1 957	33.8	0.9	9.3	—	16.1	37.2	2.7	—
		B	1 090	23.8	1.6	3.6	—	18.3	47.7	4.8	—
French Guyana	1972	A	4 134	23.8	7.0	5.9	—	57.3	3.2	2.8	—
		B	2 154	20.5	—	—	—	71.0	3.0	5.5	

Country	Year	Code	Hours per year Total	Information	Education	Culture	Sciences	Entertainment	Programmes for special audiences	Advertising	Other programmes not elsewhere classified
AMERICA, SOUTH (cont'd.)											
Guyana	1975	A	7 358	25.6	2.8	5.8	—	31.1	21.2	7.8	5.7
		B	6 604	26.4	2.6	1.2	—	33.9	21.3	7.9	6.3
Uruguay	1974	A	537 056	6.0	0.3	6.4	—	87.3	—	—	—
ASIA											
Afghanistan	1974	A	4 615	17.0	8.7	17.8	1.1	36.3	14.6	4.5	—
Bahrain	1975	A	3 301	5.8	3.6	7.3	—	62.6	9.0	—	11.7
Brunei	1974	A	12 211	20.1	1.2	4.7	0.6	58.9	10.2	—	4.3
		B	10 387	18.9	1.3	1.7	—	65.1	11.5	—	1.5
Burma	1974	A	6 512	15.7	5.3	27.7	0.4	27.6	4.7	2.0	16.6
Cyprus	1974	A	7 726	14.7	1.9	22.1	—	51.6	8.3	1.4	—
		B	7 285	15.7	1.1	22.0	—	51.7	8.8	0.7	—
Hong Kong	1974	A	33 970	16.8	3.0	16.7	0.3	58.8	2.0	0.8	1.6
		B	30 138	15.8	2.9	14.7	0.3	61.3	2.3	0.9	1.8
India	1974	A	24 978	29.7	9.6	27.5	—	23.4	9.2	—	0.6
Indonesia	1973	A	208 687	27.5	12.0 [2]	7.4	0.0 [2]	46.9	0.0 [2]	0.0 [3]	6.2 [3]
Iran	1974	A	7 600	17.8	16.0	31.7	2.1	7.8	22.2	2.4	—
		B	7 400	18.2	16.5	32.6	2.2	5.3	22.8	2.4	—
Iraq	1974	A	22 565	23.2	—	6.7	0.2	49.1	11.8	5.1	3.9
		B	3 664	—	—	—	—	85.0	15.0	—	—
Israel	1973	A	26 208	9.6	0.6	16.1	0.2	29.2	20.0	1.7	22.6
Japan	1974	A	27 613	19.4	22.7	29.1	—	28.5	—	0.2	0.1
Jordan	1973	A	8 762	21.9	2.5	7.1	0.5	50.2	16.0	1.8	—
		B	8 589	22.3	2.5	6.1	0.3	51.2	16.4	1.2	—
Korea, Rep. of	1974	A	45 762	18.4	11.0	22.5	0.9	29.8	10.1	4.4	2.9
		B	45 571	18.4	11.0	22.6	0.9	29.7	10.1	4.4	2.9
Kuwait	1974	A	18 447	5.9	3.2	0.4	2.0	46.4	42.1	—	—
		B	8 073	13.5	3.8	0.8	2.6	66.7	12.6	—	—
Lebanon	1973	A	36 513	4.8	0.3	1.4	0.1	86.1	1.3	—	6.0
		B	36 513	4.8	0.3	1.4	0.1	86.1	1.3	—	6.0
Malaysia	1974	A	24 446	21.7	5.5	2.0	2.1	59.1	8.7	0.9	—
Maldives	1973	A	6 483	13.9	12.8	2.7	—	48.9	21.7	—	—
		B	4 754	11.3	17.5	3.7	—	66.7	0.8	—	—
Nepal	1972	A	3 514	27.9	0.8	27.8	—	2.6	21.7	18.3	0.9
Pakistan	1973	A	44 720	...	...	...	...	...	...	...	...
Philippines [4]	1975	A	677 578	17.2	1.1	3.0	0.0	66.8	11.9	—	—
		B	676 870	17.3	1.1	3.0	0.0	66.8	11.8	—	—

RADIO PROGRAMMES

Country	Year	Code	Hours per year Total	Information	Education	Culture	Sciences	Entertainment	Programmes for special audiences	Advertising	Other programmes not elsewhere classified
ASIA (cont'd.)											
Qatar	1973	A	6 162	13.9	1.3	16.0	0.8	43.1	13.1	—	11.8
		B	3 692	23.2	2.1	14.1	1.4	31.0	14.1	—	14.1
Saudi Arabia	1973	A	6 105	22.8	—	22.8	—	23.9	30.5	—	—
Singapore	1974	A	25 498	19.5	0.7	10.0	0.9	58.3	9.7	0.1	0.8
Sri Lanka	1974	A	24 390	9.6	6.4	14.5	1.2	45.1	11.9	—	11.3
		B	21 479	10.7	7.1	15.1	1.2	39.6	13.5	—	12.8
Syria	1971	A	7 280	25.3	8.9	5.1	1.6	45.6	13.5	—	—
Thailand	1975	A	9 308	36.7	16.4	4.3	0.3	36.7	5.6	—	—
Turkey	1974	A	83 986	9.6	11.2	10.6	0.2	48.2	3.3	4.5	12.4
Vietnam, South	1974	A	73 460	34.3	15.9	12.5	0.8	21.8	4.5	5.4	4.8
		B	71 910	35.0	15.4	11.8	0.3	22.3	4.6	5.6	5.0
Yemen	1972	A	4 819	32.4	6.1	25.9	0.5	20.5	11.9	0.5	2.2
		B	4 801	32.5	6.1	26.0	0.2	20.6	11.9	0.5	2.2
EUROPE											
Austria	1975	A	36 786	22.8	2.4	15.8	1.6	40.2	6.6	8.5	2.1
		B	36 656	22.9	2.4	15.5	1.6	40.4	6.6	8.5	2.1
Belgium [5]	1973	A	23 130	20.7	1.9	24.5	0.1	41.0	11.5	0.2	0.1
		B	22 623	21.1	1.8	23.0	0.1	41.9	11.7	0.3	0.1
Czechoslovakia	1974	A	40 456	11.9	4.4	22.0	0.7	44.1	3.5	0.5	12.9
Denmark	1973	A	13 355	21.4	2.3	16.2	—	48.7	4.3	7.1	—
Faeroe Island	1974	A	1 800	18.4	—	25.2	—	34.7	21.7	—	—
Finland	1973	A	17 294	29.1	0.9	3.2	3.0	47.6	2.2	—	14.0
France	1973	A	28 202	9.7	—	8.5	—	81.3	0.5	—	—
German, Democratic [6]	1974	A	44 677	33.5	0.8	54.4	0.9	6.3	4.1	—	—
Gibraltar	1974	A	5 967	28.4	0.1	14.4	0.9	47.3	4.5	2.7	1.7
Greece	1973	A	32 083	17.6	0.3	22.3	0.2	42.6	4.3	12.5	0.2
		B	31 755	17.6	0.2	22.1	0.2	42.7	4.4	12.6	0.2
Holy See	1974	A	9 776	45.2	—	18.6	2.7	16.5	6.1	—	10.9
Hungary	1974	A	17 108	17.0	1.2	67.8	4.3	1.2	7.9	0.6	—
Iceland [7]	1974	A	6 062	24.4	0.4	25.0	—	30.4	4.7	9.1	6.1
Ireland	1974	A	6 348	22.0	0.5	26.4	—	29.6	6.7	14.8	—
Italy [8]	1974	A	17 775	13.7	0.6	4.3	—	72.8	5.0	2.9	0.7
Malta	1974	A	6 188	28.8	5.0	11.8	0.4	46.1	2.5	—	5.4
		B	6 188	28,8	5.0	11.8	0.4	46.1	2.5	—	5.4
Monaco	1974	A	19 098	5.7	—	0.4	—	57.5	36.3	—	0.1

Country	Year	Code	Hours per year Total	Information	Education	Culture	Sciences	Entertainment	Programmes for special audiences	Advertising	Other programmes not elsewhere classified
EUROPE (cont'd.)											
Netherlands	1974	A	21 008	...	...	...	...	...	...	...	...
Norway [9]	1974	A	6 282	29.5	2.3	22.0	0.2	25.0	16.0	3.9	1.1
Poland	1974	A	40 217	...	...	...	...	...	...	...	...
Portugal	1974	A	16 588	19.8	—	40.1	—	37.3	2.8	—	—
Romania	1972	A	27 205	13.7	1.7	32.4	0.3	42.0	8.4	0.4	1.1
		B	27 083	13.5	1.7	32.4	0.3	42.2	8.4	0.4	1.1
Spain	1974	A	1 772 572	16.3	6.4	16.4	0.3	43.2	8.2	9.2	—
		B	1 754 610	16.4	6.5	15.6	0.3	43.6	8.3	9.3	—
Sweden	1974	A	18 566	16.5	4.4	22.9	2.4	38.7	12.2	—	2.9
		B	18 397	16.6	4.4	22.2	2.4	39.1	12.3	—	3.0
Switzerland	1974	A	33 450	14.8	0.9	39.3	4.9	36.1	4.0	—	—
United Kingdom	1974	A	70 781	23.9	2.5	5.7	0.4	55.1	7.0	4.1	1.3
Yugoslavia	1974	A	298 413	14.4	5.1	9.1	—	64.1	—	7.3	—
OCEANIA											
American Samoa	1974	A	8 760	13.1	—	0.9	—	68.2	0.7	17.1	—
		B	2 502	8.8	—	—	—	29.2	2.3	59.7	—
Australia	1972	A	...	26.7	1.1	14.8	—	43.4	3.5	10.5	—
Cook Islands	1972	A	4 108	10.1	5.1	3.5	0.6	2.8	60.8	17.1	—
Fiji	1975	A	15 109	6.4	2.4	2.7	0.1	77.9	3.6	1.3	5.6
		B	2 746	27.2	13.1	0.9	—	6.2	16.2	5.7	30.7
Gilbert Islands	1974	A	2 826	31.3	6.1	11.2	—	37.3	13.7	0.4	—
		B	2 332	27.5	6.2	9.1	—	40.2	16.6	0.4	—
Guam	1974	A	8 760	14.6	—	—	—	60.4	—	25.0	—
		B	8 760	14.6	—	—	—	60.4	—	25.0	—
Nauru	1974	A	3 626	7.4	—	4.1	1.7	75.2	11.6	—	—
		B	660	27.3	—	—	—	45.4	27.3	—	—
New Caledonia	1974	A	6 194	8.2	—	30.4	—	61.2	0.2	—	—
New Hebrides (En.)	1973	A	2 340	35.0	4.4	1.1	—	55.6	2.8	1.1	—
		B	1 690	48.5	6.2	1.5	—	38.5	3.8	1.5	—
New Hebrides French	1973	A	1 170	62.2	—	2.2	—	26.7	2.2	2.2	4.5
		B	784								
New Zealand	1974	A	371 540	12.2	3.1	7.1	0.2	64.4	6.7	6.3	—
		B	294 008	14.2	3.7	5.2	0.2	61.7	7.4	7.6	—
Niue	1975	A	1 617	18.4	6.8	—	—	70.8	4.0	—	—
		B	437	43.5	12.6	—	—	32.0	11.9	—	—
Norfolk Islands	1974	A	2 288	11.2	4.6	14.7	1.1	52.8	13.6	2.3	—
		B	1 937	9.8	3.1	10.1	1.3	60.5	12.5	2.7	—

RADIO PROGRAMMES

Country	Year	Code	Hours per year Total	Information	Education	Culture	Sciences	Entertainment	Programmes for special audiences	Advertising	Other programmes not elsewhere classified
OCEANIA (cont'd.)											
Pacific Islands [10]	1974	A	6 691	28.9	14.2	1.2	1.4	40.4	12.4	1.5	—
		B	5 339	29.7	16.1	0.5	—	40.0	11.7	2.0	—
Tonga	1974	A	3 484	17.2	9.7	2.2	—	54.5	13.4	3.0	—
		B	3 237	10.8	10.5	2.4	—	58.6	14.5	3.2	—
Western Samoa	1974	A	5 789	10.8	2.9	0.1	—	77.3	4.6	4.3	—
		B	2 145	5.3	7.9	0.3	—	63.1	12.3	11.1	—

1. These data cover only 55% of all Canadian stations. 2. Data on sciences and programmes for special audiences are included with education. 3. Data on advertising are included with other programmes not elsewhere classified. 4. Data refer to radio stations located in the city of Manila and suburbs only. 5. French Broadcasting only. 6. The data which relate to the German Democratic Republic include the relevant data relating to Berlin for which separate data have not been supplied. This is without prejudice to any question of status which may be involved. 7. National stations Networks I and II. 8. Nationsl programmes only. 9. Regional programmes only. 10. Average broadcasting time of 6 district stations.

Table 15 — Radio broadcasting: programmes by type for a typical week in 1973
Number of countries and territories presented in this table: 98

| Country | Hours per year Total | Composition of domestic sound broadcasting programmes of selected countries during a typical week in 1973 ||||||||
		Information	Education	Culture	Sciences	Entertainment	Programmes for special audiences	Advertising	Other programmes not elsewhere classified
AFRICA									
Algeria	2 318	41.4	21.5	4.9	—	32.2	—	—	—
Botswana	*5 649	32.7	29.4	14.3	0.3	14.1	6.2	3.0	—
Burundi	*4 937	23.2	11.7	3.2	0.6	50.8	4.6	0.5	5.4
Comoro Island	3 577	19.1	80.9	—	—	—	—	—	—
Congo	*5 757	43.1	19.2	10.3	0.2	18.5	5.6	2.3	0.8
Djibouti	9 828	11.1	2.1	15.9	1.6	67.7	1.6	—	—
Egypt	50 636	13.0	1.3	14.3	0.7	50.8	19.5	0.4	—
Ethiopia	6 477	20.8	20.2	—	—	49.8	—	9.2	—
Ivory Coast	7 001	2.1	67.5	4.4	—	2.2	1.5	1.5	20.8
Madagascar	8 294	18.5	—	5.0	0.6	62.1	12.5	1.3	—
Malawi	6 673	18.3	19.3	36.6	—	6.7	7.4	9.4	2.3
Mauritius	6 032	16.4	5.3	23.1	0.4	52.2	2.6	—	—
Morocco	8 031	15.9	4.5	2.3	—	71.8	4.9	—	0.6
Nigeria	8 284	20.8	9.3	26.8	—	30.2	6.7	6.2	—
Reunion	5 954	15.4	0.6	8.7	1.7	63.8	6.7	3.1	—
Rwanda	*5 233	18.5	9.3	6.1	0.3	57.2	6.9	1.7	—
Seychelles	3 133	14.9	28.2	3.3	0.4	45.6	4.2	3.3	—
Sudan	9 048	21.9	1.7	14.9	1.2	33.9	24.7	1.7	—
Tunisia	6 192	12.3	15.1	16.0	0.8	52.9	2.9	—	—
United Rep. of Cameroon	9 386	21.2	3.8	60.0	0.6	8.0	—	6.4	—
Western Sahara	8 502	22.3	2.4	7.9	—	30.4	35.9	1.1	—
Zaire	5 668	54.1	6.4	4.6	1.0	22.0	6.4	5.5	—

Composition of domestic sound broadcasting programmes of selected countries during a typical week in 1973

Country	Hours per year Total	Information	Education	Culture	Sciences	Entertainment	Programmes for special audiences	Advertising	Other programmes not elsewhere classified
AMERICA, NORTH									
Barbados	7 020	18.7	3.0	2.2	0.5	55.1	11.4	7.2	1.9
Belize	*5 847	19.3	3.3	22.4	3.2	30.4	14.3	7.1	—
Bermuda	40 560	12.0	—	1.0	—	73.0	3.0	10.0	1.0
Canada [1]	3 278 236	21.4	1.7	7.9	0.1	63.2	3.4	2.1	0.2
Cuba	261 612	29.4	9.7	54.7	—	—	2.2	3.8	0.2
El Salvador	*108 165	5.4	1.4	2.9	—	81.1	4.4	0.8	4.0
Greenland	*4 072	27.5	0.6	20.3	1.4	30.6	6.7	—	12.9
Jamaica	*6 104	30.6	1.3	9.2	0.2	41.7	17.0	—	—
Panama Canal Zone	8 736	17.8	—	3.0	—	73.7	2.0	3.5	—
St Pierre & Miquelon	3 380	18.3	—	13.5	—	63.2	5.0	—	—
AMERICA, SOUTH									
Argentina	8 555 404	24.7	0.5	24.0	—	—	34.1	16.7	—
Brazil	5 298 745	15.9	4.6	1.6	0.1	52.1	3.7	19.8	2.2
Falkland Island	1 976	23.7	5.3	55.3	1.3	3.9	9.2	1.3	—
Guyana	5 832	37.8	3.3	—	—	48.4	10.5	—	—
Uruguay	*528 968	9.7	3.8	7.5	0.4	73.1	0.5	4.5	0.5
ASIA									
Bahrain	4 082	23.5	0.6	4.5	0.6	60.6	4.5	—	5.7
Brunei	9 984	18.9	0.4	3.4	0.5	61.7	14.3	—	0.8
Burma	4 917	25.2	4.0	6.4	0.5	62.6	1.3	—	—
Hong Kong	33 970	16.8	3.0	16.7	0.3	58.8	2.0	0.8	1.6
India	357 550	17.0	6.5	16.6	—	14.4	8.2	37.3	—
Indonesia	208 687	27.5	12.0 [2]	7.4	0.0 [2]	46.9	0.0 [2]	0.0 [3]	6.2 [3]
Iran	9 901	22.3	—	41.4	5.9	12.7	9.0	5.6	3.1
Iraq	*15 196	22.9	3.7	9.2	2.0	39.3	15.2	3.8	3.9
Israel	26 208	9.6	0.6	16.1	0.2	29.2	20.0	1.7	22.6
Japan	27 493	19.3	22.9	28.9	16.2	12.0	0.3	0.3	0.1
Jordan	8 762	21.9	2.5	7.1	0.5	50.2	16.0	1.8	—
Korea, Rep. of	9 551	29.6	10.9	32.1	—	20.6	0.1	—	6.7
Kuwait	17 472	5.3	4.7	0.2	1.9	46.2	41.7	—	—

Composition of domestic sound broadcasting programmes of selected countries during a typical week in 1973

Country	Hours per year Total	Information	Education	Culture	Sciences	Entertainment	Programmes for special audiences	Advertising	Other programmes not elsewhere classified
ASIA (cont'd.)									
Lebanon	36 513	4.8	0.3	1.4	0.1	36.1	1.3	—	6.0
Malaysia	8 736 [4]	19.3	0.6	11.4	0.1	49.0	15.6	4.0	—
Maldives	6 483	13.9	12.8	2.7	—	48.9	21.7	—	—
Pakistan	44 720	...	...	...	...	...	...	...	...
Philippines [5]	464 815	17.2	1.1	2.9	—	66.4	11.9	0.5	—
Qatar	6 162	13.9	1.3	16.0	0.8	43.1	13.1	—	11.8
Saudi Arabia	6 105	22.8	—	22.8	—	23.9	30.5	—	—
Singapore	26 572	21.6	0.6	19.1	0.5	49.9	8.3	—	—
Sri Lanka	22 954	13.7	6.2	—	—	12.9	5.7	—	61.5
Thailand	*7 800	24.1	14.5	6.9	0.5	44.3	5.3	4.0	0.4
Turkey	75 673	11.7	11.4	69.0	—	—	3.3	4.6	—
South Vietnam	56 628	25.7	15.0	2.4	0.9	36.2	19.5	—	0.3
EUROPE									
Austria	35 799	20.0	2.3	16.3	3.1	40.7	5.6	9.6	2.4
Belgium [6]	23 130	20.7	1.9	24.5	0.1	41.0	11.5	0.2	0.1
Czechoslovakia	40 326	11.5	4.8	22.7	0.6	43.6	2.0	0.5	14.3
Denmark	13 355	21.4	2.3	16.2	—	48.7	4.3	7.1	—
Faeroe Island	1 800	18.1	—	24.8	—	35.2	21.4	—	0.5
Finland	17 294	29.1	0.9	3.2	3.0	47.6	2.2	—	14.0
France	28 202	9.7	—	8.5	—	81.3	0.5	—	—
German, Demo. [7]	44 997	34.0	0.7	55.0	0.9	5.7	3.7	—	—
Gibraltar	5 831	28.5	—	13.3	0.9	47.4	5.4	2.7	1.8
Greece	32 083	17.6	0.3	22.3	0.2	42.6	4.3	12.5	0.2
Hungary	17 112	18.4	1.6	70.3	1.3	—	7.8	0.6	—
Iceland [8]	6 036	25.0	0.4	23.5	—	33.0	4.5	7.2	6.4
Ireland	6 254	21.4	1.3	19.3	—	35.3	7.6	15.0	0.1
Italy [9]	17 933	14.6	0.6	4.0	—	71.7	5.0	3.6	0.5
Malta	*6 161	25.8	5.9	12.2	0.2	45.5	7.7	—	2.7
Monaco	*16 885	6.1	—	0.3	—	52.8	37.7	3.0	0.1
Norway [10]	6 224	28.1	2.3	19.3	0.2	25.0	15.5	3.8	5.8
Poland	26 026	20.7	1.9	7.3	—	51.0	6.7	2.2	10.2

Composition of domestic sound broadcasting programmes of selected countries during a typical week in 1973

Country	Hours per year Total	Information	Education	Culture	Sciences	Entertainment	Programmes for special audiences	Advertising	Other programmes not elsewhere classified
EUROPE (cont'd.)									
Spain	1 696 756	16.4	6.6	16.0	0.2	45.2	8.0	7.6	—
Sweden	18 541	17.4	4.8	22.2	2.3	37.8	12.3	1.9	1.3
Switzerland	32 915	16.6	0.7	29.7	5.5	43.2	4.3	—	—
United Kingdom	44 184	33.8	3.4	3.4	—	54.4	3.1	1.9	—
Yugoslavia	286 543	14.8	5.5	9.4	—	63.4	—	6.9	—
OCEANIA									
American Samoa	6 552	23.8	—	—	—	63.5	2.4	—	10.3
Gilbert Island	*2 471	28.8	4.3	14.3	—	37.6	12.8	2.2	—
Guam	*7 656	20.6	—	—	—	65.1	—	14.3	—
New Caledonia	5 840	13.4	2.2	19.4	1.0	53.3	4.4	6.3	—
New Hebrides (Eng.)	2 340	35.0	4.4	1.1	—	55.6	2.8	1.1	—
New Hebrides (Fr.)	1 170	62.2	—	2.2	—	26.7	2.2	2.2	4.5
New Zealand	371 540	12.2	3.1	7.1	0.2	64.4	6.7	6.3	—
Niue	1 326	18.6	2.6	3.9	2.0	27.5	3.9	—	41.5
Norfolk Island	2 392	7.6	—	7.4	—	82.6	1.8	0.6	—
Pacific Island	6 734 [11]	23.4	6.8	0.8	1.4	55.0	7.7	1.4	3.5
Tonga	4 641	16.4	5.6	—	—	52.8	4.8	20.4	—
Western Samoa	5 798	13.9	4.5	4.5	0.4	59.2	4.9	12.6	—

1. These data cover only 55% of all Canadian stations. 2. Data on sciences and programmes for special audiences are included with education. 3. Data on advertising are included with other programmes not elsewhere classified. 4. The figures refer to national network only. 5. Data refer to radio stations located in the city of Manila and suburbs only. 6. French Broadcasting only. 7. The data which relate to German Democratic Republic include the relevant data relating to Berlin for which separate data have not been supplied. This is without prejudice to any question of status which may be involved. 8. National station networks I and II. 9. National programmes only. 10. Regional programmes only. 11. Average broadcasting time of 6 district stations.

Table 16 — Television broadcasting: programmes by type (1972-1974)
Number of countries and territories presented in this table: 78

Country	Year	Hours per year	Percentage distribution by type of programme							
			Information	Education	Culture	Sciences	Entertainment	Programmes for special audiences	Advertising	Other promes not elsewhere classified
AFRICA										
Algeria	1973	2 668	26.0	13.0	34.1	3.4	15.1	8.3	—	—
	1974	2 863	22.3	14.5	36.5	—	17.0	9.6	0.1	—
Djibouti	1973	2 184	23.8	7.1	21.4	4.8	42.9	—	—	—
	1974	2 120	38.7	5.3	25.4	0.5	17.0	7.1	—	6.0
Egypt	1972	5 369	13.4	1.8	35.1	—	27.7	18.4	3.5	—
	1973	6 188	17.4	10.2	34.3	—	23.2	14.6	0.4	—
	1974	6 483	12.4	9.3	38.0	—	19.6	18.0	2.7	—
Ethiopia	1974	1 521	33.3	—	27.4	1.7	14.5	22.2	0.9	—
	1975	1 750	21.3	31.4	23.7	—	4.2	3.0	1.8	14.6
Ghana	1974	2 838	17.0	34.5	23.8	1.8	8.2	7.3	7.3	—
Madagascar	1973	845	32.3	1.5	44.6	6.2	12.3	3.1	—	—
	1974	949	30.1	—	50.7	5.5	11.0	2.7	—	—
Mauritius	1973	2 613	24.8	9.9	39.6	—	24.9	1.0	—	—
	1974	2 656	28.8	9.1	37.2	—	23.8	1.1	—	—
	1975	2 694	32.8	8.4	35.0	—	22.7	1.1	—	—
Nigeria	1973	2 782	15.4	26.2	29.5	—	11.2	14.0	3.7	—
	1974	2 275 [1]	18.9	11.4	34.3	—	13.7	17.1	4.6	—
Reunion	1973	1 926	18.2	5.4	42.5	4.9	19.8	9.2	—	—
Senegal	1974	1 300	22.0	2.0	54.0	—	12.0	10.0	—	—
Sudan	1973	2 600	12.0	8.0	26.0	—	18.0	22.0	4.0	10.0
Tunisia	1973	12 610	19.9	12.4	25.4	5.2	24.7	12.4	—	—
Zaire	1973	3 094	31.9	7.6	23.9	3.4	22.3	10.9	—	—
	1974	3 160	27.3	22.9	36.3	3.0	7.1	3.3	—	—
AMERICA, NORTH										
Barbados	1974	2 492	12.7	12.5	37.6	—	14.6	19.8	1.6	1.2
Bermuda	1973	3 617	14.6	10.8	5.4	—	13.7	27.7	12.0	15.8
Canada	1973	53 246	24.4	1.9	4.1	0.1	65.4	4.0	0.1	—
	1974	81 696	27.5	20.2	4.7	0.9	44.0	2.8	—	—

Country	Year	Hours per year	Percentage distribution by type of programme							
			Information	Education	Culture	Sciences	Entertainment	Programmes for special audiences	Advertising	Other prommes not elsewhere classified
AMERICA, NORTH (cont'd.)										
Cuba	1973	9 160	29.0	4.2.	60.8	—	—	4.9	—	1.1
Jamaica	1974	2 860	28.7	15.1	40.8	—	7.8	7.6	—	—
Panama Canal Zone	1973	3 566	23.2	—	1.5	—	64.9	8.7	1.7	—
	1974	3 640	22.7	—	1.4	—	65.6	8.6	4.7	—
	1975	3 640	22.5	—	1.4	—	63.6	10.7	1.8	—
St Pierre & Miquelon	1973	1 362	30.1	—	47.4	—	13.5	9.0	—	—
	1974	1 911	10.5	3.3	54.3	—	26.6	5.2	—	—
St Vincent	1974	2 725	31.6	5.5	25.2	1.5	7.3	3.8	4.4	20.7
Trinidad & Tobago	1973	3 847	11.8	18.2	54.2	—	4.7	6.2	4.8	—
	1974	3 848	11.8	18.3	54.2	—	4.7	6.2	4.8	—
Virgin Islands (U.S.)	1973	2 631	11.6	—	45.9	1.0	21.7	5.6	14.3	—
AMERICA, SOUTH										
Argentina	1972	131 946	12.8	1.0	6.3	—	49.8	13.7	16.4	—
	1973	141 374	12.5	1.9	6.1	—	52.7	12.6	14.3	—
	1974	145 220	10.7	2.4	3.1	—	59.1	10.4	14.3	—
Brazil	1972	260 161	8.6	10.6	24.4	0.5	31.5	11.4	12.3	0.7
	1973	243 610	15.8	9.0	25.2	0.3	24.6	10.2	13.3	1.6
Chile	1975	4 025	9.2	0.7	34.5	—	10.4	26.9	18.3	—
Ecuador	1973	16 973	19.5	5.0	51.8	—	13.9	9.8	—	—
	1974	27 987	13.6	3.9	40.8	1.3	17.4	11.7	9.5	—
ASIA										
Bahrain	1973	1 820	21.4	—	54.3	1.4	8.6	8.6	5.7	—
	1974	1 949	23.1	0.8	27.6	0.7	32.7	10.9	4.2	—
	1975	2 080	24.6	1.4	4.3	—	53.8	12.9	2.9	—
Cyprus	1972	1 794	25.1	4.3	45.1	0.1	8.2	4.6	12.6	—
	1973	1 807	26.2	4.0	51.1	0.4	6.9	3.0	8.4	—
	1974	1 820	27.2	3.6	57.1	0.7	5.7	1.4	4.3	—
Hong Kong	1973	18 819	14.1	15.6	22.3	—	32.5	11.0	3.9	0.6
	1974	18 438	12.1	15.9	43.8	0.5	11.6	11.8	3.9	0.5
	1975	18 285	9.8	12.7	50.9	0.3	12.2	9.0	4.9	0.3
India	1973	5 217	16.3	7.0	32.9	2.0	17.9	16.9	—	7.0
	1974	6 485	28.4	7.8	12.5	3.8	38.1	9.4	—	—
Iran	1973	3 429	30.9	9.2	29.3	1.5	11.3	10.0	3.3	4.5
	1974	4 140	20.2	2.2	48.4	0.7	14.7	11.1	2.8	—
Iraq	1974	4 130	20.0	5.9	30.7	1.8	22.2	12.1	5.5	1.8
Israel	1973	3 237	8.6	41.8	12.4	—	5.6	30.9 [2]	—	0.8
Japan	1973	18 890	14.4	35.2	26.8	—	23.2	—	0.2	0.2
	1974	18 690	14.4	38.0	23.1	—	24.1	—	0.2	0.2
	1975	18 081	16.2	37.6	22.5	—	23.4	—	0.1	0.1

Country	Year	Hours per year	Percentage distribution by type of programme							
			Information	Education	Culture	Sciences	Entertainment	Programmes for special audiences	Advertising	Other progremmes not elsewhere classified
ASIA (cont'd.)										
Jordan	1973	3 168	20.9	—	53.3	2.5	14.0	6.6	2.7	—
	1974	3 367	22.4	7.7	49.8	2.3	10.8	4.6	2.3	—
	1975	3 367	22.2	7.8	49.9	2.0	10.9	4.7	2.0	—
Korea, Rep. of	1972	2 721	23.9	34.5	15.3	—	23.7	—	—	2.5
	1973	5 836	19.6	10.0	25.0	0.4	29.1	9.1	3.8	3.0
	1974	8 954	18.3	2.6	27.9	0.5	30.7	11.9	4.9	3.2
Kuwait	1972	2 089	16.6	—	57.3	1.2	17.6	6.4	0.8	—
	1973	2 305	23.9	—	18.0	2.3	24.8	27.1	3.9	—
	1974	4 230	12.3	22.3	38.2	0.9	14.3	9.1	2.9	—
Malaysia	1972	4 434	29.2	3.3	29.6	1.6	18.3	12.1	5.9	—
	1973	4 623	26.7	2.2	43.7	0.3	10.4	9.2	7.4	—
	1974	5 083	31.7	4.6	35.8	0.2	12.3	7.7	7.7	—
Pakistan	1973	9 399	22.9	8.7	37.1	2.8	10.2	12.9	5.4	—
Philippines	1975	68 466	15.3	0.8	54.0	0.2	23.4	6.4	—	—
Qatar	1973	1 339	13.3	—	58.2	—	9.4	19.1	—	—
Saudi Arabia	1973	2 080	26.2	12.5	35.0	1.3	6.2	18.8	—	—
Singapore	1973	5 538	23.5	—	54.9	1.9	9.4	10.3	—	—
	1974	5 378	26.9	—	33.3	—	28.2	11.6	—	—
Syrian Arab Republik	1974	2 018	8.4	27.8	—	—	46.0	—	17.8	—
Thailand	1974	3 183	18.5	8.9	43.8	—	19.8	5.0	4.0	—
Turkey	1973	2 302	14.2	6.0	9.0	1.2	51.8	16.3	1.5	—
	1974	2 596	21.2	26.5	16.7	—	17.3	—	5.8	12.6
Viet-Nam, Rep. of	1974	2 400	31.3	16.8	34.9	1.4	2.5	2.2	—	10.8
EUROPE										
Austria	1973	4 553	32.9	11.2	30.7	5.0	6.0	8.4	3.8	2.0
	1974	4 654	29.8	11.0	31.6	4.5	7.9	11.2	2.6	1.5
	1975	4 357	27.4	12.7	33.0	5.4	8.6	8.1	3.7	—
Belgium	1973	5 448	27.5	10.2	35.0	0.7	13.0	11.9	0.3	1.4
	1974	5 856	23.4	9.4	44.4	3.4	8.3	8.8	0.1	2.2
Czechoslovakia	1972	5 132	32.9	14.1	24.1	—	8.3	5.2	15.4	—
	1973	5 272	32.5	12.1	31.8	—	18.7	—	4.8	0.1
	1974	5 275	26.8	8.5	33.7	4.5	16.4	—	10.4	—
Denmark	1973	2 336	29.6	7.0	25.0	2.2	19.4	15.4	—	1.4
	1974	2 322	19.6	8.7	32.2	—	20.7	14.1	—	4.7
Finland	1972	2 394	45.1	1.9	46.5	5.0	—	1.5	—	—
	1973	2 885	37.4	1.6	31.2	4.2	7.5	1.2	—	17.0
France	1972	6 189	18.5	12.0	41.3	—	19.6	6.4	2.2	—
German, Democratic	1973	6 360	30.3	5.1	30.9	3.0	9.2	9.4	1.2	10.9
	1974	6 634	34.9	4.9	27.1	—	25.8	6.0	1.2	—

Country	Year	Hours per year	Percentage distribution by type of programme							
			Information	Education	Culture	Sciences	Entertainment	Programmes for special audiences	Advertising	Other prommes not elsewhere classified
EUROPE (cont'd.)										
Gibraltar	1972	1 807	18.0	2.9	40.3	0.7	14.4	13.7	10.0	—
	1973	2 090	19.9	2.5	39.8	—	12.9	15.4	9.5	—
	1974	2 483	28.3	2.1	32.7	—	12.6	14.7	9.7	—
Greece	1974	3 293	22.5	11.0	11.0	1.3	40.4	10.1	3.7	—
Hungary	1972	3 352	37.0	15.3	35.9	2.7	—	5.7	3.4	—
	1973	3 692	32.4	16.9	35.2	7.0	—	7.0	1.4	—
	1974	3 692	26.8	16.9	38.0	6.3	—	9.9	2.1	—
	1975	3 692	21.1	16.9	40.8	5.6	—	12.7	2.8	—
Iceland	1973	1 122	36.6	2.2	32.8	—	17.4	7.8	3.2	—
	1974	1 181	36.5	2.9	30.0	—	19.0	7.4	4.3	—
Ireland	1972	2 652	31.4	2.5	24.5	—	21.7	14.0	5.9	—
	1973	2 877	19.6	4.8	9.9	—	40.6	14.7	10.4	—
	1974	2 995	30.7	5.2	28.4	—	11.0	24.8	—	—
Italy [3]	1973	5 136	32.6	17.6	4.9	...	18.5	16.2	4.0	6.2
	1974	5 252	32.9	15.3	6.6 [4]	./.	20.4	15.0	3.7	6.1
Malta	1972	1 774	30.2	4.0	35.8	—	10.8	13.1	6.1	—
Monaco	1974	2 696	6.5	—	84.7	—	0.7	4.5	2.7	1.0
Netherlands	1974	4 056	31.0	13.0	24.0	—	15.0	12.0	5.0	—
Norway	1972	2 387	29.4	11.3	19.4	0.8	26.1	10.7	2.2	—
	1973	2 283	30.3	10.9	23.5	0.5	19.6	13.0	2.3	—
	1974	2 279	26.7	9.9	20.9	—	19.0	12.1	2.8	8.5
Poland	1972	7 002	27.3	11.4	6.9	5.9	33.6	5.3	—	9.6
	1973	7 378	22.3	11.3	9.0	2.6	31.9	9.2	—	13.6
	1974	7 773	23.1	12.7	11.4	2.1	35.6	5.3	2.5	7.2
Portugal	1974	5 304	22.3	22.5	23.9	—	3.1	14.2	2.7	11.3
Romania	1972	6 378	11.0	12.5	38.4	4.1	12.8	16.2	1.5	3.5
Spain	1974	3 519	21.7	—	25.6	—	21.8	15.0	7.6	8.3
Sweden	1973	5 231	21.8	9.6	28.8	2.3	24.2	13.3	—	—
	1974	4 836	22.8	10.4	23.1	2.5	24.5	13.4	3.1	0.1
	1975	4 786	23.1	11.4	22.2	2.8	17.1	14.8	—	8.7
Switzerland	1973	9 135	14.1	7.3	23.2	1.7	15.7	13.5	16.8	7.7
	1974	9 453	21.7	7.8	21.8	1.7	19.7	14.3	12.2	0.7
United Kingdom	1972	13 555	20.7	14.4	19.0	0.2	20.3	11.5	5.6	8.3
	1973	13 652	34.0	13.5	16.6	0.2	23.4	12.3	—	—
	1974	13 838	33.6	14.9	15.4	0.1	23.6	12.4	—	—
	1975	21 086	20.0	46.2	10.1	0.1	15.5	8.1	—	—
Yugoslavia	1972	11 265	32.6	11.2	30.8	—	17.3	—	8.1	—
	1973	11 388	29.7	8.7	38.8	1.4	9.1	—	12.3	—
	1974	11 600	33.3	12.1	23.7	1.0	18.4	6.8	4.8	—

Country	Year	Hours per year	Percentage distribution by type of programme							
			Information	Education	Culture	Sciences	Entertainment	Programmes for special audiences	Advertising	Other prommes not elsewhere classified
OCEANIA										
American Samoa	1972	10 452	13.7	53.0	12.9	2.0	10.4	6.0	1.0	1.0
	1973	13 009	3.5	79.1	7.4	—	6.4	3.6	—	—
	1974	13 480	4.6	64.0	28.0	0.2	2.4	0.7	—	—
Guam	1974	6 535	5.6	—	23.9	—	45.9	24.7	—	—
New Caledonia	1972	1 690	38.5	—	20.5	6.2	23.8	11.0	—	—
	1973	1 740	25.0	—	72.5	—	1.4	1.1	—	—
	1974	1 924	22.4	3.4	36.2	3.1	24.6	9.7	0.5	—
New Zealand	1973	3 380	20.6	1.0	43.0	0.5	12.7	18.0	4.2	—
	1974	3 380	19.1	8.8	3.4	0.8	50.5	13.3	4.1	—
	1975	9 077	44.0	—	18.1	3.0	8.5	21.7	4.7	—
Pacific Islands	1972	2 184	4.8	17.9	67.8	—	9.5	—	—	—
	1973	2 600	15.0	15.0	—	—	68.0	—	2.0	—

1. The figures relate to Nigerian Broadcasting Corporation only and do not cover the whole country. 2. Broadcasts in Arabic only, including different types of programmes (news, bulletins, light entertainment, broadcasts for women, children etc.). 3. National programmes only. 4. Data on sciences are included with culture.

Table 17 — Television broadcasting: programmes by type
Number of countries and territories presented in this table: 77
A = total hours of broadcasting per year and percentage distribution by type of programme
B = of which: national production

Country	Year	Hours per year	PERCENTAGE DISTRIBUTION BY TYPE OF PROGRAMME							
			Information	Education	Culture	Sciences	Entertainment	Programmes for special audiences	Advertising	Other programmes not elsewhere classified
		(1)	(2)	(3)	(4)	(5)	(6)	(7)	(8)	(9)
AFRICA										
Algeria	1974 A	2 863	22.3	14.5	36.5	—	17.0	9.6	0.1	—
	B	1 513	29.7	27.4	13.7	—	16.6	12.3	0.2	—
Egypt	1974 A	6 483	12.4	9.3	38.0	—	19.6	18.0	2.7	—
Ethiopia	1975 A	1 750	21.3	31.4	23.7	—	4.2	3.0	1.8	14.6
	B	1 318	28.2	41.7	2.7	—	1.7	4.0	2.4	19.3
Djibouti	1973 A	2 184	23.8	7.1	21.4	4.8	42.9	—	—	—
Ghana	1974 A	2 838	17.0	34.5	23.8	1.8	8.2	7.3	7.3	—
	B	2 448	19.6	40.0	14.9	2.1	6.4	8.5	8.5	—
Madagascar	1974 A	949	30.1	—	50.7	5.5	11.0	2.7	—	—
	B	260	70.0	—	—	—	20.0	10.0	—	—
Mauritius	1975 A	2 694	32.8	8.4	35.0	—	22.7	1.1	—	—
	B	810	64.0	28.0	1.2	—	3.1	3.7	—	—
Nigeria	1973 A	2 782	15.4	26.2	29.5	—	11.2	14.0	3.7	—
	B	1 430	5.5	50.9	21.8	—	21.8	—	—	—
Reunion	1973 A	*1 926	18.2	5.4	42.5	4.9	19.8	9.2	—	—
Senegal	1974 A	1 300	22.0	2.0	54.0	—	12.0	10.0	—	—
Sudan	1973 A	2 600	12.0	8.0	26.0	—	18.0	22.0	4.0	10.0
	B	1 820	14.3	5.7	2.9	—	25.7	31.4	5.7	14.3
Tunisia	1973 A	12 610	19.9	12.4	25.4	5.2	24.7	12.4	—	—
	B	*10 306	22.3	13.9	12.1	6.3	30.3	15.1	—	—
Zaire	1974 A	3 160	27.3	22.9	36.3	3.0	7.1	3.3	—	—
AMERICA, NORTH										
Barbados	1974 A	2 492	12.7	12.5	37.6	—	14.6	19.8	1.6	1.2
	B	299	59.5	17.4	—	—	—	—	13.0	10.1
Bermuda	1973 A	*3 617	14.6	10.8	5.4	—	13.7	27.7	12.0	15.8
	B	*740	57.2	—	1.9	—	14.3	26.4	—	—

Country	Year	Hours per year (1)	PERCENTAGE DISTRIBUTION BY TYPE OF PROGRAMME							
			Information (2)	Education (3)	Culture (4)	Sciences (5)	Entertainment (6)	Programmes for special audiences (7)	Advertising (8)	Other programmes not elsewhere classified (9)
AMERICA, NORTH (cont'd.)										
Canada	1974 A	81 696	27.5	20.2	4.7	0.9	44.0	2.8	—	—
	B	5 345	34.2	20.8	3.7	1.1	36.6	3.5	—	—
Cuba	1973 A	*9 160	29.0	4.2	60.8	—	—	4.9	—	1.1
Jamaica	1974 A	2 860	28.7	15.1	40.8	—	7.8	7.6	—	—
	B	*879	78.5	5.9	—	—	5.7	9.9	—	—
Panama Canal Zone	1974 A	3 640	22.5	—	1.4	—	63.6	10.7	1.8	—
	B	3 640	22.5	—	1.4	—	63.6	10.7	1.8	—
St Pierre & Miquelon	1974 A	1 911	10.5	3.3	54.3	—	26.6	5.2	—	—
St Vincent	1974 A	2 725	31.6	5.5	25.2	1.5	7.3	3.8	4.4	20.7
	B	1 365	54.9	11.0	11.7	—	13.2	1.8	7.3	—
Trinidad & Tobago	1974 A	3 848	11.8	18.3	54.2	—	4.7	6.2	4.8	—
	B	*264	49.7	—	3.3	—	23.2	23.8	—	—
U.S. Virgin Islands	1973 A	*2 631	11.6	—	45.9	1.0	21.7	5.6	14.3	—
	B	*2 273	4.2	—	53.0	1.1	25.2	3.3	13.2	—
AMERICA, SOUTH										
Argentina	1974 A	145 220	10.7	2.4	3.1	—	59.1	10.4	14.3	—
Brazil	1973 A	243 610	15.8	9.0	25.2	0.3	24.6	10.2	13.3	1.6
	B	188 490	19.6	11.2	10.8	0.2	31.1	8.6	17.2	1.2
Chile	1975 A	4 025	9.2	0.7	34.5	—	10.4	26.9	18.3	—
	B	1 587	22.7	1.7	5.6	—	26.4	43.7	—	—
Ecuador	1974 A	*27 987	13.6	3.9	40.8	1.3	17.4	11.7	9.5	—
ASIA										
Bahrain	1975 A	2 080	24.6	1.4	4.3	—	53.8	12.9	2.9	—
	B	665	69.2	—	13.5	—	6.0	9.0	2.3	—
Cyprus	1974 A	1 820	27.2	3.6	57.1	0.7	5.7	1.4	4.3	—
	B	728	53.6	1.8	21.4	1.8	7.1	3.6	10.7	—
Hong Kong	1974 A	18 285	9.8	12.7	50.9	0.3	12.2	9.0	4.9	0.3
	B	9 731	15.0	21.5	43.2	—	13.2	1.3	5.8	—
India	1974 A	6 485	28.4	7.8	12.5	3.8	38.1	9.4	—	—
	B	6 070	27.9	8.1	12.4	3.4	39.0	9.2	—	—
Iran	1974 A	4 140	20.2	2.2	48.4	0.7	14.7	11.1	2.8	—
	B	2 272	26.9	2.9	23.9	0.3	23.9	17.1	5.1	—
Iraq	1974 A	4 130	20.0	5.9	30.7	1.8	22.2	12.1	5.5	1.8
	B	1 596	—	0.7	57.1	—	30.2	12.0	—	—
Israel	1973 A	3 237	8.6	41.8	12.4	—	5.5	30.9	—	0.8
	B	2 184	10.7	57.1	1.8	—	3.4	25.8	—	1.2

Country	Year	Hours per year	PERCENTAGE DISTRIBUTION BY TYPE OF PROGRAMME							
			Infor-mation	Education	Culture	Sciences	Entertain-ment	Programmes for special audiences	Adverti-sing	Other programmes not elsewhere classified
		(1)	(2)	(3)	(4)	(5)	(6)	(7)	(8)	(9)

ASIA (cont'd.)

Country	Year	Hours per year	Information	Education	Culture	Sciences	Entertainment	Prog. special aud.	Advertising	Other
Japan	1975 A	18 081	16.2	37.6	22.5	—	23.4	—	0.1	0.1
Jordan	1974 A	3 367	22.4	7.7	49.8	2.3	10.8	4.6	2.3	—
	B	1 511	38.5	17.1	12.8	1.7	15.4	10.3	4.3	—
Korea, Republic of	1974 A	8 954	18.3	2.6	27.9	0.5	30.7	11.9	4.9	3.2
	B	7 132	22.9	3.3	16.4	0.6	37.5	9.0	6.2	4.0
Kuwait	1974 A	4 230	12.3	22.3	38.2	0.9	14.3	9.1	2.9	—
	B	2 345	19.9	40.3	8.3	1.5	15.1	14.8	—	—
Malaysia	1974 A	*5 083	31.7	4.6	35.8	0.2	12.3	7.7	7.7	—
	B	2 548	49.0	8.2	14.3	—	8.2	6.1	14.3	—
Pakistan	1973 A	9 399	22.9	8.7	37.1	2.8	10.2	12.9	5.4	—
	B	6 608	31.6	9.4	21.4	1.9	14.6	13.8	7.3	—
Philippines	1975 A	68 466	15.3	0.8	54.0	0.2	23.4	6.4	—	—
	B	32 574	22.2	1.6	26.6	0.4	42.5	6.7	—	—
Qatar	1973 A	1 339	13.3	—	58.2	—	9.4	19.1	—	—
	B	*1 177	2.2	—	65.7	—	10.6	21.5	—	—
Saudi Arabia	1973 A	2 080	26.2	12.5	35.0	1.3	6.2	18.8	—	—
	B	1 040	27.5	15.0	20.0	—	12.5	25.0	—	—
Singapore	1974 A	5 378	26.9	—	33.3	—	28.2	11.6	—	—
	B	1 882	58.7	—	4.6	—	30.2	6.4	—	—
Syrian Arab Republic	1974 A	2 018	8.4	27.8	—	—	46.0	—	17.8	—
	B	1 606	10.6	35.0	—	—	32.1	—	22.4	—
Thailand	1974 A	3 183	18.5	8.9	43.8	—	19.8	5.0	4.0	—
Turkey	1974 A	2 596	21.2	26.5	16.7	—	17.3	—	5.8	12.6
Viet-Nam, Rep. of	1974 A	2 400	31.3	16.8	34.9	1.4	2.5	2.2	—	10.8
	B	2 177	29.4	17.4	36.5	—	2.4	2.4	—	11.9

EUROPE

Country	Year	Hours per year	Information	Education	Culture	Sciences	Entertainment	Prog. special aud.	Advertising	Other
Austria	1975 A	*4 357	27.4	12.7	33.0	5.4	8.6	8.1	3.7	—
	B	*2 788	42.7	19.0	11.0	3.0	8.4	10.1	5.7	—
Belgium	1974 A	5 856	23.4	9.4	44.4	3.4	8.3	8.8	0.1	2.2
	B	3 502	30.3	13.4	23.0	3.2	11.8	14.5	0.1	3.7
Czechoslovakia	1974 A	5 275	26.8	8.5	33.7	4.5	16.4	—	10.4	—
Denmark	1974 A	2 322	19.6	8.7	32.2	—	20.7	14.1	—	4.7
Finland	1973 A	2 885	37.4	1.6	31.2	4.2	7.5	1.2	—	17.0
France	1972 A	6 189	18.5	12.0	41.3	—	19.6	6.4	2.2	—
	B	5 513	20.8	13.5	34.1	—	21.9	7.2	2.5	—
German Democratic Republic	1974 A	6 634	34.9	4.9	27.1	—	25.8	6.0	1.2	—

Country	Year	Hours per year	PERCENTAGE DISTRIBUTION BY TYPE OF PROGRAMME							
			Information	Education	Culture	Sciences	Entertainment	Programmes for special audiences	Advertising	Other programmes not elsewhere classified
		(1)	(2)	(3)	(4)	(5)	(6)	(7)	(8)	(9)
EUROPE (cont'd.)										
Gibraltar	1974 A	2 483	28.3	2.1	32.7	—	12.6	14.7	9.7	—
Greece	1974 A	3 293	22.5	11.0	11.0	1.3	40.4	10.1	3.7	—
Hungary	1975 A	*3 692	21.1	16.9	40.8	5.6	—	12.7	2.8	—
	B	*2 496	31.3	20.8	22.9	6.3	—	14.6	4.2	—
Iceland	1974 A	*1 181	36.5	2.9	30.0	—	19.0	7.4	4.3	—
	B	*497	53.6	3.7	4.8	—	24.3	6.3	7.3	—
Ireland	1974 A	2 995	30.7	5.2	28.4	—	11.0	24.8	—	—
	B	1 347	55.2	6.5	4.1	—	9.7	24.6	—	—
Italy [2]	1974 A	5 252	32.9	15.3	6.6 [3]	./. [3]	20.4	15.0	3.7	6.1
Malta	1972 A	1 774	30.2	4.0	35.8	—	10.8	13.1	6.1	—
Monaco	1974 A	2 696	6.5	—	84.7	—	0.7	4.5	2.7	1.0
	B	392	44.6	—	7.7	—	1.3	28.1	11.5	6.9
Netherlands	1974 A	4 056	31.0	13.0	24.0	—	15.0	12.2	5.0	—
	B	2 339	30.1	15.3	10.6	—	21.7	14.6	7.7	—
Norway	1974 A	2 279	26.7	9.9	20.9	—	19.0	12.1	2.8	8.5
Poland	1974 A	7 773	23.1	12.7	11.4	2.1	35.6	5.3	2.5	7.2
	B	6 687	26.9	14.8	13.3	2.5	25.0	6.2	2.9	8.4
Portugal	1974 A	5 304	22.3	22.5	23.9	—	3.1	14.2	2.7	11.3
Romania	1972 A	*6 378	11.0	12.5	38.4	4.1	12.8	16.2	1.5	3.5
	B	*4 178	15.1	15.0	18.0	4.6	16.6	22.9	2.3	5.4
Spain	1974 A	3 519	21.7	—	25.6	—	21.8	15.0	7.6	8.3
	B	2 637	26.3	—	14.9	—	22.8	15.9	10.1	10.1
Sweden	1975 A	4 786	23.1	11.4	22.2	2.8	17.1	14.8	—	8.7
	B	3 019	30.6	15.9	15.9	2.3	10.4	14.0	—	10.8
Switzerland	1974 A	9 453	21.7	7.8	21.8	1.7	19.7	14.3	12.2	0.7
United Kingdom	1975 A	21 086	20.0	46.2	10.1	0.1	15.5	8.1	—	—
Yugoslavia	1974 A	116 001	33.3	12.1	23.7	1.0	18.4	6.8	4.8	—
	B	116 001	33.3	12.1	23.7	1.0	18.4	6.8	4.8	—
OCEANIA										
American Samoa	1974 A	13 480	4.6	64.0	28.0	0.2	2.4	0.7	—	—
	B	7 100	7.0	92.2	0.2	—	0.4	0.2	—	—
Guam	1974 A	6 535	5.6	—	23.9	—	45.9	24.7	—	—
New Caledonia	1974 A	1 924	22.4	3.4	36.2	3.1	24.6	9.7	0.5	—
New Zealand	1974 A	3 380	19.1	8.8	3.4	0.8	50.5	13.3	4.1	—
	B	*1 081	26.5	14.4	5.8	1.2	30.5	14.0	7.6	—
Pacific Islands	1973 A	2 600	15.0	15.0	—	—	68.0	—	2.0	—
	B	234	88.9	—	—	—	—	—	11.1	—

Table 18 - Television broadcasting: programmes by type during a typical week in 1973
Number of countries and territories presented in this table: 56

Country	Composition of television broadcasting programme during a typical week in 1973								
	Hours per year	Information	Education	Culture	Sciences	Entertainment	Programmes for special audiences	Advertising	Other programmes elsewhere classified
AFRICA									
Algeria	2 668	26.0	13.0	34.1	3.4	15.1	8.3	–	–
Djibouti	2 184	23.8	7.1	21.4	4.8	42.9	–	–	–
Egypt	6 188	17.4	10.2	34.3	–	23.2	14.6	0.4	–
Madagascar	845	32.3	1.5	44.6	6.2	12.3	3.1	–	–
Mauritius	2 613	24.8	9.9	39.6	–	24.9	1.0	–	–
Nigeria	2 782	15.4	26.2	29.5	–	11.2	14.0	3.7	–
Reunion	1 926	18.2	5.4	42.5	4.9	19.8	9.2	–	–
Sudan	2 600	12.0	8.0	26.0	–	18.0	22.0	4.0	10.0
Tunisia	12 610	19.9	12.4	25.4	5.2	24.7	12.4	–	–
Zaire	3 094	31.9	7.6	23.9	3.4	22.3	10.9	–	–
AMERICA, NORTH									
Bermuda	3 617	14.6	10.8	5.4	–	13.7	27.7	12.0	15.8
Canada	53 246	24.4	1.9	4.1	0.1	65.4	4.0	0.1	–
Cuba	9 160	29.0	4.2	60.8	–	–	4.9	–	1.1
Panama Canal Zone	3 566	23.2	–	1.5	–	64.9	8.7	1.7	–
St Pierre & Miquelon	1 362	30.1	–	47.4	–	13.5	9.0	–	–
Trinidad & Tobago	3 847	11.8	18.2	54.2	–	4.7	6.2	4.8	–
Virgin Island (U.S.)	2 631	11.6	–	45.9	1.0	21.7	5.6	14.3	–
AMERICA, SOUTH									
Argentina	141 374	12.5	1.9	6.1	–	52.7	12.6	14.3	–
Brazil	243 610	15.8	9.0	25.2	0.3	24.6	10.2	13.3	1.6
Ecuador	16 973	19.5	5.0	51.8	–	13.9	9.8	–	–

Country	Composition of television broadcasting programme during a typical week in 1973							
	Hours per year	Information	Education	Culture	Sciences	Entertainment	Programmes for special audiences	Advertising	Other programmes elsewhere classified
ASIA									
Bahrain	1 820	21.4	—	54.3	1.4	8.6	8.6	5.7	—
Cyprus	1 807	26.2	4.0	51.1	0.4	6.9	3.0	8.4	—
Hong Kong	18 819	14.1	15.6	22.3	—	32.5	11.0	3.9	0.6
India	5 217	16.3	7.0	32.9	2.0	17.9	16.9	—	7.0
Iran	3 429	30.9	9.2	29.3	1.5	11.3	10.0	3.3	4.5
Israel	3 237	8.6	41.8	12.4	—	5.5	30.9 [1]	—	0.8
Japan	18 890	14.4	35.2	26.8	—	23.2	—	0.2	0.2
Jordan	3 168	20.9	—	53.3	2.5	14.0	6.6	2.7	—
Korea, Republic of	5 836	19.6	10.0	25.0	0.4	29.1	9.1	3.8	3.0
Kuwait	2 305	23.9	—	18.0	2.3	24.8	27.1	3.9	—
Malaysia	4 623	26.7	2.2	43.7	0.3	10.4	9.2	7.4	—
Pakistan	9 399	22.9	8.7	37.1	2.8	10.2	12.9	5.4	—
Qatar	2 080	26.2	12.5	35.0	1.3	6.2	18.8	—	—
Singapore	5 538	23.5	—	54.9	1.9	9.4	10.3	—	—
Turkey	2 302	14.2	6.0	9.0	1.2	51.8	16.3	1.5	—
EUROPE									
Austria	4 553	32.9	11.2	30.7	5.0	6.0	8.4	3.8	2.0
Belgium	5 448	27.5	10.2	35.0	0.7	13.0	11.9	0.3	1.4
Czechoslovakia	5 272	32.5	12.1	31.8	—	18.7	—	4.8	0.1
Denmark	2 336	29.6	7.0	25.0	2.2	19.4	15.4	—	1.4
Finland	2 885	37.4	1.6	31.2	4.2	7.5	1.2	—	17.0
German, Democratic	6 360	30.3	5.1	30.9	3.0	9.2	9.4	1.2	10.9
Gibraltar	2 090	19.9	2.5	39.8	—	12.9	15.4	9.5	—
Hungary	3 692	32.4	16.9	35.2	7.0	—	7.0	1.4	—
Iceland	1 122	36.6	2.2	32.8	—	17.4	7.8	3.2	—
Ireland	2 877	19.6	4.8	9.9	—	40.6	14.7	10.4	—
Italy [2]	5 136	32.6	17.6	4.9	...	18.5	16.2	4.0	6.2
Norway	2 283	30.3	10.9	23.5	0.5	19.6	13.0	2.3	—
Poland	7 378	22.3	11.3	9.0	2.6	31.9	9.2	—	13.6
Sweden	5 231	21.8	9.6	28.5	2.3	24.2	13.3	—	—

Country	Composition of television broadcasting programme during a typical week in 1973								
	Hours per year	Information	Education	Culture	Sciences	Entertainment	Programmes for special audiences	Advertising	Other programmes elsewhere classified
EUROPE (cont'd.)									
Switzerland	9 135	14.1	7.3	23.2	1.7	15.7	13.5	16.8	7.7
United Kingdom	13 652	34.0	13.5	16.6	0.2	23.4	12.3	—	—
Yugoslavia	11 388	29.7	8.7	38.8	1.4	9.1	—	12.3	—
OCEANIA									
American Samoa	13 009	3.5	79.1	7.4	—	6.4	3.6	—	—
New Caledonia	1 740	25.0	—	72.5	—	1.4	1.1	—	—
New Zealand	3 380	20.6	1.0	43.0	0.5	12.7	18.0	4.2	—
Pacific Islands	2 600	15.0	15.0	—	—	68.0	—	2.0	—

1. Broadcasts in Arabic only, including different types of programmes (news, bulletins, light entertainment, broadcasts for women, children, etc.).
2. National programmes only.

Recommendation concerning the international standardization of statistics on radio and television
adopted by the General Conference at its nineteenth session
Nairobi, 22 November 1976

The General Conference of the United Nations Educational, Scientific and Cultural Organization, meeting in Nairobi from 26 October to 30 November 1976, at its nineteenth session,

Considering that, by virtue of Article IV, paragraph 4, of the Constitution, it is for the Organization to draw up and adopt instruments for the international regulation of questions falling within its competence,

Considering that Article VIII of the Constitution provides *inter allia* that "each Member State shall submit to the Organization, at such times and in such manners as shall be determined by the General Conference, reports on... statistics relating to its educational, scientific and cultural institutions and activities...",

Convinced that it is highly desirable for the national authorities responsible for collecting and communicating radio and television statistics to be guided by certain standards in the matter of definitions, classifications and presentation, in order to improve the international comparability of such statistics,

Having before it, as item 30 of the agenda of the session, proposals concerning the international standardization of statistics on radio and television,

Having decided at its eighteenth session that this question should be made the subject of an international regulation, to take the form of a recommendation to Member States within the meaning of Article IV, paragraph 4, of the Constitution,

Adopts, this twenty-second day of November 1976, the present recommendation.

The General Conference recommends that Member States should apply the following provisions concerning international standardization of statistics on radio and television by taking whatever legislative measures or other steps may be required, in conformity with the constitutional practice of each State, to give effect, within their respective territories, to the standards and principles formulated in this recommendation.

The General Conference recommends that Member States bring this recommendation to the attention of authorities and services responsible for collecting and communicating radio and television statistics.

The General Conference recommends that Member States forward to it, by the dates and in the form which it shall prescribe, reports concerning action taken by them upon this recommendation.

I. SCOPE AND DEFINITIONS

Scope

1. The statistics referred to in this recommendation are intended to provide, in respect of each Member State, information on a standardized basis about:
   (a) domestic broadcasting;
   (b) external broadcasting.

Definitions

2. In compiling the statistics covered by this recommendation, the following definitions should be used:
   (a) *Broadcasting institution:* an organization legally authorized to provide a broadcasting service.
   (b) *Broadcasting service:* a radiocommunication service un which the transmissions are intended for direct reception by the general public. This service may include sound transmissions, television transmissions, or other types of transmissions.
   (c) *Radiocommunication:* telecommunication by means of electromagnetic waves of frequencies lower than 3,000 GHz propagated in space without artificial guide.
   (d) *Telecommunication:* any transmission, emission or reception of signs, signals, writing, images and sounds or intelligence of any nature by wire, radio, visual or other electromagnetic systems.
   (e) *Domestic broadcasting:* a broadcasting service primarily intended for general reception within the country in which the broadcasting institution is authorized to operate.
   (f) *External broadcasting:* a broadcasting service primarily intended for reception outside the boundaries of the country in which the broadcasting institution is authorized to operate.
   (g) *Sound broadcasting (radio):* broadcasting of sound only signals.
   (h) *Television:* broadcasting of transient images of fixed or moving objects, with or without sound.
   (i) *Transmitter:* an apparatus producing radio-frequency energy for the purpose of broadcasting radio or television programmes.
   (j) *Power of a broadcast transmitter:* the radio frequency power that the transmitter normally supplies to the aerial system, being the unmodulated carrier power for a sound transmitter, and the power generated during the peaks of the modulation envelope for a television transmitter.

(k) *Maximum effective radiated power (Maximum ERP):* the product of the power supplied to the aerial and the gain of the aerial relative to a half-wave dipole in the direction of maximum radiation.

(l) *Broadcast frequency band:* a continuous group of frequencies allocated to broadcasting by international regulations.

(m) *Programme:* a self-contained item, either with a title or otherwise indicated, broadcast during a pre-announced period.

(n) *Broadcasting time:* time during which programmes are broadcast by one or more transmitters.

(o) *Programme service:* a sequence of radio or television programmes broadcast regularly by one or more transmitters and forming a distinct named entity within the broadcasting service of a broadcasting institution.

(p) *Sound broadcasting (radio) receiver:* a receiver connected to an aerial or other source of radio signals in order to reconstitute in an audible form the elements of a particular sound programme service conveyed by such signals.

(q) *Television receiver:* a receiver connected to an aerial or other source of radio signals in order to reconstitute in an audible and visual form the elements of a particular television broadcast available to the viewer.

(r) *Receiving licence:* an authorization or a contract needed, usually in return for payment, to use sound broadcasting (radio) and/or television receivers.

II. CLASSIFICATION OF DATA

3. For the different aspects of domestic broadcasting covered by this recommendation, the following classifications should be used:

Broadcasting institutions

4. Broadcasting institutions should be classified:
   (a) by their constitutional status:
       (i) *Government broadcasting institution:* a broadcasting institution operated in all respects by a government (central or federal, State, provincial, local, etc.) either directly or through a separate institution created by it;
       (ii) *Public service broadcasting institution:* a broadcasting institution created or licensed by a legislative act or regulation (central or federal, State, provincial, local, etc.) and which constitutes an autonomous body;
       (iii) *Commercial broadcasting institutions:* a broadcasting institution corporately or privately owned and which is primarily profit oriented.
   (b) by their geographical coverage:
       (i) *National broadcasting institution:* a broadcasting institution which provides a broadcasting service intended to cover the country as a whole;
       (ii) *Regional broadcasting institution:* a broadcasting institution which within a country provides a regional broadcasting service;
       (iii) *Local broadcasting institution:* a broadcasting institution which provides a local broadcasting service.

5. Sources of revenue of broadcasting institutions should be classified according to their origin in the following categories:
   (a) *Government funds:* revenue received directly, or indirectly, from normal government funds (central or federal, State, provincial, local, etc.);
   (b) *Licence fees:* revenue from the proceeds of a broadcast receiving licence payable by users;
   (c) *Private endowments:* private funds made available for a broadcasting institution's use;
   (d) *Advertising:* revenue received in return for the advertiser's right to draw the audience's attention to his goods or services;
   (e) *Other income:* revenue from sources other than those defined in (a) to (d) above.

6. Current expenditure of broadcastin institutions should be classified into the following categories:
   (a) *Programme costs*
       All real costs directly attributable to planning, production and acquisition of programmes, including personnel costs, but excluding the fixed costs of keeping installations running:
       (i) Costs of a broadcasting institution's own productions;
       (ii) Costs incurred in the purchasing of programmes between broadcasting institutions.
   (b) *Costs of production, transmission and other facilities*
       All real costs not directly attributable to programmes.
       (i) Costs incurred in the upkeep of production facilities;
       (ii) Operating costs of transmission;
       (iii) Personnel, management and administration costs.

7. Personnel permanently employed in broadcasting institutions should be classified as follows:
   (a) *Programme and journalistic staff:*
       (i) *Programme staff:* planning, creative-writing and programme-producung personnel, excluding journalists;
       (ii) *Journalistic staff:* personnel engaged in the preparation of news bulletins, etc.
   (b) *Technical staff:*
       (i) *Technical production staff:* personnel employed on the operation and maintenance of the technical equipment necessary for programme production;
       (ii) *Technical transmission staff:* personnel employed on the operation and maintenance of transmitters and links between production centres and transmitters;
       (iii) *Other technical staff:* personnel employed on the design and installation of technical equipment or of buildings; study and research personnel, etc.
   (c) *Administrative staff:* personnel employed on the management or organization of a broadcasting institution and providing central services.
   (d) *Other staff:* personnel other than those defined in (a) to (c) above.

Transmitting facilities

8. Statistics on transmitters should distinguish between sound broadcasting transmitters and television transmitters.

   (a) *Sound broadcasting transmitters* should be classified by frequency band:
   - LF (Low frequency) also known as the long-wave band;
   - MF (Medium frequency) also known as the medium-wave band;
   - HF (High frequency) also known as the short-wave band;
   - VHF (Very high frequency);
   - SHF (Super high frequency).

   Transmitter power should be specified in terms of carrier power in LF, MF and HF, and Maximum ERP in VHF and SHF.

   (b) *Television transmitters* should be classified by frequency band:
   - VHF (Very high frequency) Bands 1, 2 and 3;
   - UHF (Ultra high frequency) Bands 4 and 5;
   - SHF (Super high frequency).

   Maximum ERP should be specified and a distinction made between black and white transmitters and colour transmitters.

Programmes

9. Statistics relating to programme services of domestic broadcasting should be classified as follows:

   (a) *National programme service:* a programme service broadcast natiowide;
   (b) *Regional programme service:* a programme service broadcast to regional audiences normally differentiated by language, ethnic or other cultural differences;
   (c) *Local programme service:* a programme service broadcast to audiences which, geographically, are conveniently grouped, e.g. cities and towns.

10. Statistics relating to programmes should be classified as follows:

    (a) *By function:* a programme characterized by its intended purpose.

    (i) *Informative programmes:* programmes intended primarily to inform about facts, events, theories or forecasts or to provide explanatory background information:
    - News bulletins and news commentaries including sports news);
    - Other informative programmes, e.g. programmes dealing with political, economic, scientific, cultural and social matters, special events, etc.

    (ii) *Educational, cultural and religious programmes*
    Educational programmes: programmes intended primarily to educate and in which the pedagogical element is fundamental:
    - Educational programmes related to a specific curriculum (e.g. schools, university, etc.); excluding programmes for rural development purposes;
    - Educational programmes for rural development purposes;
    - Other educational programmes.

    Cultural programmes: programmes intended primailry to stimulate artistic and/or intellectual curiosity:
    - Programmes which can be regarded as cultural performances or activities in themselves;
    - Programmes which are intended primarily to enrich the audience's knowledge in a non-didactic way regarding various spheres and phenomena of culture.

    Religious programmes: programmes based on different forms of religious service or similarly inspirational programmes intended to edify the audience.

    (iii) *Advertisements:* commercial or other advertisements in respect of which payment is made.

    (iv) *Entertainment programmes and unclassified programmes*
    Entertainment programmes: programmes intended primarily to entertain:
    - Cinema films;
    - Programmes produced as plays, whether as single complete programmes or as serials;
    - Programmes of which the predominant content is music, whether "live" or recorded;
    - Sports programmes (but excluding sports news);
    - Other entertainment programmes.

    Unclassified programmes: programmes not otherwise classified.

    (b) *By language of programme:*
    (i) Programmes broadcast in the official language(s);
    (ii) Programmes in dialects of the official language(s);
    (iii) Programmes in the languages of ethnic minorities;
    (iv) Programmes broadcast in languages other than (i), (ii) and (iii) above.

    (c) *By origin of programme:*
    (i) *National production:* programmes produced in the country, whether by the broadcasting institutions or otherwise;
    (ii) *Imported programmes:* programmes produced by organizations outside the reporting country;
    (iii) *International co-production:* programmes produced jointly by broadcasting institutions in the country and organizations outside the reporting country.

Listeners and viewers

11. (a) *Potential audience:* number of people as a percentage of the total population having access to a radio or television receiver, either in their own homes or in a listening group.

    (b) Statistics on the *estimated number of receivers* should be classified as follows:
    (i) *Sound broadcasting receivers,* distinguishing, if possible, between:
    - VHF receivers with frequency modulation;
    - LF, MF, HF, VHF and SHF receivers with amplitude modulation;
    - receivers equipped with both frequency and amplitude modulation.

(ii) *Television receivers,* distinguishing, if possible, between:
- Black and white receivers;
- Colour receivers.

(c) Statistics on *receiving licences* should be classified as follows:
(i) Licences for sound only (radio);
(ii) Licences for television;
(iii) Combined sound only (radio) and television licences.

External broadcasting

12. For the different aspects of external broadcasting covered by this recommendation, the following items should be included:

(a) Number of transmitters and their transmitting power;
(b) Total annual broadcasting time (in hours) of all languages and by individual languages as a percentage of the total.

III. REPORTING OF STATISTICAL DATA

13. The statistics covered by this recommendation should be drawn up desirably every year, but if this is not possible, every two years and refer to the latter year of the biennial period. The requested information should be presented in conformity with the definitions and classifications set out in paragraphs 2 to 12 above. Attention should be drawn to any differences between these definitions and classifications and those customarily used at the national level. These statistics should be presented separately for radio and television and should as far as possible cover all the following types of data:

Domestic broadcasting
Broadcasting institutions

14. Number of institutions legally authorized

(a) By constitutional status:
(i) Government broadcasting institution;
(ii) Public service broadcasting institution;
(iii) Commercial broadcasting institution.
(b) By geographical coverage:
(i) National broadcasting institution;
(ii) Regional broadcasting institution;
(iii) Local broadcasting institution.

15. Sources of revenue of broadcasting institutions referred to in paragraph 14 (a)
Total annual revenue and as a percentage of that total:

(a) Government funds
(b) Licence fees
(c) Private endowments
(d) Advertising
(e) Other income

16. Current expenditure of broadcasting institutions referred to in paragraph 14 (a)
Total annual current expenditure and as a percentage of that total:

(a) Programme costs:
(i) Programme production costs
(ii) Programme purchase costs

(b) Costs of production, transmission and other facilities:
(i) Production facilities costs
(ii) Transmission facilities costs
(iii) Personnel, management and administrative costs

17. Personnel employed in broadcasting institutions referred to in paragraph 14(a)
Total number of staff

(a) Programme staff:
(i) Programme staff excluding journalists
(ii) Journalists
(b) Technical staff:
(i) Production staff
(ii) Transmission staff
(iii) Other technical staff
(c) Administrative staff
(d) Other staff

Transmitting facilities

18. Total number of radio transmitters and their transmitting power expressed in carrier power or in maximum ERP for each of the under-mentioned categories:

(a) Low frequency (LF)
(b) Medium frequency (MF)
(c) High frequency (HF)
(d) Very high frequency (VHF)
(e) Super high frequency (SHF)

19. Total number of television transmitters and their transmitting power expressed in maximum ERP for each of the under-mentioned categories:

(a) Very high frequency (VHF)
(b) Ultra high frequency (UHF)
(c) Super high frequency (SHF)

Programmes

20. Number of programme services of broadcasting institutions referred to in paragraph 14(a)

(a) National programme services
(b) Regional programme services
(c) Local programme services

21. Total annual broadcasting time (in hours) of broadcasting institutions referred to in paragraph 14(a)

(a) By function, as percentage of total broadcasting time:
(i) Informative programmes:
News bulletins and news commentaries (including sports news)
Other informative programmes
(ii) Educational, cultural and religious programmes:
Educational programmes:
- Educational programmes related to a specific curriculum (excluding those for rural development purposes)
- Educational programmes for rural development purposes
- Other educational programmes
Cultural programmes:
- Cultural programmes or activities
- Programmes about culture
Religious programmes
(iii) Advertisements

(iv) Entertainment programmes and unclassified programmes
  Entertainment programmes
  - Cinema films
  - Plays
  - Music
  - Sport programmes (but excluding sports news)
  - Other entertainment programmes
  Unclassified programmes
(b) By language of programme, as percentage of total broadcasting time
  (i) Official language(s)
  (ii) Dialects of the official language(s)
  (iii) Languages of ethnic minorities
  (iv) Other languages
(c) By origin of programme, as percentage of total broadcasting time
  (i) National production
  (ii) Imported programmes
  (iii) International co-productions

Listeners and viewers

22.(a) Potential audience
   (b) Estimated number of receivers in use:
     (i) Radio receivers:
       - Receivers with amplitude modulation only
       - Receivers also equipped for frequency modulation
     (ii) Television receivers:
       Black and white receivers
       Colour receivers
   (c) Number of receiving licences in force:
     Sound only (radio)
     Television
     Combined

External broadcasting

23. Statistics on external radio broadcasting should include:
   (a) Number of transmitters and their transmitting power
   (b) Total annual broadcasting time (in hours) of all languages and by individual languages as a percentage of the total.

UNITED NATIONS EDUCATIONAL, SCIENTIFIC AND CULTURAL ORGANIZATION

Questionnaire on Statistics of Communication
Part three: Radio and television broadcasting
1977

1. The present questionnaire is intended for the international collection of statistics on radio and television broadcasting. Unesco has been compiling statistics on selected aspects of broadcasting since 1959 by means of a questionnaire on mass media which in 1976 was split up in order to cover the different media separately. The present questionnaire has been prepared in accordance with the *Recommendation concerning the international standardization of statistics on radio and television,* adopted by the General Conference of Unesco at its nineteenth session, 22 November 1976 in Nairobi.

2. The purpose of this Recommendation is to guide national authorities responsible for collecting and communicating radio and television statistics, through the adoption of certain standards, in order to improve the quality, completeness and the international comparability of such statistics. To meet these objectives, the definitions proposed in the Recommendation should be carefully read before completing the various tables. For ease of reference these definitions accompany the relevant tables.

3. The data to be supplied should refer to the calendar year 1977 or to the financial year 1976/77 depending on the accounting and information arrangements in your country. If statistics for that year are not available those for the latest year for which they are available should be entered in the questionnaire. The data thus obtained will be used for publication in the Unesco Statistical Yearbook, the United Nations Statistical Yearbook and in other publications.

4. Section I of this questionnaire relates to Domestic Sound Broadcasting and consists of nine tables requesting data on broadcasting institutions (tables 1-4), transmitting facilities (table 5), programmes (tables 6-8) and access to domestic sound broadcasting (table 9). Section II deals with External Broadcasting. Section III and the nine tables contained in it refer to Television Broadcasting and request statistical information on broadcasting institutions (tables 11-14), transmitters (table 15), programmes (tables 16-18) and access to television broadcasting (table 19).

5. In completing the questionnaire, please indicate cases where no data are available, and where the quantity is nil or negligible and *do not leave any space blank.* The following symbols are recommended for your use:

    Data not available   ...
    Quantity nil or negligible   -
    Estimates or provisional figures   *

6. In countries where several autonomous broadcasting institutions are operating, it is necessary that one central agency - either the Unesco National Commission or any other official body - function as a clearing house for the consolidation of the statistical information submitted by the different broadcasting institutions. Please give here the name and address of the organization or agency responsible for consolidation of the data: _____

_____

_____

7. The completed questionnaire should be returned before 30 June 1978 to the following address:

    Division of Statistics
    on Culture and Communication
    Office of Statistics
    Unesco
    Place de Fontenoy
    75700 Paris, France

SECTION I: DOMESTIC SOUND BROADCASTING
— BROADCASTING INSTITUTION —

a) Data requested in this chapter relate to the total number of sound broadcasting institutions in your country which are defined in the Recommendation as organizations legally authorized to provide a broadcasting service primarily intended for general reception within the country in which they operate.

Cable distribution systems are not included in the statistics required.

In accordance with the Recommendation it is requested that in cases where the same broadcasting institution is providing both radio and television broadcasting services separate data, based on estimates if necessary, should be reported for each. Please indicate how many of the total number of broadcasting institutions as referred to in table 1 provide both radio and television broadcasting services: . . . . .

b) The figures to be provided in tables 1 and 2 should refer to 31 December 1977 or to the end of the financial year 1976/77. Please indicate the date to which your data refer. Date: . . . . .

c) The figures to be provided for the tables 3 and 4 should refer to the entire year 1977 or to the financial year 1976/77 respectively. Please indicate the year to which your data refer: 19 ....

Table 1: Sound broadcasting institutions
by constitutional status and by geographical coverage

Geographical coverage[2]	Total number of sound broadcasting institutions	Constitutional status[1]		
		Government	Public service	Commercial
TOTAL				
of which:				
National				
Regional				
Local				

1. For the different types of broadcasting institutions the following definitions should be applied:

    Government broadcasting institution: a broadcasting institution operated in all respects by a government (central or federal, State, provincial, local, etc.) either directly or through a separate institution created by it;

    Public service broadcasting institution: a broadcasting institution created or licensed by a legislative act or regulation (central or federal, State, provincial, local, etc.) and which constitutes an autonomous body;
    (This category includes cases of private ownership where the purpose is not profit making and which qualify for the status of a public utility);

    Commercial broadcasting institution: a broadcasting institution corporately or privately owned and operating for financial profit.

2. Geographical coverage:

    National broadcasting institution: a broadcasting institution which provides a broadcasting service intended to cover the country as a whole;

    Regional broadcasting institution: a broadcasting institution which within a country provides a regional broadcasting service;

    Local broadcasting institution: a broadcasting institution which provides a local broadcasting service.

    Broadcasting institutions which provide not only national but also regional and/or local broadcasting services should be considered as national broadcasting institutions. Broadcasting institutions which provide regional as well as local broadcasting services should be considered as regional broadcasting institutions.

Table 2: Personnel permanently employed in sound broadcasting institutions
by type and by broadcasting institution

Type of personnel [1]	Total number of personnel	Type of sound broadcasting institution		
		Government	Public service	Commercial
TOTAL				
of which:				
1. Programme staff				
1.1. Programme staff (excl. journalists)				
1.2 Journalistic staff				
2. Technical staff:				
2.1 Technical production staff				
2.2 Technical transmission staff				
2.3 Other technical staff				
3. Administrative staff				
4. Other staff				

1. For the different types of personnel the following definitions are given in the Recommendation:

   Programme staff: planning, creative-writing and programme-producing personnel.

   Journalistic staff: personnel engaged in the preparation of news bulletins (and similar programmes such as news magazines, sports news etc. as referred to in point 1.1. on page 6).

   Technical production staff: personnel employed on the operation and maintenance of the technical equipment necessary for programme production;

   Technical transmission staff: personnel employed on the operation and maintenance of transmitters and links between production centres and transmitters;

   Other technical staff: personnel employed on the design and installation of technical equipment or of buildings; study and research personnel, etc.;

   Administrative staff: personnel employed on the management or organization of a broadcasting institution and providing central services such as research, training etc.

   Other staff: personnel other than those defined in one of the categories above.

Table 3: Annual revenue of sound broadcasting institutions
by source of revenue and by type of broadcasting institution

Source of annual revenue[1]	Total annual revenue	Type of sound broadcasting institution		
		Government	Public service	Commercial
TOTAL (in millions of national currency) . .				
of which as a percentage:	100%	100%	100%	100%
Government funds				
Licence fees				
Private endowments				
Advertising				
Other income				

1. For the different types of revenue the following definitions are given in the Recommendation:

    Government funds: revenue received directly, or indirectly, from normal government funds (central or federal, State, provincial, local, etc.);

    Licence fees: revenue from the proceeds of a broadcast receiving licence payable by users:

    Private endowments: private funds made available for a broadcasting institution's use;

    Advertising: revenue received in return for the advertiser's right to draw the audience's attention to his goods or services;

    Other income: revenue from sources other than those defined in one of the four categories above.

Table 4. Annual current expenditure of sound broadcasting institutions
by purpose of current expenditure and by type of broadcasting institution

Purpose[1]	Total annual current expenditure	Type of sound broadcasting institution		
		Government	Public service	Commercial
TOTAL (in millions of national currency) . .				
of which as a percentage:	100%	100%	100%	100%
1. Programme costs				
1.1 Programme production costs . . .				
1.2 Programme purchasing costs . . .				
2. Costs of production, transmission and other facilities				
2.1 Production facilities costs				
2.2 Transmission facilities costs				
2.3 Personnel, management and administration costs				

1. For the different types of current expenditure the following definitions are given in the Recommendation:

    Programme costs: All real costs directly attributable to planning ... (see Recommendation);

    Programme production costs: costs of a broadcasting institution's own productions;

    Programme purchasing costs: costs incurred in the purchasing of programmes, in co-productions and in the exchange of programmes between broadcasting institutions;

    Costs of production, transmission and other facilities: all real costs not directly attributable to programmes;

    Productions facilities costs: costs incurred in the upkeep of production facilities;

    Transmission facilities costs: operating costs of transmission.

— TRANSMITTING FACILITIES FOR DOMESTIC SOUND BROADCASTING —

a) Data requested in this chapter should relate to the total number of sound broadcasting transmitters[1] regularly operated in your country regardless of whether the responsibility for them lies with broadcasting institutions or with other bodies such as Posts and Telegraphs. The *transmitting power of* a sound broadcasting transmitter should be specified in terms of *carrier power* for LF, MF and HF transmitters and *maximum ERP*[2] for VHF and SHF transmitters.

b) The figures to be provided should refer to *31 December 1977* to the end of the financial year 1976/77 or to the latest date for which they are available. Please indicate date: ......

Table 5: Sound broadcasting (radio) transmitters
by frequency band, transmitting power and type of broadcasting institution

Frequency band[3]	Type of broadcasting institution using the transmitters								
	All transmitters		Government		Public service		Commercial	
	Number	Total transmitting power in kW	Number	Total transmitting power in kW	Number	Total transmitting power in kW	Number	Total transmitting power in kW
TOTAL of which:								
Low frequency (LF) (long-wave band)								
Medium frequency (MF) (medium-wave band)								
High frequency (HF) (short wave band)								
Very high frequency (VHF)								
Super high frequency (SHF)								

1. *Transmitter:* an apparatus producing radio-frequency energy for the purpose of broadcasting radio or television programmes;
2. *Maximum effective radiated power (Maximum ERP):* the product of the power supplied to the aerial and the gain of the aerial relative to a half-wave dipole in the direction of maximum radiation;
3. *Broadcast frequency band:* a continuous group of frequencies allocated to broadcasting by international regulations.

— PROGRAMMES OF DOMESTIC SOUND BROADCASTING —

The figures to be provided in the table 6 should refer to 31 December 1977 or to the end of the financial year 1976/77. Please indicate the date to which your data refer: ....

Table 6: Programme services by geographical coverage
and by type of broadcasting institution providing the programme service

Geographical coverage	Total number of programme services	Type of sound broadcasting institution		
		Government	Public service	Commercial
TOTAL				
of which:				
National programme service				
Regional programme service				
Local programme service				

A programme service is defined in the Recommendation as a sequence of radio or television programmes broadcast regularly by one or more transmitters and forming a distinct named entity *within the broadcasting service of a broadcasting institution.* The following categories should be applied:

National programme service: a programme service broadcast nationwide;

Regional programme service: a programme service broadcast to regional audiences (e.g. audiences of states, provinces, etc. within a country, often differentiated by language, culture, etc.);

Local programme service: a programme service broadcast to audiences which, geographically, are conveniently grouped, e.g. cities and towns.

The information required on radio programmes relates to a number of broad types of programmes according to their function and which are defined in the Recommendation as follows:

1. *Informative programmes:* programmes intended primarily to inform about facts, events, theories or forecasts or to provide explanatory background information:

    1.1   News bulletins and news commentaries (including sports news);

    1.2   Other informative programmes, e.g. programmes dealing with political, economic, scientitic, cultural and social matters, special events, etc.

2. *Educational programmes:* programmes intended primarily to educate and in which the pedagogical element is fundamental, and classified as follows:

    2.1   Educational programmes related to a specific curriculum (e.g. schools, university, etc.); excluding programmes for rural development purposes;

    2.2   Educational programmes for rural development purposes;

    2.3   Other educational programmes.

3. *Cultural programmes:* programmes intended primarily to stimulate artistic and/or intellectuel curiosity, and classified as follows:

    3.1   Programmes which can be regarded as cultural performances or activities in themselves[1];

    3.2   Programmes which are intended primarily to enrich the audience's knowledge in a non-didactic way regarding various spheres and phenomena of culture.

4. *Religious programmes:* programmes based on different forms of religious service or similarly inspirational programmes intended to edify the audience.

5. *Advertisements:* commercial or other advertisements in respect of which payment is made.

6. *Entertainment programmes:* programmes intended primarily to entertain, and classified as follows:

    6.1   Programmes produced as plays, whether as single complete programmes or as serials;

    6.2   Programmes *of which the predominant content is music,* whether "live" or recorded;

    6.3   Sports programmes (but excluding sports news);

    6.4   Other entertainment programmes.

7. *Unclassified programmes:* programmes not otherwise classified.

---

1. In this first survey following the adoption of the Recommendation this sub-category of cultural programmes will be omitted as overlapping occurs between this sub-category and some sub-categories under point 6 (Entertainment programmes). For future surveys this sub-category might be reintroduced after further elaboration on the strength of comments received and on the experience gained through this first survey.

a) The figures requested in tables 7 and 8 should refer to the entire year 1977 or to the financial year 1976/77, please indicate the year to which they refer: 19 ....

b) The figures to be provided in tables 7 and 8 should relate to the *total annual broadcasting time* (in hours) for the *total number of sound broadcasting institutions* in your country.

Table 7: Sound broadcasting programmes
by function and by type of broadcasting institution

Type of programme by function	Total *annual* broadcasting time (in hours)[1]	Type of broadcasting institution		
		Government	Public service	Commercial
TOTAL				
of which:				
1. Informative programmes				
of which:				
1.1 News bulletins, news commentaries (including sports news)				
1.2 Other informative programmes				
2. Educational programmes				
of which:				
2.1 Educational programmes related to a specific curriculum (schools, university, etc.)				
2.2 Educational programmes for rural development purposes				
2.3 Other educational programmes				
3. Cultural programmes				
of which:				
3.1 (see note 1 on previous page)				
3.2 Programmes regarding various spheres and phenomena of culture				
4. Religious programmes				
5. Advertisements				
6. Entertainment				
of which:				
6.1 Plays				
6.2 Music				
6.3 Sport programmes (exclusive sport news) . .				
6.4 Other entertainment programmes				
7. Other programmes not elsewhere classified . . .				

1. The total shown in this table should be identical to the total given in table 8.

Table 8: Sound broadcasting programmes by function and by origin of programme

Type of programme by function	Total *annual* broadcasting time (in hours)[1]	Origin of programme[2]		
		National production	Imported programmes	International co-production
TOTAL				
of which:				
1. Informative programmes				
of which:				
1.1 News bulletins, news commentaries (including sports news)				
1.2 Other informative programmes				
2. Educational programmes				
of which:				
2.1 Educational programmes related to a specific curriculum (schools, university, etc.)				
2.2 Educational programmes for rural development purposes				
2.3 Other educational programmes				
3. Cultural programmes				
of which:				
3.1 (See note on page 7)				
3.2 Programmes regarding various spheres and phenomena of culture				
4. Religious programmes				
5. Advertisements				
6. Entertainment				
of which:				
6.1 Plays				
6.2 Music				
6.3 Sport programmes (exclusive sports news)				
6.4 Other entertainment programmes				
7. Other programmes not elsewhere classified				

1. The total shown in this table should be identical to the total given in table 7.
2. For the different types of origin of programme the following definitions are given in the Recommendation:

    National production: programmes produced in the country, whether by the broadcasting institutions or otherwise;

    Imported programmes: programmes produced by organizations outside the reporting country;

    International co-production: programmes produced jointly by broadcasting institutions in the country and organizations outside the reporting country.

– ACCESS TO DOMESTIC SOUND BROADCASTING –

The figures requested should refer either to the specific dates as indicated in the table or to the end of the respective financial years.

Table 9: Potential audience, estimated number of receivers and number of receiving licences

Audience, receivers and licences	Dates		
	31.12.1975	31.12.1976	31.12.1977
Potential audience [1] en %			
Estimated *total* number of radio receivers[2] in use . . of which:			
Receivers with amplitude modulation (am) only . .			
Total number of existing receiving licences[3] for radio only			
Number of combined radio and television licences, if applicable			

1. *Potential audience:* number of people as a percentage of the total population, having access to a radio receiver, either in their own homes or in a listening group;
2. *Sound broadcasting (radio) receiver:* a receiver connected to an aerial or other source of radio signals in order to reconstitute in an audible form the elements of a particular sound programme service conveyed by such signals;
3. *Receiving licence:* an authorization or a contract needed, usually in return for payment, to use sound broadcasting (radio) and/or television receivers.

SECTION II: EXTERNAL BROADCASTING

a) Data requested in this section relate to external broadcasting which in the Recommendation is defined as a broadcasting service primarily intended for reception outside the country in which the broadcasting institution is authorized to operate.

b) The figures to be provided should refer to 31 December 1977 or *to the end* of the financial year 1976/77 for table 10a. and to the entire year for table 10b. Please indicate the date or year to which your data refer:

Date: ....   Year ....

Table 10a.: Number of transmitters used for external broadcasting and their transmitting power

Number of transmitters	Total transmitting power (in kW)

Table 10b.: Annual broadcasting time by individual languages

Language of programme	Annual broadcasting time (in hours)
TOTAL	
of which in:	
1. English	
2. French	
3. Spanish	
4.	
5.	
6.	
7.	
8.	
9.	
10.	
11. Other languages	

SECTION III: TELEVISION BROADCASTING
— BROADCASTING INSTITUTIONS —

a) Data requested in this chapter relate to the total number of television broadcasting institutions in your country which are defined in the Recommendation as organizations legally authorized to provide a broadcasting service primarily intended for general reception within the country in which they operate.

Cable distribution systems are not included in the statistics required.

In accordance with the Recommendation it is requested that in cases where the same broadcasting institution is providing both radio and television broadcasting services separate data, based on estimates if necessary, should be reported for each. Please indicate how many of the total number of broadcasting institutions as referred to in table 11 provide both radio and television broadcasting services. Numbers: . . .

b) The figures to be provided in tables 11 and 12 should refer to 31 December 1977 or to the end of the financial year 1976/77. Please indicate the date to which your data refer: . . . .

c) The figures to be provided in tables 13 and 14 should refer to the entire year 1977 or to the financial year 1976/77 respectively. Please indicate the year to which your data refer: 19 ...

Table 11: Television broadcasting institutions
by constitutional status and by geographical coverage

Geographical coverage[2]	Total number of television broadcasting institutions	Constitutional status[1]		
		Government	Public service	Commercial
TOTAL				
of which:				
National				
Regional				
Local				

1. For the different types of broadcasting institutions the following definitions should be applied:

    Government broadcasting institution: a broadcasting institution operated in all respects by a government (central or federal, State, provincial, local, etc.) either directly or through a separate institution created by it;

    Public service broadcasting institution: a broadcasting institution created or licensed by a legislative act or regulation (central or federal, State, provincial, local, etc.) and which constitutes an autono.nous body; (This category includes cases of private ownership where the purpose is not profit making and which qualify for the status of a public utility);

    Commercial broadcasting institution: a broadcasting institution corporately or privately owned and operating for financial profit.

2. Geographical coverage:

    National broadcasting institution: a broadcasting institution which provides a broadcasting service intended to cover the country as a whole;

    Regional broadcasting institution: a broadcasting institution which within a country provides a regional broadcasting service;

    Local broadcasting institution: a broadcasting institution which provides a local broadcasting service.

    Broadcasting institutions which provide not only national but also regional and/or local broadcasting services should be considered as national broadcasting institutions. Broadcasting institutions which provide regional as well as local broadcasting services should be considered as regional broadcasting institutions.

Table 12: Personnel permanently employed in television broadcasting institutions
by type and by broadcasting institution

Type of personnel [1]	Total number of personnel	Type of television broadcasting institution		
		Government	Public service	Commercial
TOTAL				
of which:				
1. Programme staff:				
1.1 Programme staff (excl. journalists)				
1.2 Journalistic staff				
2. Technical staff				
2.1 Technical production staff				
2.2 Technical transmission staff				
2.3 Other technical staff				
3. Administrative staff				
4. Other staff				

1. For the different types of personnel the following definitions are given in the Recommendation:

   Programme staff: planning, creative-writing and programme-producing personnel.

   Journalistic staff: personnel engaged in the preparation of news bulletins (and similar programmes such as news magazines, sports news etc. as referred to in point 1.1 on page 17);

   Technical production staff: personnel employed on the operation and maintenance of the technical equipment necessary for programme production;

   Technical transmission staff: personnel employed on the operation and maintenance of transmitters and links between production centres and transmitters;

   Other technical staff: personnel employed on the design and installation of technical equipment or of buildings; study and research personnel, etc;

   Administrative staff: personnel employed on the management or organization of a broadcasting institution and providing central services such as research, training, etc;

   Other staff: personnel other than those defined in one of the categories above.

Table 13: Annual revenue of television broadcasting institutions
by source of revenue and type of broadcasting institution

Source of annual revenue[1]	Total annual revenue	Type of television broadcasting institution		
		Government	Public service	Commercial
TOTAL (in millions of national currency)...				
of which as a percentage:	100%	100%	100%	100%
Government funds..........				
Licence fees............				
Private endowments.........				
Advertising............				
Other income...........				

1. For the different types of revenue the following definitions are given in the Recommendation:

   Government funds: revenue received directly, or indirectly, from normal government funds (central or federal, State, provincial, local, etc.);

   Licence fees: revenue from the proceeds of a broadcast receiving licence payable by users;

   Private endowments: private funds made available for a broadcasting institution's use;

   Advertising: revenue received in return for the advertiser's right to draw the audience's attention to his goods or services;

   Other income: revenue from sources other than those defined in one of the four categories above.

Table 14: Annual current expenditure of television broadcasting institutions
by purpose of expenditure and type of broadcasting institution

Purpose[1]	Total annual current expenditure	Type of television broadcasting institution		
		Government	Public service	Commercial
TOTAL (in millions of national currency)....				
of which as a percentage:	100%	100%	100%	100%
1. Programme costs...........				
1.1 Programme production costs.....				
1.2 Programme purchasing costs.....				
2. Costs of production, transmission and other facilities.............				
2.1 Production facilities costs......				
2.2 Transmission facilities costs......				
2.3 Personnel, management and administration costs................				

1. For the different types of current expenditure the following definitions are given in the Recommendation:

   Programme costs: All real costs directly attributable to planning, production and acquisition of programmes, including personnel costs, but excluding the fixed costs of keeping installations running;

   Programme production costs: costs of a broadcasting institution's own productions;

   Programme purchasing costs: costs incurred in the purchasing of programmes, in co-productions and in the exchange of programmes between broadcasting institutions;

   Costs of production, transmission and other facilities: All real costs not directly attributable to programmes;

   Production facilities costs: costs incurred in the upkeep of production facilities;

   Transmission facilities costs: operating costs of transmission.

— TRANSMITTING FACILITIES FOR TELEVISION BROADCASTING —

a) Data requested in this chapter should relate to the total number of television broadcasting transmitters[1] regularly operated in your country regardless of whether the responsibility for them lies with broadcasting institutions or with other bodies such as Posts and Telegraphs. The *transmitting power* of a television broadcasting transmitter should be specified in terms of *maximum ERP*.[2]

b) The figures to be provided should refer to *31 December 1977* to the end of the financial year 1976/77 or to the latest date for which they are available. Please indicate date: ....

Table 15: Television broadcasting transmitters
by frequency band, transmitting power and type of broadcasting institution

Frequency band[3]	All transmitters		Type of broadcasting institution using the transmitters					
			Government		Public service		Commercial	
	Number	Total transmitting power in kW	Number	Total transmitting power in kW	Number	Total transmitting power in kW	Number	Total transmitting power in kW
TOTAL of which:								
Very high frequency (VHF)								
of which: for colour transmissions								
Ultra high frequency (UHF)								
of which: for colour transmissions								
Super high frequency (SHF)								
of which: for colour transmissions								

1. *Transmitter:* An apparatus producing radio-frequency energy for the purpose of broadcasting radio or television programmes;
2. *Maximum effective radiated power (Maximum ERP):* The product of the power supplied to the aerial and the gain of the aerial relative to a half-wave dipole in the direction of maximum radiation;
3. *Broadcast frequency band:* A continuous group of frequencies allocated to broadcasting by international regulations.

— PROGRAMMES OF TELEVISION BROADCASTING —

The figures to be provided in table 16 should refer to 31 December 1977 or to the end of the financial year 1976/77. Please indicate the date to which your data refer: . . . . . .

Table 16: Programme services
by geographical coverage and by type of broadcasting institution providing the programme service

Geographical coverage	Total number of programme services	Type of television broadcasting institution		
		Government	Public service	Commercial
TOTAL				
of which:				
National programme service				
Regional programme service				
Local programme service				

A programme service is given in the Recommendation as a sequence of radio or television programmes broadcast regularly by one or more transmitters and forming a distinct named entity *within the broadcasting service of a broadcasting institution*. The following definitions should be applied:

National programme service: a programme service broadcast nationwide;

Regional programme service: a programme service broadcast to regional audiences (e.g. audiences of states, provinces, etc., within a country, often differentiated by language culture, etc.);

Local programme service: a programme service broadcast to audiences which, geographically, are conveniently grouped, e.g. cities and towns.

The information required on television programmes relates to a number of broad types of programmes according to their function and which are defined in the Recommendation as follows:

1. *Informative programmes:* programmes intended primarily to inform about facts, events, theories or forecasts or to provide explanatory background information:

    1.1   News bulletins and news commentaries (including sports news);

    1.2   Other informative programmes, e.g. programmes dealing with political, economic, scientific, cultural and social matters, special events, etc.

2. *Educational programmes:* programmes intended primarily to educate and in which the pedagogical element is fundamental, and classified as follows:

    2.1   Educational programmes related to a specific curriculum (e.g. schools, university, etc.); excluding programmes for rural development purposes;

    2.2   Educational programmes for rural development purposes;

    2.3. Other educational programmes.

3. *Cultural programmes:* programmes intended primarily to stimulate artistic and/or intellectual curiosity, and classified as follows:

    3.1   Programmes which can be regarded as cultural performances or activities in themselves[1];

    3.2   Programmes which are intended primarily to enrich the audience's knowledge in a non-didactic way regarding various spheres and phenomena of culture.

4. *Religious programmes:* programmes based on different forms of religious service or similarly inspirational programmes intended to edify the audience.

5. *Advertisements:* commercial or other advertisements in respect of which payment is made.

6. *Entertainment programmes:* programmes intended primarily to entertain, and classified as follows:

    6.1   Cinema films;

    6.2   Programmes produced as plays, whether as single complete programmes or as serials;

    6.3   Programmes *of which the predominant content is music,* whether "live" or recorded;

    6.4   Sports programmes (but excluding sports news);

    6.5   Other entertainment programmes.

7. *Unclassified programmes:* programmes not otherwise classified.

---

1. In the first survey following the adoption of the Recommendation in 1976 this sub-category of cultural programmes will be omitted as overlapping occurs between this sub-category and some sub-categories under point 6 (Entertainment programmes). For future surveys this sub-category might be reintroduced after further elaboration on the strength of comments received and on the experience gained through this first survey.

a) The figures requested in the tables 17 and 18 should refer to the entire year 1977 or to the financial year 1976/77. Please indicate the year to which they refer: 19 ....

b) The figures to be provided in tables 17 and 18 should relate to the *total annual broadcasting time* (in hours) for the *total number of television broadcasting institutions* in your country.

Table 17: Television broadcasting programmes
by function and by type of broadcasting institution

Type of programme by function	Total *annual* broadcasting time (in hours)[1]	Type of broadcasting institution		
		Government	Public service	Commercial
TOTAL				
of which:				
1. Informative programmes				
of which:				
1.1 News bulletins, news commentaries (including sports news)				
1.2 Other informative programmes				
2. Educational programmes				
of which:				
2.1 Educational programmes related to a specific curriculum (schools, university, etc.)				
2.2. Educational programmes for rural development purposes				
2.3. Other educational programmes				
3. Cultural programmes				
of which:				
3.1 (See note 1 on previous page)				
3.2 Programmes regarding various spheres and phenomena of culture				
4. Religious programmes				
5. Advertisements				
6. Entertainment				
of which:				
6.1 Cinema films				
6.2 Plays				
6.3 Music				
6.4 Sport programmes (exclusive sports news)				
6.5 Other entertainment programmes				
7. Other programmes not elsewhere classified				

1. The total shown in this table should be identical to the total given in table 18.

Table 18: Television broadcasting programmes
by function and by origin of programme

Type of programme by function	Total *annual* broadcasting time (in hours)[1]	Origin of programme[2]		
		National production	Imported programmes	International co-production
TOTAL				
of which:				
1. Informative programmes				
of which:				
1.1 News bulletins, news commentaries (including sports news)				
1.2 Other informative programmes				
2. Educational programmes				
of which:				
2.1 Educational programmes related to a specific curriculum (schools, university, etc.)				
2.2 Educational programmes for rural development purposes				
2.3 Other educational programmes				
3. Cultural programmes				
of which:				
3.1 (See note on page 17)				
3.2 Programmes regarding various spheres and phenomena of culture				
4. Religious programmes				
5. Advertisements				
6. Entertainment				
of which:				
6.1 Cinema films				
6.2 Plays				
6.3 Music				
6.4 Sport programmes (exclusive sports news)				
6.5 Other entertainment programmes				
7. Other programmes not elsewhere classified				

1. The total shown in this table should be identical to the total given in table 17.

2. For the different types of origin of programme the following definitions are given in the Recommendation:

   National production: programmes produced in the country, whether by the broadcasting institutions or otherwise;

   Imported programmes: programmes produced by organizations outside the reporting country;

   International co-production: programmes produced jointly by broadcasting institutions in the country and organizations outside the reporting country.

— ACCESS TO TELEVISION BROADCASTING —

The figures requested should refer either to the specific dates as indicated in the table or to the end of the respective financial years.

Table 19: Potential audience, estimated number of receivers and number of receiving licences

Audience, receivers and licences	Dates		
	31.12.1975	31.12.1976	31.12.1977
Potential audience[1] in %			
Estimated *total* number of television receivers[2] in use . of which: Colour receivers			
Total number of existing receiving licences[3] for television . . . . of which: Number of licences for colour television receivers . .			

1. *Potential audience:* number of people, as a percentage of the total population having access to a television receiver, either in their own homes or in a listening group;

2. *Television receiver:* a receiver connected to an aerial or other source of radio signals in order to reconstitute in an audible and visible form the elements of a particular television broadcast available to the viewer;

3. *Receiving licence:* an authorization or a contract needed, usually in return for payment, to use sound broadcasting (radio) and/or television receivers.

For Reference

Not to be taken from this room